The Bedside
'GUARDIAN'
35

The Bedside 'GUARDIAN' 35

A selection from *The Guardian* 1985–6
Edited by
W. L. WEBB

With an Introduction by
Salman Rushdie

Cartoons by

Gibbard
Bryan McAllister
Steve Bell

COLLINS
8 Grafton Street London WI
1986

William Collins Sons & Co. Ltd
London · Glasgow · Sydney · Auckland
Toronto · Johannesburg

British Library Cataloguing in Publication Data

The Bedside Guardian.—35 : 1985–6
1. English essays—Periodicals
I. Webb, W. L.   II. The Guardian
        082'.05   PR1361

ISBN 0-00-217702-1

First published 1986
© Guardian Newspapers 1986

Photoset in Plantin by
Rowland Phototypesetting Ltd, Bury St Edmunds, Suffolk
Printed and bound in Great Britain by
Robert Hartnoll (1985) Ltd.,
Bodmin Cornwall

Introduction

"Bedside Guardian": the name conjures up a stern, corseted figure, some sort of Victorian chaperone, guarding the boudoirs of young girls against thin-silk-ripping chaps. It could also, I suppose, be a dog, a burglar alarm or a chastity belt. It is, of course, none of these things.

The Bedside Guardian is an unusual book. It aims to place by your bedside what is more traditionally discovered on your doormat. (Well, my doormat, anyway.) Is this wise? What does it mean, that the very stuff that was originally supposed to wake one up in the morning is now offered as a way of lulling us to sleep? Furthermore, are yesterday's papers not better employed lining drawers, lighting fires, cleaning muddy boots? Do we actually want our journalists immortalized in such literary preserves, such nocturnal pickles as *Bedside Guardians?* Sufficient unto the day (it may be argued) is *The Guardian* thereof.

Obviously, however, as I'm here to introduce the book, I come (on the whole) to praise the thing, not to bury it. And, as a matter of fact, one of the best recommendations for the *Bedside Guardian* is precisely that it does demonstrate that good journalism, like all good writing, is built to last. In these days of increasingly disposable novels, it may be that we are wrapping fish and packing china in the wrong kind of printed matter.

Which is not to say that I do not have my dissatisfactions, with the paper as well as the anthology; what self-respecting *Guardian* reader would not? But if I complain that this book contains not a single Doonesbury strip, another reader will feel relieved; if I mention my aversion to this or that Guardian writer (Waldemar Januszczak, to name but a few; a Grauniad miszczprint if ever I saw one), then it's a good bet that for some other reader, the same person is the paper's greatest asset.

Enough carping; this year's selection does contain most of

the pieces I remember best, and plenty I missed first time round that I was glad to discover. At the lighter end, Polly Toynbee's portrait of Mr James Whitaker, the gossip journalist whose claim to immortality is that he took the notorious photograph of Princess Diana pregnant in a bikini, shows that the nation's love affair with the Windsors depends upon some pretty weird go-betweens. In Tom Nairn's marvellous phrase, the basis of the Royals' popularity is "the glamour of backwardness". But do the Royals know this? Princess Diana confided recently to what I ought to call an "unimpeachable source" of my own that her favourite TV programme was *Dynasty*, which she liked "because of the escapism". This joke is almost as funny as Nancy Banks-Smith's columns on the Carringtons, to say nothing of the Ewings, and as a fervent Banks-Smith fan I'm delighted to see her given pole position here.

(Incidentally, if Ms Banks-Smith thinks Mountbatten had no neck in *The Last Viceroy*, she should check out the England fast bowler, Gladstone Small. He makes Nicol Williamson look like a giraffe.)

I was pleased, too, to read again Richard Boston's piece on an "orgy of complacent self-congratulation" at a College reunion at King's, Cambridge, a piece that is all dinner-jackets and Brideshead until the chill, dark shadow of its last lines; and David Rose's superb analysis of the reporting of the Handsworth troubles. Matthew Engel's contribution from the West Indies is good because it sticks to the cricket; when he wrote about the Troubles of Goochy, he was less convincing, seeming at times not to understand just why those Caribbean politicos were making such a fuss about Graham's South African venture.

To mention South Africa is to remember that it's been another ugly year in the big wide world, and that one of the ugliest sights on display has been the spectacle of the British Prime Minister, her mind lacquered rigid, explaining to the South African black majority that theirs is the immoral position. That Mrs Thatcher is a racist can no longer be doubted (the *New Statesman* said so in a leader, so it must be true). Her interview with Hugo Young, reprinted here, shows perfectly the smug contempt with which she treats all those who disagree

"Here, want a taste?"

30 April, 1986

with her. One day we will not believe we tolerated such a leader
for so long; or, believing, we will feel ashamed.

In the year of Chernobyl, of the attack on Libya, of the
continuing campaign of disinformation about Nicaragua, it
hasn't been easy to believe what one reads in the free world's
free press. *The Guardian* hasn't been perfect. Like all the other
papers, it swallowed the US figures about the thousands who
"died" at Chernobyl, and recanted in much smaller print later;
like all the other papers, it initially failed to question the official
Western version, that the Chernobyl reactor was much less safe
than Western models, that such a disaster could not have
happened here. Only later did we discover that Chernobyl was
very far from being some sort of Heath Robinson contraption,
but pretty up to date, and that the West was littered with
reactors of comparable levels of "safety", that is, unsafety.

But at least *The Guardian* has subsequently refused to let the
issue die; the Jill Tweedie piece in this selection, with its
radioactively babbling brook, is one example of that. At least

9

The Guardian did print Edward Thompson's polemic against the US bombing of Libya (also reprinted here). At least, in *The Guardian*, the Reagan-Thatcher description of Central America, of South Africa, of the world, is subjected to regular and disenchanted scrutiny.

These are not small mercies, and one is grateful for them. This is, after all, also the year of the Murdoching, or Wapping, of Fleet Street. The destruction of the *Sunday Times*, and the continued decline of *The Times*, means that this country no longer has much in the way of a quality press. New papers, we are told, are on the way, and it is possible that the situation may improve. In the meanwhile, in the Britain of 1986, a society whose most radical voices are heard in the Church of England, the House of Lords, and even, it is rumoured, Buckingham Palace, *The Guardian* deserves at least two cheers, and is welcome to my bedside. It may not help me to sleep, but I can always read a novel instead.

SALMAN RUSHDIE

Over Bobby's dead body

Last night I dreamt I returned to Southfork again. After all these years the dear old homestead is just the same. The same scruffy grass – how one suffers for the poor horses – Miss Ellie in her large selection of simple smocks, Ray still having trouble with joined-up writing, Sue Ellen still falling down in public places, Cliff Barnes perfecting his remarkable impression of Donald Duck. All in the same old familiar pickle. Or, in the case of Sue Ellen, pickled.

And on the same old channel. In the last *Dallas* (BBC-1), you will faintly recall, Bobby was hit amidships by Katharine Wentworth's car and his body has been in cold storage ever since while the BBC and Thames disputed custody of the corpse.

It all took time. None of us are any younger and few now have even the faintest recollection why Bobby bit the dust. 'But what was Katharine Wentworth *doing* in Dallas, Momma?' Gary asked last night, understandably at sea. Miss Ellie was repressive: 'We're not sure and I don't think it really matters.'

Her son slaughtered and she doesn't think it really matters? The fact is that Miss Ellie was not in Dallas at the time, having been mysteriously replaced by another woman altogether, and knows nothing whatsoever about the matter.

So, collecting our scattered thoughts as best we can, here is the story so far. Bobby (of Ewing Oil) had spent the night with Pam (of Grayson Oil). They had been separated by the jealous wiles of Katharine Wentworth (of Wentworth Tool and Die), Pam's mad half-sister or half-mad sister. Pretty miffed at being the only one in Dallas with no oil, she first shot Bobby then, finding that did not serve, hit him with a Cadillac in the small of the back. Bobby expired forgiving his family at some length in Dallas Memorial Hospital. Meanwhile, back at the ranch, JR is madly in love with a woman in satin camiknickers, Cliff Barnes has married Jamie because she is rich, and Ray, who always gets it a bit wrong, is divorcing Donna because she is rich.

And there's a chap called Jack whom nobody alive can remember a darn thing about.

If there is one deeply endearing thing about Southfork it is the homeliness. Just ordinary millionaires a-setting around the microwave in the kitchen, worrying whether to report Sue Ellen missing again. 'Let's do the show right here' is their family motto. If they have a wedding, they hold it in the front drive. But even their staunchest fans will feel they have gone too far burying Bobby in the back garden like a budgie. As Pammy said tearfully, 'I couldn't bring myself to go to Southfork. There's just too much of Bobby there.' Not to put too fine a point on it, there's *all* of Bobby there, underneath the old oak tree.

Never was a feuding family so united as the Ewings at Bobby's funeral – 'I love you, boy'. . . 'I love you too, Daddy' . . . 'I love you, Momma' . . . 'I love you, Gary' . . . 'I love you, Sue Ellen' – culminating in JR's moving monologue over Bobby's body: 'I love you, Bobby. Tell Daddy I love him too.' (Daddy vanished in the South American jungle in mysterious circumstances.) Only Little Lucy rang to say she couldn't get a flight back in time for the funeral. A likely story. She could have circumnavigated Mars and grown six inches in the time between Bobby's death and his funeral but Little Lucy has been given the boot and tossed her last ringlet at Southfork.

All this togetherness disintegrated with the reading of the will. It occurred to me that under his wholesome crust, Bobby may have concealed a wholly unsuspected sense of humour. Among various unsuitable bequests like a high spirited horse to his brother, Gary, who lives in a suburban cul-de-sac called Knotts Landing, was the gift of 'Cedar Ridge, adjacent to Southfork' to his brother, Ray. Ray, who uses his head solely as somewhere to park his stetson, has not noticed that the topography of Southfork lies open to every eye, resembling nothing so much as a well-scuffed snooker table. There is no ridge.

6 March, 1986   **Nancy Banks-Smith**

Awaiting events

The next few days seem certain to witness events in the Mediterranean, sponsored jointly by Ronald Reagan and Muammar al-Gadafy. If not they will witness events on one or other sector of our revolving stage like South Africa or Northern Ireland. I don't think it is wrong to harbour ambiguous feelings towards events, wishing they would not happen, but taking an interest when they do.

On misdialling a number some time ago I found myself connected to an answering machine. It did not identify itself or its owner but, after several moments' silence, a deep masculine voice announced: 'There has been an event.' After another long pause it started to transmit a series of electronic signals. It then disconnected itself.

By altering various digits in the number I had first tried to dial, I rediscovered the number which stirred this sinister apparatus into action. Some days it had nothing to report. You could tell it was there because it sounded just like another person who was keeping silent. There was heavy breathing without the breath. On other days something had happened, and a passable imitation of Valentine Dyall would give the word: 'There has been an event . . .'

Now these events were important enough to be worth recording, and for somebody to want to know about them by ringing up. On the other hand no evidence was offered about what they related to. Were they, I wondered, weird but innocent scientific events like anti-neutrinos with negative mass striking a detector deep in a Cheshire saltmine? Was somebody monitoring flying saucers? Had Menwith Hill tracked a highly disturbing signal from a Russian agent to his Moscow control, as it does in Frederick Forsyth?

I never found the answer. Nor do I know whether the events changed the course of history because I don't know what the course of history would have been if they hadn't occurred, if you take my meaning.

I mention this because events are at their most interesting when least is known about them. Once all is clear, they become banal. It seems a pity so much space in newspapers and time on the air is devoted to events – in some papers non-events – rather than ideas. Is not the contemplation of an unknown event a richer experience than the completed thing?

One's political colleagues surely believe it is. For the next two years they will be fully occupied in assessing the likely results of the next general election. Indeed that process began on June 10, 1983. Then, on a given night, two years of adventure with ideas will be abruptly ended in the space of a few hours. There will have been an event.

At one time I used to find the preoccupation with events a source of great irritation. A new item falls into one of three categories: interesting and immediate; interesting but not immediate; and immediate but not interesting. The dispute used to turn on baskets two and three.

I would go to some pains to promote an item in basket two. It might be a philosophical difference emerging within the French Communist Party, or the success in the United States of a hitherto untested cosmological theory. Then, just before edition time, some oaf would lose his way in the Lake District and the rescue services would all be called out. Hard news. Big deal. Bang goes cosmological phenomenon.

Events are a serious distraction from the business in hand. On overseas visits, now increasingly rare, I confess to have had a profoundly unprofessional instinct. I would earnestly hope that no basket three events took place while I was there because they would divert attention from long-term developments, which would certainly be in basket two and possibly basket one.

I did not in the least resent discovering a large-scale massacre in the central African Republic of Rwanda, of which I can, without immodesty, say I provided the first full account. It was not what I was there to look for, but it was interesting and it had implications. It is the events without implications – the one-off pot-hole, the burst gas main, even for most of the time the air crash – which exercise so baleful a tyranny over what is judged to be news.

This, of course, is where one has to envy as well as take issue with academics. Their term of abuse for early publications is 'mere journalism'. Yet it is surprising how often the laborious academic thesis, pored over for months and with not a reference left uncited, says what a political commentator discovered with only half an hour to collect his thoughts.

Here, then, is one of the great dichotomies. The world is not divided only between left and right, breakfasters and non-breakfasters, zealots and decent chaps, joggers and sedentarians. It can be divided between those who need to listen to *The World at One* and watch *Newsnight*, and those who can afford to pick it all up as the days go by; or not at all, as the case may be.

Penguin says on the cover of its edition of *The Imitation of Christ*, by Thomas à Kempis, that after the Bible it has probably been the best-loved book in Christendom since Thomas died in 1471. That did not prevent other publishers writing to T. A. Kempis, Esq, saying they were impressed with his work and asking him to write a follow-up.

T. A. Kempis, Esq, has valuable advice for those who would like to reflect unhindered by the onrush of events: 'Avoid public gatherings as far as possible, for the discussion of worldly affairs becomes a great hindrance.' I know a seconder, if one is needed: 'Avoid unnecessary talk and aimless visits, listening to news and gossip.' Motion carried.

Tonight's panel includes Garret FitzGerald, Hosni Mubarak, Derek Hatton, and Tom Kempis. Lines are open from 6 o'clock on 091-212-46 . . . sorry, wrong number.

14 April, 1986   **Geoffrey Taylor**

Another Stassinopoulos phenomenon

Miss Arianna Stassinopoulos, the most upwardly mobile Greek since Icarus, finally outdid her compatriot on Saturday night. At fashionable St Bartholomew's Episcopalian Church on Park Avenue she pledged to oilman Michael Huffington the hand and heart which were once on loan to Bernard Levin, John Selwyn Gummer and the presidency of the Cambridge Union, though not all at the same time. What was more, in a notoriously cynical world, the whole thing could be presented as a true romance. It is one thing to meet the heir to a $300 million Texas oil fortune in September and become engaged in January, but quite another to go ahead and marry him in a month when US petrol prices have fallen 21.9 per cent at the pumps. It must be love. The passion they share is music.

The groom, who is also tall, is said to be 'charming'. His grandfather died from a poisoned arrow while searching the jungles of South America for the oil his father eventually found in Indonesia. They are respectable Texans.

Whether it was because of this or because the late seven o'clock kick-off meant a crowded schedule (a reception and a dinner-dance to fit in before lunch), the guests turned up in black tie or evening dress, as for the Hollywood Oscars, which in some respects the scene resembled.

All was enthusiastically reported in the tabloid *Daily News*, but the event warranted only six bland paragraphs on page 63 of the *New York Times*, a commendably unsensational publication. Students of the Stassinopoulos phenomenon will take satisfaction from the fact that the report was the longest on yesterday's social pages, where the new Mrs Huffington's name appears (last sighting: Friday) with impressive regularity.

By general agreement of those who worry about these things, it was definitely this week's social wedding of the year. Conducted by the Bishop of New York in basic C. of E. with a nod towards Greek rites (Greek Unorthodox?) and undeniably

Byzantine architecture, it boasted as its sort-of-bridesmaids Barbara Walters, the million-dollar CBS anchorperson, and Selwa 'Lucky' Roosevelt, the White House Chief of Protocol, as well as the happy couple's sisters. Mrs Ann Getty, cultured and vivacious wife of Gordon (the Getty who stood up to Dad), and Arianna's fairy godmother in American society, was matron of honour. Norman Parkinson (aged 72) brought his camera.

Not bad going for the author of an indistinguished, if lucrative, biography of Maria Callas and sometime disciple (with Mr Levin) of the upwardly and horizontally mobile Bhagwan Rajneesh, a woman who set out in 1981 to conquer New York with a couple of letters of introduction and the less than unanimous good wishes of polite society in London.

'Sweet' said some, 'pushy' said others, and transparently so. In New York these traits do not go unnoticed. 'Hers is the sort of intimacy that always supports your values, no matter how hideous they may be,' one admirer told *New York Magazine*.

But so many people are at it that it causes less offence. To be a 'Socialite author' here is not a political position in the sense that George Bernard Shaw was a leftwing socialite author. It is a way of life which includes writing (an overdue biography of Picasso in the bride's case). And Miss Stassinopoulos ('rhymes with Acropolis,' explained the man from the *Daily Express*) proved an assiduous Big League player in the social whirl – as Saturday's disposition underlines.

Despite reports that the bride (35) and groom (38) had agreed on a private wedding – steps had been taken to ensure that their nuptial will reverberate through the glossy prints for some time. The Tinas, the Suzis and the Lizes who command the gossip columns here, had all been invited, along with many of New York's beautiful people and Dr Henry Kissinger. The 370-strong guest list was thus sufficiently rich, powerful and decorative to impress even the universal matrons in headscarves who love weddings and just happened to be passing. 'Dunna whose geddin' married,' said one New Yorker whom Arianna had evidently not got round to inviting to a soirée, 'but there's a lot of celebrities in there. I just seen Henry Kissinger and Gregory Peck.'

Actually, Mr Peck was a likely mis-sighting. But that is the great thing about being famous and famous for it, as the bride's previous career in Cambridge and Covent Garden circles brilliantly demonstrated: celebrity begets celebrity. Once you have spotted Shirley MacLaine on the church step, a clutch of Gettys, or Dr K. and Norman Mailer, failed to spot Lord Gowrie and mistaken Princess Michael of Kent for someone else, anything goes. And besides, American beautiful people of a certain age aspire to look like Gregory Peck – even some of the women.

So everyone got their money's worth. The bride arrived on time (ahead of many of her guests) and revealed that she was not nervous. Dr Kissinger's security man refused to reveal his mental condition or the name of his employer. Mr Levin, one of several invited ex-beaux, arrived with a blonde on his arm. Mr Gummer, that modest stepping-stone of yesteryear, was evidently detained by important business at the Ministry of Agriculture.

Fortunately, a Runyonesque photographer called Hy, who wore his ageing baseball cap backwards and looked like one of New York's homeless, knew everyone who mattered. 'Mr Myler, look this way, Nawm, pleeze,' he would cry, a democratic touch which found embodiment in the Huffington employee who said 'Michael, may I be the first to congratulate you, sir?'

Otherwise, in the reassuring shadow of the Waldorf Astoria Hotel, where the wine cellar is on the sixth floor to stop the subway trains rattling the sediment, plutocracy was much in evidence.

It will be argued, as it was among the media peasantry on the pavement (Harold Evans, Andrew Neil and the Rothermeres being inside), that this kind of carry-on would never have occurred at home. But this is a fairy story with a reassuring moral for both sides of the Atlantic. Never mind the spoilsports complaining that Reagan's America spawns a shallow, narcissistic culture. Un-British it may be, but for those who play by its rules and work hard it can still be a land of opportunity. Ask Mrs Huffington.

14 April, 1986   **Michael White**

Diamond Brill

At the far end of Manhattan, hanging plants, the badge of the middle classes, have appeared in the windows of the industrial buildings of a century ago. A blue velvet rope goes up nightly on the sidewalk outside Bar Lui, the cavernous and block-long restaurant (wood-grilled wild mushrooms, buck-wheat fettucine with grilled duck and black olives, etc.). Neon lights, woodsy Maine shirts, screaming yellows on wax models, Spandex dancewear in studio entrances: Downtown is the new Uptown.

Downtown goes to bed at dawn: here are the huge new nightclubs, Area, Palladium, El International – seven floors of milling night, dancing in a drained aquarium, men in dresses, women in bits of glittering lurex, sequins and shaven heads, rock stars, slumber and yacht parties, all the wild fantasies of rock videos.

Inevitably, there is money to be made packaging the outrageous, smoothing it out for the mainstream. Klein, Lauren, Blass, even Perry Ellis – old and institutionalized now – stand by as younger stars fizzle for a moment or two. Enter Dianne Brill, Queen of the Night, creator of the New Millionaires' Club fashion range for men: silk lurex tuxedos, moon-glow cotton suit ensembles with big gold pennies on the cuff, black rayon spy jackets, all worn with gold chains and dollar bills, silver spatless boots and golden jewellery. The line has been launched at the Palladium – it will be on Columbus Avenue in time for Christmas.

Next door to Bar Lui, in the Cable Building, along Diva-ish clanging corridors and empty spaces, Dianne Brill has installed her showroom. Opposite her firmly and thickly closed door, another stands open. Some old-timer, padded and creased, veteran of Lower Broadway before it became Downtown, waits for the sight of his neighbours coming to work. The star of Cars' videos, of parties, clubs, openings, galas, balls and Andy

Warhol's MTV show, *15 Minutes*, Dianne Brill, the Mae West and Jayne Mansfield look-alike, taps along the corridor on her five-inch stiletto heels.

She is 5ft 9in tall; down her ample back tumbles a mane of peroxide blonde hair. ('A bit Louis XIV and a bit Western.') She is a very large woman squeezed into a skin-tight scarlet jersey dress that rides up and involves much wriggling to straighten. The make-up is bright, the jewellery glitters. 'I'm me,' she says cheerfully. 'I do me. I look like me. Maybe I look frightening – this six foot, big-breasted blonde – but this is me. Cars crash. People react. It's fun.'

She is cheery and harmless, all good clean fun for the eighties. 'It's the New Money theory. If I want it: goddamit, let's do it. There's no tomorrow. If we need something we just work and do it. If you want that jacket, no matter that it's a week's wages. If you need it – go for it. It's not sensible: it's fun. I love the flash, the opulence. This isn't the sixties – we're more geared to the positive. People OD-ing, lining up to throw up, all the ugliness – I have no time for that, it was a dark time. The sixties I want to remember is *The Man from Uncle*, James Bond, Dean Martin . . .'

To imagine, though, that Dianne Brill is quite the air-head she appears, would be to miss the point entirely. She is Miss Gung-ho America. Her visual, as she calls it, is 'totally theatre'. As the daughter of a shrewd real estate developer from Racine, Wisconsin and Tampa, Florida, she has what she likes to term 'a buying and selling merchant mentality'.

This is the girl who hired Cuban wedding halls in Tampa, brought in reggae bands and charged the kids $3 a head. ('I was a Chiefette and to be a Chiefette at Camberlain High was *wonderful*. I was supposed to be the Prom Queen but I was accused of kissing some guy when he was doing something footballish and I was kicked off the squad. The point is this: I'm still a cheerleader. Do you know what I'm saying?')

She is also the canny trader who tottered into small Cuban stores and bought up the entire stock – forties, fifties, basements full. A wink here, a big, open smile there. 'I've always been good at schmoozing.' She changed the clothes along the way:

a leather collar on a fat man's suit, studs, tucks, natty Dianne embellishments.

Moving to Manhattan was the obvious step. 'I might be big and blonde which is a Los Angeles thing, but my head is pure New York. Do you know what I'm saying? It's the survivor mentality, I won't stop, I won't go down with the ship. New York embraces that. I didn't plan to become this Queen of the Night thing. Work is part of me so I've made me part of my work. I give a lot, I really work at having fun. I'm a vegetarian, I don't drink and I don't do drugs – that probably helps. And sexuality is a good soother – but not sleazy. You don't find me sleeping around.'

What you have to know about the eighties and Downtown, says Dianne Brill, is that it is about having fun. 'If you can buy a diamond for $500 as big as a pin head or a zircon for $500 as big as a chestnut, the new money will buy the zircon because it's bright and it flashes.' Miss Brill's lurex tuxedos are full of shiny zircon buttons.

'The work I do is brilliant – I'm so proud of what I'm doing. It's a woman designing clothes for a man she sees as a hero.' And in case you still do not know what she is saying: 'I think I am America. It's America's time again. That's where the streets are paved in gold.'

Ronald Reagan's America, maybe – hardly Louis Farrakhan's.

7 November, 1985   **Linda Blandford**

Opening our eyes to Tripoli

It floated down into a wet, misty English morning, more like a dove descending than the bat out of hell we knew it to be. This was the first F-111 to be filmed returning to base, splashing down at Lakenheath at 7.30 a.m. The BBC had counted them out, and now it was counting them back.

Though when they had done their counting on Monday, and filmed the bombs going aboard, the truck carefully positioned to block the camera's view, the story was still – as it was on ITN's *News at 10* – that this was probably the NATO exercise it was said to be. Only the presence of so many KC-10 tanker aircraft at Upper Heyford alerted the TV crews that the exercise story might be a blind.

The key images kept changing. But just after nine, in the BBC's extended *Breakfast Time* we had the first film of casualties in a Tripoli hospital, with wounded children, and one grotesque figure, missing his left arm, his – or her – face wound in bandages like a fencing mask.

It was an image that clearly upset the unhappy Sir John Biggs-Davison, doggedly saying we would have to wait for the Prime Minister's statement, but admitting that he wanted surgery on terrorism, not butchery. And which was this? asked Peter Snow. 'I am deeply disturbed by the nature of this operation . . .'

16 April, 1986 **Hugh Hebert**

Notes on the nature of American blood

I have long had difficulties with that very large term, the Third World. So I have been attending very carefully to our broadcasting media, in the hope of being instructed.

I now understand that there is no simple category, a unified Third World, stretching from Guatemala to Indonesia. On the contrary, there are three distinct categories: 1) deserving wogs; (2) loyal wogs; and (3) bad wogs.

The first are a proper object for our concern. They have pot-bellies, running sores, and they are deserving objects for our charity. They are too demoralized and hungry to cause us any more bother than a vague sense of guilt, and it is merit-worthy to save some of them from starving.

Loyal wogs are those whom we help in other ways, but especially by sending them machine-guns, tanks, fighter air-craft, helicopters, handcuffs, explosives and military advisers. They pay for these either with oil or by taxing their own deserving wogs into deeper poverty. We give this help on condition that they use these weapons only against their own people.

Bad wogs are another matter. They may buy weapons from the Other Side or each other, and they point them at loyal wogs. They have even been known to point them at us.

They do not defend the values of the Free World. In fact, they don't take much interest in our world at all. They are descendants of those archetypal wogs, the Senyussi of the Libyan desert, who, in the midst of World War II, would steal the uniforms of the rival armies from the washing-lines, not caring if they were British khaki or German field-grey. After the war they became scrap merchants, and made a profit from the burned-out tanks littering the desert.

Bad wogs can be assumed to be terrorists. A few of them are. Most of that few come from the miserable enclosures in which, for three generations, Palestinians have lived an embattled existence. Others may have been Libyans, usually in pursuit of Libyans of other factions, carelessly killing anyone else who might get in the way.

But it is not necessary to *prove* that any Libyan was behind any particular act of terror. For their guilt is self-evident from their bad woggishness. This consists in *not* asking us for our charity, in buying arms from the Other Side, and in making windy speeches in which they say they don't give a fart for the Free World.

Such behaviour could be contagious. Clearly, it must be punished.

One way might have been through process of international law, followed by sanctions. But there is a difficulty here. Both the United Nations and the international court at the Hague might wish to proceed to a verdict by way of some evidence. An indictment of bad woggishness would not be enough. But the United States had not yet been able to come up with (or manufacture?) anything better than that.

There is a trouble also with sanctions. These might have been bloodless, but they would have occasioned extreme anguish inside the stock market, and the twisting of the guts of Western finance. Libyans belong to the sub-species of wogs known as

Arabs, whose oil revenues now float the little barks of Western banks and property markets. If the Arabs drew the plug, how many Western financiers would be flapping about in the tank like sharks out of water?

Sanctions would hurt 'us' more than it hurt 'them'. They are therefore unthinkable. They would constitute a Threat to Property, Banking and Order. It is much better to go out after wog blood.

Wog blood, it should be understood, is of a different colour and quality to Western blood. This has been clear for several centuries. It is an inferior sort of stuff.

This was demonstrated recently in the Gulf of Sirte. The Americans sank two patrol boats, full of wogs. Twelve survivors from one were picked up, several days later, from a drifting raft by Spanish fishermen. (You can count on dagos or wops to come to the aid of wogs.) Twelve more – if I remember rightly – may be drifting dead on a raft to this day. They were never found.

I write, 'if I remember rightly'. The reason I do not recall these matters clearly is that our media – and especially the BBC news programmes – say almost nothing about them. This week's bombing of Tripoli and Benghazi (we are told) was in 'self-defence', and in 'retaliation' for the killing of one American serviceman in a West Berlin disco. I am sorry about that American death (in which there may or may not have been Libyan complicity) but I do not understand why that death required the bombing of a sleeping city, whereas those twelve other deaths have now been dumped in the memory-hole.

Well, in fact, *I do* understand. Just as there are three categories of Third Worlders, so there are three categories of human blood. 1) US citizens' blood; 2) Allied blood; 3) Commie and wog blood.

Commie and wog blood has so low a value it does not even merit a quotation on the Wall Street exchange. Allied blood rises and falls according to the state of the diplomatic market. But American blood has a supreme and sacred value, and it is always way up there, right at the top of the market. One single drop of American blood – or even one American hostage whose blood might be at risk – licenses the sacrificial bombardment of any number of wogs or gooks.

The Americans behave today as if they were awarded by God some unique privilege above all other nations, just as the British once did in high Palmerstonian days. To mention this self-evident fact results in everyone clucking their tongues and saying one is 'anti-American'.

I like many Americans very much, and I like the gutsy and capable American peace movement most of all. But insofar as Reagan and Weinberger *are* the public face of 'America', I am decidedly anti-American.

Even the loyal Sir Robin Day, on Tuesday's *World at One*, went so far as to suggest that the bombing of residential Tripoli was, maybe, 'clumsy'? I think it was bloody-minded, barbaric, racist, blindly arrogant, and will breed nothing in the world but ill. I don't know by what right the Americans bombard and bomb around the Mediterranean. I think that West Europe has got to get out from under American domination, just as East Europe must get out from under the Soviet Union, and we should work on common strategies to do it. I wish that – not 'Americans' – but their bombers, battleships and bases would go home.

Mrs Thatcher and her lot astonish me. I knew they were destroying Britain but I did not know that the loss of any sense of national honour had gone that far. After selling out British industry and high technology with a secret 'Memorandum of Understanding' to Star Wars, they now let the scraggy wog-hunting US eagle roost on our pastures and lime our fields.

It is not only that Mrs Thatcher signed away the last shred of our sovereignty. She also consigned, in that 'clumsy' moment, 5000 British citizens in Libya to a potential hostage situation, and doomed British diplomatic and commercial relations with great parts of the Arab and Moslem world.

I knew this nation was sick, but not as sick as that. CND is calling out a sit-down demonstration, at 12 on Saturday, in Grosvenor Square. I don't know whether the traditions of our people have crumbled away into nothing but cynicism and the hunt for money. Maybe a jolt could stir us up again. In 1956, when Eden went wog-hunting at Suez, protesting people packed into Trafalgar Square and (after a diplomatic pause) Eden retired 'ill'. But, then, on that occasion, the United States took the side of upholding a rule of international law.

This time both lots (American and British) of self-styled upholders of the 'Rule of Law' have chosen to exchange it for the arbitrary Rule of War. The British part is the more shameful part of the two. The American eagle flies off from our land, and returns, satiate and gorged with blood. We don't even get any blood; we just get bloodied with the guilt. Is there no way to make Mrs Thatcher follow Eden, and retire 'ill'?

18 April, 1986   **E. P. Thompson**

Don't travel to Moldavia

The basic mistake, and I make no bones about this, was to hold the royal wedding in a greenhouse.

The Ewings of Dallas, in their homely Texan fashion, held their weddings in the garage driveway, a fact which used to make Terry Wogan, who is as *comme il faut* as they come, to draw in his breath a bit smartish.

One liked to think that the Carringtons of *Dynasty* (BBC-1) were a cut above this kind of thing. No windswept Weetabix on gale-lashed patio for them. No frenzied attempts to drown in the bijou pool. The Carringtons live in a style which would knock spots off Suleiman the Magnificent. The *mice* eat brie in what everyone calls The Carrington Mansion.

It must have been all the more a blow, arriving in Moldavia for the wedding of Amanda Carrington and Crown Prince Michael, to find the ceremony was being held in some kind of lean-to conservatory.

Well, one could have warned them. If it's not the greenfly, it will be the press lightly disguised as potted palms. In the event it was the Moldavian Popular Front, swinging through the glass, firing from the hip.

The Archbishop of Moldavia (looking divine in crushed loganberry and gold) was celebrating the marriage in a form unfamiliar to me and had just got to an interesting bit about 'Give them the dew of heaven on high and the fatness of the earth. Fill their houses with wheat and oil . . .'

Meanwhile, in a Moldavian hovel, Dex was lashed to a rude stool, the prisoner of the chap in the black eye-patch who spends so much time peering through palace keyholes, a vocation for which one feels he was physically ill-fitted. 'What do you want?' asked Dex, straining at his bonds. 'I shampooed it in one word. Destiny!' replied the peeper, flashing his remaining eye.

Terrorists in camouflage jackets were flitting rather conspicuously among the potted royal azaleas . . . Dex strained at his stool . . . they tip-toed along the palace tiles . . . with one

"I'd love to direct you to Buckingham Palace but I'm afraid one of your F-111s was even more off target than has previously been admitted . . ."

17 April, 1986

27

mighty bound he was free . . . they crashed through the conservatory windows . . . Dex was coming strongly up the straight but was evidently not going to be among the first three.

When the Moldavian Popular Front arrives uninvited, that's when you know who your friends are. Stephen, Denver's leading gay, flung the Archbishop to the floor. Luke, Stephen's lover, threw himself on Claudia, Stephen's wife. Blake crawled on to Krystle. Prince Michael did a dramatic backward crash on to Amanda. Jeff pulled down Lady Ashley, who, game girl, was taking pictures of it all. Dex was engaged in mortal combat with the eye-patch. And the King of Moldavia, seizing an unrepeatable opportunity, hurled himself on Joan Collins.

There they lay, two by two, dead to the world or, of course, just dead. It looked a scene of marked impropriety, like something out of *The Last Days of Pompeii*.

We will pause here while I pay a deserved tribute to shoulder pads. Shoulders are being worn wide in Denver this year. The inspiration seems to be American football and all the leading ladies of Dynasty have difficulty coming through a door head on. This fashionable whim was gloriously vindicated in Moldavia. You could see the force of the bullets being absorbed by the shoulder pads or harmlessly deflected on to some minor, male member of the cast.

Personally I think it is all for the best. A girl like Amanda, accustomed to The Carrington Mansion, would never have been happy in a house filled with wheat and oil.

Those of you who are tearing out your hair in handfuls over the problem of Christmas presents can replace the tufts right now. Amaze and delight your friends with a video of Bobby Ewing's Funeral, a seasonal and acceptable present and, at £6.99, cheap, thank God.

The new series of *Dallas*, which Thames TV and the BBC have been snarling over for twelve months, has been snatched from under their noses by a very cheeky dog indeed, Prestwich Holdings, and a video of the first two episodes, *Bobby's Obsequies* and *The Reading of the Will*, is on sale at Woolworth.

You will be delighted to know that Miss Ellie, Barbara Bel Geddes, looks just the way she used to and Little Christopher (accurately described by the defunct Bobby on *The Wogan*

Show as 'That homely mutt') is changed out of all recognition and can now be viewed without pain.

'No one can replace him,' said JR as they buried Bobby in the back garden. I wouldn't be too sure about that. There's a new Ewing in the cast list – Jack, played, if you can believe me, by someone called Dack Rambo.

14 December, 1985   **Nancy Banks-Smith**

Getting away from it all

So. Well, well. Long time no see. And how are *you*, fresh from your first communion with a nuclear cloud? None the worse for it, are we, aside from a temporary tremor of the hands and a quite controllable facial tic. Didn't do us a bit of harm, silly old us.

Soon they'll be telling us there's nothing like a burst of radiation for pepping up the system. A great all-round tonic. 'Dear Comrades, I have found your Eau de Chernobyl a most efficacious laxative and have been more than regular in my habits ever since.' But we mustn't depend on Russia for free hand-outs. Next dose: Sellafield. Buy British, I say.

Besides, what's a bit of radiation when we've got Colonel Gadafy prowling the planet? Mad Dog Gadafy, from whence all terrors come. Mr Reagan said so in Bali while the Indonesian army handcuffed his journalists and dragged them away. He said so in Tokyo, while rockets knitted in some Japanese suburb whistled past his left ear. Mrs Thatcher said so in Seoul, while Korean policemen played skittles with Korean students.

She's got herself a brand-new coiffure, did you notice? A sort of hairy Britannia's helmet, bullet-proof I dare say. It fits snuggly down over her shell-likes to block out all the whingeing from us wimps. Oh, those Winds of Freedom – they've given me *shocking* heartburn.

What a spring. I bet you didn't know the Yanks knew they were going to use our bases to hit Tripoli. Not the Pentagon Yanks, the ordinary ones, like you and me. I got two phone

If . . .

Steve Bell

calls the evening before, one from New Mexico, one from California. It'll be tonight, they said, get your earplugs in. Come *on*, I said, you've got it wrong, guys. Mrs T may be trigger-happy, but she hasn't completely mislaid her marbles. She's gaga about him, yes, but she's not going to let him have all his own way.

Next morning, switch on the telly, *wumph*, she had. My American mates phoned again. They've promised to let me know earlier next time, so I can keep that poor Sir Geoffrey informed. Now my daughter's phoned from Italy. Nothing in the shops but bread and eggs, all veg and milk banned, everyone's sitting in the bath all day washing radiation out of their pores. I tell you, I wouldn't know anything if it weren't for me little black blower.

I've already suffered one side-effect from it all – the rendering down of my vocabulary to the approximate dimensions of a baby's shrunk sock. To our leaders, as seen on TV, I have shouted 'You're all mad, insane, barking, mad, barking, insane' at least 1000 times daily over the past few weeks – is this a record? Chernobyl required the stretching of these meagre resources to include Russian leaders who, like men who have let off a lethal fart, stood about fanning themselves and hoping nobody'd notice. What's Russian for barking?

But it's a silver cloud that has no fall-out. The Soviet vow of silence gave our own apparatchiks a heaven-sent chance to look positively chatty. 'Couldn't happen here in this open society,' they rabbited on, 'and do shut up, with all due respect, about Dungeness.'

One of them announced on the radio: 'We are in a nuclear-safety situation.' Ah, I thought, so that's our trouble, I should have known. Help, I've had a high-level dose of toxic safety, thank you and goodnight. For the last little while we've all been trapped inside a Raymond Briggs cartoon. 'What's 500 times the usual radiation level, dear?' 'I'm not sure, dear, but they'd tell us if it was bad.' 'Shall I boil the water, dear?' 'Yes dear, why not.'

Meanwhile, there's always the Royals to cheer us up when the going gets a tiny bit critical. We can watch Poland on the news, banning all leaf veggies, issuing iodine pills, but then, two items down, there's our lovely Princess Di planting a tree. God bless this sceptred isle. We can rush about all day, pulling our forelocks to Mr America, stoking up his fires, massaging unguents into his body politic and throwing ourselves across the Atlantic puddle so he doesn't have to get his tootsies wet. But, on our day off, we're allowed to look at pictures of Randy Andy and wait with bated breath for this summer's biggest treat – Miss Fergie's wedding dress. And we're still all a-tingle from singing Happy Birthday, dear Ma'am. How much more excitement can the human frame take?

The thing is, what I've been wondering is, what's it like if you live in the heart of the country? Does all that Nature everywhere make you feel better? Do Mr Vole and Mrs Squirrel and flocks of feathered friends have a calming effect on the stomach ulcers? Perhaps if I read Marcus Aurelius while nothing more dangerous than robins fly overhead I could become the Patience Strong of the Nuclear Age, composing ditties on the age-old wisdom of country folk. Aargh oi, we do be saying, Strontium 90 at night, shepherd's delight. That kind of thing.

Anyway, I'm going to try it out. Next week, arising as a phoenix from the London ashes of finger-licking chicken boxes and old pizza wrappers, I shall wend my way to the back of beyond, to a remote cottage at the edge of a forest at the foot of moors, far from the reach of mains gas or electricity or water or even mains telly. From thence, I shall send weekly summer bulletins to you in the front line, informing you of whether or not the world looks a saner, more comprehensible and rather less impermanent residence there, away from it all.

Come to think of it, what do we drink if we don't drink mains water? Oh yes, I can hear the sound of that babbling brook now. Click click click click . . .

13 May, 1986   **Jill Tweedie**

Chernobyl and market forces

The withered old crone in a floral headscarf gazed blankly at us across the counter piled high with succulent red strawberries. They glistened in the thin light of the covered market as we asked her where they had been grown. 'Krasnodar,' she muttered.

Her neighbour, an ebullient young Georgian with a thick stubble, chuckled villainously and said, 'Tell them the truth, Granny. They're from Chernobyl.'

Across the aisle, a Japanese family was waving a portable geiger counter over some plump tomatoes. In the Moscow free markets, the Japanese are called the 'tiki-tiki' these days from the characteristic clicking of the little radiation monitors they carry.

Until Chernobyl, the free markets were one of the great pleasures of living in Moscow. At the big central market, beside the old circus, you could smell the flowers as you pushed through the doors from the street, and then you walked into a blaze of colour. Past the flowers, you realized anew each time that the Soviet Union was a vast continent of a country, so big that something was always in season somewhere. There were the huge apples from Alma-Ata near the Chinese frontier, the little sweet tomatoes from the Black Sea coast, the pomegranates from Georgia, and the heaped mountains of raw honey and fresh thick cream and the pickled garlic from the collective farms around Moscow.

It is the kind of sight to stun any tourist into total silence. Our preconceptions about the Soviet Union do not prepare us for this sudden evidence of plenty where the rationing works by the good old capitalist method of price. In winter the tomatoes are £20 a kilo and a single cucumber can cost £8. And you pay the money readily for the sudden delight of crunching something fresh and green after weeks of potatoes and cabbage.

Our own favourite market is a relatively new building of

aggressive concrete, looking a bit like a flying saucer. It is known as the Cherry Tree Market, after the traditional name of this suburb of Moscow, which has now been burdened with the formal title of Brezhnev Borough. Muscovites, being a nostalgic and deeply romantic folk, pay about as much attention to the new name as the British do to the monstrous names bestowed on our old counties by local government reorganization.

We like the Cheremyshinski market because of the long lines of suckling pigs and the arrays of fresh-skinned rabbits of all sizes. 'Listen, comrade, buy the mum and dad and I'll throw in the two little ones for free,' they say.

There was the day we haggled to buy half a cow, to take it home and carve it up ourselves and put the joints in the freezer. That was when we got to know Misha the cripple, the uncrowned king of the market, who could get anything at a price. He hobbled arrogantly into the crowd of stall-holders around us as we poked and punched at the various carcasses, informed us that the price per kilo was fixed, but the weight was subject to negotiation, and winked hugely. After the crackdown on the black marketeers, Misha has been lying low lately.

This is the market where the little old men pull beautifully-painted wooden eggs from the pockets of their old army greatcoats and show you the half-forbidden religious images they have painstakingly inscribed.

The chickens here taste the way chickens do in dreams of childhood, and there is one stall where you can buy old medicine bottles filled with *adjika*, the fiery tomato purée they make down in Georgia. For a feast, buy a chicken and some *adjika* and some salads, and then go to the back door of the Pitsunda restaurant and get some fresh, hot *lavash*, the flat Georgian bread.

They know our children in the market, and Katie skips down the aisles to the women who call her Katyusha and give her tastes of honey and cream. And when they weigh vegetables, they usually throw in an extra one 'for the baby'.

But the markets now are sombre places. Prices have never been so low, as the foreigners stay away and even the Russians are being cautious. The stalls are filled with cherries and strawberries, and the sellers point to the labels on the boxes that say they come from Bulgaria, or swear that they were grown in the Moscow region.

The newspapers say that everything is being tested before being allowed on sale, and the police check the passports of the sellers to see if they come from the 'special zones'. But then we have all seen the discreet transactions that take place behind the market or near the Kievsky station where the Moscow salesmen buy boxes of produce, no questions asked.

The free markets have been little oases of colourful, care-free capitalism in the Soviet Union, and the entrepreneurial instinct is not going to be crushed by a little thing like radiation. So for months to come, one of the delights of living in Moscow will have to be forgone.

16 June, 1986   **Martin Walker**

Back room boys

It is 7.15 a.m. in Los Angeles and the sun is just rising behind the bland curved form of the Century Plaza Hotel. On the Avenue of the Stars a compact man with a neatly trimmed fair beard stands poised in his uniform of blue blazer, buttoned down shirt and khaki pants.

It's Gary Wright's job to squeeze 267 rebellious hacks, forty or so secret service agents and a dozen press aides on to four buses lined up at the kerb. Running like a whippet, he darts from bus to bus with the anxious look of a man who carries the weight of the world on his shoulders.

Wright and his colleagues in the White House travel office are the logistics whizzes of presidential trips, marshalling their clients with sergeant-major like cruelty.

Baggage calls are sadistically arranged for 5 a.m. (often five or six hours before planes are airborne), travellers are squeezed into buses like sardines with their luggage on their laps and made to stand in queues on sizzling airport aprons from Honolulu to Bali while pedestrian security men, with eyes in the back of their heads and hearing aids crackling in their ears, gingerly open deodorant aerosols with the delicacy of plastic explosive.

The Reagans and their entourage travel in a style which would make a medieval court seem modest and the Field of the Cloth of Gold look like a sodden church picnic in Margate. When the president goes on the road so does the whole of the White House. Most of the secret service, its own immigration and Customs officials, medics, and great chunks of the State Department, too.

When the First Lady, Nancy Reagan, has her own schedule the planes and staff double, too. A quick perusal of a White House phone list in Bali – which included everyone from Gary Wright to the tanned and testy Secretary of State, Mr George Shultz – revealed no fewer than 250 names, excluding the secret service contingent.

After all, if a nuclear reactor goes up in Chernobyl (or as one White House wit put it, an experiment to cook Chicken Kiev gone wrong) the President must respond. The electronic ears of the television networks flapped excitedly when they caught sight of Admiral John Poindexter when the dreadful news from north of Kiev crackled across their receivers beneath the shining wings of Air Force One at Honolulu.

Poindexter, a phlegmatic man hiding behind wire glasses, has been begged, cajoled and told by the blond, blow-dried deputy press secretary, Larry Speakes, and his balding, round-faced Armenian right-hand man, Ed Djerejian, to perform for the White House press or at least take their phone calls. 'But John's just not comfortable with that,' said one official.

In answer to the Kiev questions, Poindexter, a nuclear physicist turned White House insider, answered in characteristic verbose style with a disingenuous shrug of the shoulders even as Tass was reporting the incident.

Back on the press freedom express, the Pan American charter carrying two reluctant Australian broadcasters to their destiny with the American networks, Ed Djerejian shows no such reluctance to talk.

A career diplomat, who moved from State to the White House eighteen months ago, Djerejian has taken up foreign

"We have sought advice from the United Kingdom and they suggest we change the name."

30 April, 1986

policy communications in the Reagan Administration. He has put the White House press office into the national security net, providing it with access to the confidential intelligence and cables which are at the core of policy-making. With this tool his boss Speakes, an accented Mississippian who treats foreigners as if they are from another planet, has managed a power grab from the State Department spokesman, Bernard Kalb, an NBC man who has demonstrated that a coiffed TV correspondent without his camera and producer is as inarticulate as the next man. Kalb's sole contribution on the Reagan island-hopping across the Pacific was to intrigue fellow travellers by wearing a high-collared sleeveless jacket borrowed from Chairman Mao's wardrobe.

Djerejian, dapper in long double-breasted blazer and pleated trousers, briefs on Chernobyl by the 'First Class Only' lavatories. Where Poindexter feared to tread Djerejian jumps in, chicken Kiev and all. He is also point man in dealing with the Australians, who are suddenly beginning to relish their fame.

At Guam, home to the gung-ho Vietnam B-52s, the smallest and shabbiest Marine band in the United States beats out 'Hail to the Chief' as a typhoon plays havoc with the flags. Down the steps of Air Force One behind Shultz and Regan, waddle their lumpy white-haired wives, followed by Rawhide (the secret service code for Reagan) and the anorexic First Lady whose face, in the words of one network correspondent 'simply won't take any more lifts'.

On the plane the mobile White House, with its travelling communications complex, has been in national security mode with Reagan, Regan, Poindexter and Shultz conferring and throwing out hints to the travelling death-watch pool.

Between Guam and Bali, Billy Dale, the transportation chief, and his team panic. There is a danger that Air Force One will arrive before the press charter. The pilot opens the throttle, the rattling jumbo soars to 35,000 feet, races to 620 mph at an extra fuel cost of $700,000. Inside the cabin panting network crews, lights ablaze, are almost sitting on the laps of the Australians – Evelyn Waugh's scoop lives on as Baliburg hits the inside pages around the world.

Gaston Sigur, the inept assistant secretary of state for Far Eastern affairs, a short man with the charm of a British Rail porter, seeks to show that the human rights in Indonesia are all right after all. The Balinese gods extract their revenge. Sigur emerges from Air Force One in Tokyo sporting a large bandage on his head, having slipped and fallen in the bath. Maybe it was a Suharto plot.

In the press office boiler room the work never stops. Connie Romero, large-framed and friendly, is the champion of the transcripts, whipping Shultz briefings off the presses at Olympic speeds. Joan Trumps, the sexy blonde stenographer, turns the heads at poolside in the briefest of bikinis. Jeannie Winnick, blonde, with bright pink cheeks and always friendly, marshals the press troops, with good humour, through a maze of events with radio receivers at the ready.

These are the visible heroes and heroines of the Reagan entourage. But there are also the unseen. These range from the pilots of the C-140 Starlifter transports carrying Huey helicopters and armoured limousines to remote staging posts across the Pacific to the army of secret servicemen who make sure that the local security forces are doing their job. As secret serviceman Bob Snow puts it, 'the rustic stop in Bali is infinitely more manageable than the urban jungle of Tokyo'.

As for the Gipper (the football hero movie character Reagan has melded into his own), he's looking good. With the help of a slow jet across the Pacific, the days of sand, surf and coconut tossing in Hawaii, Bali high, with 250 aides and their briefing books, he's ready for the fray, or as ready as he will ever be.

5 May, 1986 **Alex Brummer**

A sudden accident in Smolensk Square

As far as the Soviet Foreign Ministry is concerned, the British Empire is alive and well and has a white skin. After all, what else do Britain, Canada, New Zealand and Australia have in common, that they should still all come under the responsibility of what the Soviet Ministry of International Affairs calls its second European department?

This is an internal administrative arrangement of the Soviet Foreign Ministry that is unchanged from Tsarist days. And one sees the pre-revolutionary inheritance in the way the rest of Europe is organized for Soviet diplomats. In the third European department, which brings in East and West Germany and Austria, we recognize the old Reich of Bismarck's day, with Austria tacked on after it lost the Habsburg empire.

But the Habsburg empire still lives in the fifth European department which covers Hungary and Yugoslavia and the long Balkan tail stretching through Romania and Bulgaria and down to Cyprus. The fourth department is made up of the Czechs and the Poles, and the first department has an old Bourbon empire feel about it, with France and Spain and Italy and the Benelux lands.

This would be so much historical curiosity were it not for the way that bureaucracies, particularly Soviet bureaucracies, tend to work. When a bright young Soviet graduate begins his career in the Foreign Ministry, he becomes a member of one of these departments, much in the way that Oxbridge undergraduates become members of particular colleges, with all the loyalties and personal contacts and house spirit that tend to accrue.

Bright young men look for go-getting patrons in their own departments, and rising administrators look for teams of loyal aides who will rise with them.

The British Foreign Office has something of the same, in the way the place sometimes feels like the Arabists versus the rest, and we are starting to realize how much impact the house spirit of the Foreign Office Arabists has had on British Middle East policy.

For Britain's Arabists, the bond is the language, which most of them earned at that curious little school in the Lebanon which has probably played a more formative role in British policy than the think-tank of St Antony's College, Oxford.

It is much the same in Moscow. The complexities of European languages and the specialist language courses for aspiring diplomats strongly reinforce the house spirit. And just now, house spirit is in pretty good form among the Soviet Euro-dips.

Take the German mafia, the boys from the third department. The official Soviet spokesman and the man who gives the regular briefings for the foreign press is German-speaking Vladimir Lomeiko, former head of the Novosti news agency in Bonn. The new head of Novosti, the main features press agency for the Soviet Union, and the organization which sponsors the guides for visiting western journalists, is Valentin Falin, the former Soviet ambassador in Bonn.

Then there is one of the new first deputy foreign ministers, Anatoly Kovalyov. His career is instructive. He joined the foreign service in 1948, and spent his first seven formative years in the third department, and also serving on the staff of the Soviet military administration in occupied Germany, and in the embassy in East Berlin. Back to Moscow as a counsellor in the third department before receiving the key promotion to the ranks of Gromyko's personal advisers.

The pattern is not entirely frozen. Kovalyov went on to run the first department in the late 1960s, concentrating on France as De Gaulle sidled away from Nato and began his own slightly premature ostpolitik with Moscow.

But the other newly promoted member of the German mafia, the forty-nine-year-old Yuri Kvitsinsky, was being groomed for his new job as ambassador to Bonn from his beginnings as a translator in the embassy in East Berlin back in 1962. For the next nineteen years he worked exclusively either in the third department in Moscow, or in the embassies in Bonn and East Berlin. An expert on Euro-missile negotiations, Kvitsinsky was the Soviet participant in the famous 'walk in the woods' that very nearly secured a deal back in 1982.

But it is not only the German mafia who have emerged well from the flurry of new appointments that is shaking up the Soviet Foreign Ministry. Another new Deputy Foreign Minister is Yuli Vorontsov, trained as a British specialist in the second department back in the 1950s, before going to the UN with the Soviet Mission, and then heading back to Moscow to work in the International Organizations Department as Moscow boosted its links with the UN and its agencies. He can now claim to be one of the few genuine generalists of Soviet diplomacy, having since served in the embassy in Washington, and as a highly successful ambassador in both India and France.

If there is anything in the recurrent rumour that President Andrei Gromyko will soon retire, to be replaced by current foreign minister Eduard Shevarnadze, then Vorontsov, still only fifty-six, will be one of the strongest in-house candidates from the professional diplomats, to succeed him. This is the reason, runs the gossip in Smolensk Square, home of the Foreign Ministry, why Vorontsov came back to Moscow as First Deputy Foreign Minister, rather than getting the Washington Embassy, the most prestigious ambassador's post of them all.

Significantly, the new Soviet ambassador to Washington, Yuri Dubinin, is himself part of the European mafia, from the first department, who spent most of his career in France and

Spain. He did his training at the Paris embassy, and stayed in Paris to work for Unesco, then shuttled back and forth between the Paris embassy and the first department staff in Moscow before being promoted ambassador to Madrid in 1978.

The rise of the European experts in Soviet diplomacy has been spectacular, after so many years when the specialists on America were the elite of the Foreign Ministry. Mr Gorbachev is known to think that Andrei Gromyko's long obsession with American affairs led to serious distortions in foreign policy. The pendulum is now swinging sharply in the other direction.

This is worth recalling as Mikhail Gorbachev makes his new proposals for European disarmament at the Warsaw Pact session in Budapest this week. Inevitably, Western commentators will make their ritual noises about 'Soviet strategy to divide Nato', and probably add that the Soviet leader is trying to repair the damage done by Chernobyl.

They may be right, but the recent reshuffles in the Soviet Foreign Ministry mean that we should start to look at Mr Gorbachev's European policy very much more seriously. After all, he is putting his best men where his mouth is.

11 June, 1986   **Martin Walker**

Congress for the contras

President Reagan, the great manipulator, has done it again. In spite of persistent majorities in the opinion polls against the arming of the Nicaraguan contras, he has persuaded more than half the United States Congress to go along with the plan. Perhaps it would have been different if Western European governments which disagree with his Central American policy had been less timid in declaring their views publicly. The feeling that Central America is the United States' backyard, in which it must be allowed to do what it likes, dies hard in the corridors of Whitehall, the Quai d'Orsay, and the Auswaertiges Amt. Chancellor Kohl, at least, might have said something, since it is only two weeks since twelve West Germans, kidnapped by the 'contras', were finally released. (Had twelve Americans been held hostage by guerrillas organized, financed, and armed by West Germany, one can imagine the cries of 'terrorism' which would have resounded from Washington.)

Perhaps protests from Europe would not have worked anyway. The mood in which the Congress and the President view Central America is now irredeemably suffused with the perceived need to stand tall against Communism, particularly Communism of the invisible variety, since that is the most dangerous kind. The less that other people seem to see the danger, the firmer and quicker the long trigger-finger must be.

By arming the contras the Congress has effectively declared war on Nicaragua. One of the smallest states on the continent is now under mortal threat from the largest. More young Nicaraguans will now be killed. Its economy will be further ravaged, and the pathetically low standard of living of its people will be reduced. At the diplomatic level the Congressional vote will snuff out the last flickering signs of life in the Contadora negotiations.

Nicaragua is in no way a threat to the United States. It has held elections which were freer of violence and less spoiled by intimidation, and which offered a wider range of ideological choices than most elections in the region. It has pledged not to accept foreign bases, either for nuclear or conventional weapons, on its territory and has offered to sign a treaty with the United States to that effect. Its only danger to Washington is that it sets an example of independence which has been lacking for decades in the Central American isthmus.

The definition of independence is that countries be able to choose forms of government which their neighbours object to. That is the fundamental principle which a majority in Congress has been unable or unwilling to understand or accept. Looked at in this light, it is hardly surprising that Mr Reagan was able to win his money for the contras. Most Congressmen have opposed him on pragmatic grounds. Will aid to the contras drive the Sandinistas into Moscow's arms? Is it the best way to put pressure on Managua? Should economic sanctions be allowed more time to take effect? Will American troops eventually be sucked in? Few Congressmen have dared to take a stand on

44

the basic issue of whether the United States has the right to interfere in a far-away country's internal affairs. Few have dared to say that Reagan is wrong.

27 June, 1986   **Leader**

US dismisses World Court ruling

The International Court of Justice yesterday ruled that US support to the contras in Nicaragua is illegal, and demanded that the US pay reparations to the Sandinistas . . .

In a sixteen-point ruling on a complaint lodged by Nicaragua, the judges rejected American claims of collective self-defence and found the US guilty of breaches of international law and the 1956 treaty of friendship between the two countries.

Three judges submitted dissenting opinions: Judge Oda (Japan), Judge Schwebel (US) and Sir Robert Jennings (Britain).

The US rejected the judgment, claiming that the Managua regime is a Soviet puppet . . .

28 June, 1986   **Martin Cleaver**

Nuclear steam source

These are trying times for Lord Marshall of Goring, chairman of the CEGB and supremo of most British nuclear power operations. It seems only yesterday that plain Walter Marshall was insisting that the American-designed Pressurized Water Reactors he so passionately advocates for Sizewell and elsewhere were quite different from the belching plant at Three Mile Island. Now he is putting as much distance as possible between Kiev and himself.

The other day he argued that the Russian reactor would never get a licence in Britain. In fact it was his paper in 1975 which gave the go-ahead to the Steam Generating Heavy Water Reactor, which shares a number of features with the Russian design. That was killed two years later – coincidentally at the time he lost his job as chief scientist at the Department of Energy under Tony Benn.

Brian Sedgemore, who was Benn's PPS, gave an extraordinary account of Marshall's rift with Benn in his book *Secret Constitution* (1980). According to this story, Benn was somewhat surprised to discover that Marshall had secured orders for twenty PWRs from the Shah of Iran on condition that Britain adopted the PWR as its first choice. Marshall reportedly spoke of Iran's new maturity and revealed that he was the Shah's nuclear adviser.

Marshall was returned to his old job as deputy chairman of the UK Atomic Energy Authority, where he gathered dust until his zeal for PWRs was recognized by the newly triumphant Conservative government. This infatuation had occurred a few years previously, by his own account, when his scepticism was swept aside after a lengthy investigation in the US.

This unshakeable attachment to an unproven concept – the US is looking to Sizewell to restore confidence – has a curious echo in his guttural Welsh account. While he was swatting for a first in mathematics at Birmingham University, he had told colleagues, he was so taken with the vocal tones of his East European contemporaries that he had adopted them ever since.

Benn once asked Marshall about the pro-nuclear lobby and, when his subordinate pleaded ignorance, is reputed to have remarked: 'Walter, you shave its chin every morning.' His relationship with Westinghouse, the PWR manufacturer, led to accusations in the House of Commons that he had a conflict of interest. Admirers of his persuasiveness point to his recent drink with Dr John Cunningham, who announced two days later that Labour could live with nuclear power.

Even his detractors do not doubt the sincerity of his belief in nuclear power. 'The trouble is he doesn't want the facts to intervene,' says one. 'He is not exactly known for his humility.' His aphorisms, however are legendary: 'It is a very dangerous thing to listen. If one listens one may be convinced' and 'Usually I say what I really think. It makes one so liable to be misunderstood.'

1 May, 1986   **Stuart Wavell**

Secret servant recants

To the sound of splintering closet doors, Sir Frank Cooper, the former Permanent Secretary of Defence, has come out for freedom of information and against Mrs Thatcher's conviction politics. Ninety and nine just persons shall rejoice that one sinner hath repented.

They will tearfully greet his indictment of the British political system as 'confrontational and evasive', fondly recalling that such epithets once mistakenly clung to Sir Frank himself. There was the misunderstanding during the Falklands conflict when he told the press on the eve of the San Carlos landings that there would be no D-Day operation. Later he explained that he meant an opposed landing, and anyway the speculation had been jolly helpful.

They will smite their foreheads joyfully at his utterance that media participation in the lobby system is 'a public disgrace', perhaps recollecting that as chairman of the D-Notice Committee he lauded the 'uniquely British' practice of journalists and civil servants sitting down to agree what to keep from the British public.

They will toast his call for a commission that will re-emphasize the integrity of civil servants and facilitate their movement to and from the Civil Service. Sir Frank, of course, did not enhance the service's reputation when he joined the board of Westland, one of the MoD's suppliers, barely nine months after his retirement in 1982.

Matters were not helped last year, when he became chairman of United Scientific Holdings in succession to Peter Levene, Michael Heseltine's controversial nominee for defence procurement. He is also deputy chairman of Babcock International and a director of N. M. Rothschild.

There is an assumption that, in common with other retired, instantly sweet mandarins, Sir Frank scorns the lower-middle-class upstarts now pulling the levers of power. However, he is the son of an area manager for Terry's chocolate and his scorn has been reserved for the inept. He regards himself as a Manchester radical and a provincial.

Short, stocky, pugnacious yet amiable, he set up talks with Provisional Sinn Fein in Northern Ireland, where Loyalists complained that Merlyn Rees gave him too much power. It was said that Rees had been his fitter when he was flying Spitfires and that their relationship had not altered. The truth was that Rees was his desk-bound squadron leader. Sir Frank, aged sixty-three, still seems immune to the G-forces of a violent turn.

13 March, 1986   **Stuart Wavell**

Remembering what lies beneath the Somme farmland

An officious, wavy-haired gentleman from the BBC yelled at a couple strolling along the lip of the crater: 'You! Move out of the way. We're filming.'

TV gentlemen do that the world over, unscathed. But an old Scotsman in full kilt roared at this one: 'Say please when you talk to people – and get your hair cut!'

We were with the army now, the stoop-shouldered remnants of Kitchener's Army, in the most intimate of yesterday's events forming the last big commemoration of the dead of the Somme battlefield in the lifetimes of its survivors.

Seconds later, a maroon went up in the summer sky, as it did at the same time seventy years ago, at 7.30 a.m. on July 1, 1916. In 1916, that was a signal for the detonation of four 60,000 lb landmines, one of which blasted the 90ft deep, 300ft wide crater on which the four hundred of us stood at La Boiselle. The explosion in turn was a signal for the offensive which brought 60,000 British casualties in its first hour and 1.2 million dead on both sides in four months.

That landmine did little good. Although the explosives for it were taken down the secret 250-yard tunnel, this was a few

48

dozen yards too far away to collapse the front line German trenches. But that was the story of the Somme.

Recently the great hole, in which brambles now grow, was bought by an Englishman, Richard Dunning, of Guildford, who did not want houses built on ground in which so many bits of human beings still lie. And yesterday a plain cross made from Tyneside wood was unveiled in homage to the regiment which perished around the village. A brief service began with a reading from the diary of Tom Easton, a nineteen-year-old, 'The great mine exploded at 7.30 a.m. . . . men fell on every side screaming from the severity of their wounds. Had they lived, would they ever have forgiven?'

A twelve-year-old boy, David Southworth, stared down at us and most sternly spoke two lines from the anti-war poet Siegfried Sassoon: 'Look down and swear by the green of the spring that you will never forget. Look down and swear by the slain of the war that you will never forget.' After this, the open-air congregation threw poppy petals into the crater and placed little wooden remembrance crosses all along its perimeter.

David's declamation was the closest anybody came yesterday to trying deliberately to make us feel chastened. The big event, led by the Duke of Kent, three and a half hours later beneath the great arch in the British Commonwealth cemetery at Thiepval was, if anything, upbeat in tone. Reading from the Funeral Oration of Pericles, the Duke said: 'In the hour of trial, the one thing they feared was dishonour . . . for the whole earth is the sepulchre of heroes. Monuments may rise, tablets be set up to them in their own lands, but there is an abiding memorial that no pen or chisel has traced. It is not on stone or brass, but on the living hearts of humanity.'

The seventy British and French veterans seated in places of honour in front of the Duke, Mr George Younger, the Defence Secretary, and French VIPs, had feared many more things than dishonour: death, mutilation, rats, separation from their loved ones and – as happened to them – the slaughter of much of their generation. But they looked on impassively and politely.

The service paper said: 'Tout le monde chante O God Our Help in Ages Past', and for a few moments it was possible to believe that much of Europe was here in spirit at least, reflecting on one of the twentieth century's great Golgothas.

Lutyens' 141ft high triple arch, inscribed with the names of 73,000 soldiers with no known grave, is flanked by sycamores, poplars, copper beeches and silver birches. But it still stands out starkly among the undulating folds of Somme farmland, waist high with young corn. A layman might say that the countryside was like Norfolk, rather flat. But to the veterans it teems with bridges, salients and redoubts and stumps of trees. 'The Somme doesn't look like anything terrestrial any more,' the French writer, Pierre Loti recorded at the time . . . 'a squashed brown mush into which everything sinks.'

In the past two days the little group of veterans with which I have travelled have found a live, earth-caked hand grenade in a potato field and enough serviceable barbed wire for Mr Rupert Murdoch to double his fortifications at Wapping. Two weeks ago another First World War body was discovered and the granddaughter was told that her missing relative had been traced at last.

'It is almost beyond comprehension,' the Army's Chaplain General, Archdeacon Frank Johnston, said in his sermon at Thiepval, 'the enormity of the losses, the horrendous suffering, the confusion, the awesome effect on those of us who stand here. What a person remembers makes him the kind of person he is.'

The Last Post, from the sound chamber of the arch, was played as perfectly as most of us will hear it in our lifetimes. But this congregation contained experts. 'It was a bit too slow at the beginning,' one veteran said afterwards. A piper followed with 'The Flowers of the Forest Are All Gang Awa', a lament written for the loss of the flower of Scots chivalry in the Battle of Flodden Field, in 1415. But it proved just as evocative of the flower of 1916.

It sent tears coursing down the faces of three old soldiers sitting in front of the Duke, then two ninety-year-old British survivors took two minutes to toil and sweat up the memorial's twenty-five steep steps alongside their French counterparts to lay a wreath 'To Our Comrades'.

The the war fractured other lives too. For the first time

yesterday Mrs Betty Bower, aged seventy-five, of Newcastle, laid the wreath at the foot of the arch bearing the name of her brother Ted killed at the Somme at the age of eighteen. She had only just found his name. 'It has been the dream of my life to do this,' she said. A few feet away another Newcastle woman, Mrs Annie Patterson, aged seventy-three, discovered the name of her father, Will Coulson, killed seventy years ago yesterday at the age of thirty-two, when she was three years old. 'I have found you,' she said to the name on the memorial bearing the names of 73,000 others. 'I have found you at last.'

She has the dimmest memory of her father going off to war. 'I remember I fell down the front doorstep and he ran and picked me up,' she said. 'You can tell from photographs that he loved holding me on his knee. To think of all the love and comfort I have missed all these years.'

2 July, 1986   **John Ezard**

Let the dead bury their dead . . .

Our text today is mass graves. Local authorities have to tell the Home Office by the end of the year where they would bury the dead millions in a nuclear war, but only the Isle of Wight, it seems, has conscientiously consulted people. This has landed Mr George Killoran of the IoW County Council in arguments. The Rev Colin Slough says: 'When I asked this interviewer whether he was really serious, and who would be left to do the burying, he replied that I was "one of the loony left CND mob" and got really upset. I told him to go.' Mary Winch, clerk in charge of Sandown and Shanklin cemeteries: 'I told him the whole idea was ludicrous, then he said something about my being in the CND and loony, so I showed him out smartish.' Peter Sheppard, superintendent-registrar of the Whippingham Crematorium: 'I had to point out that if there was a nuclear war there would be no gas, and we run on gas.' Mr Killoran: 'I am entitled to my opinion and I told them what I thought of them.' Most councils, it seems, have just shoved a pin in open spaces away from water supplies.

30 November, 1985 **Stephen Cook**

A hush all over the Wold

Though I regard my chunk of South Cotswolds – don't we all? – as a rare surviving stretch of authentic countryside, your authentic countryman is a rarer bird still to get in your sights. We are mostly cuckoos who have moved in. There's a poet with a loud and insistent call at the bottom of my valley; a tele-presenter haunts the old mill house; the casual drinker in the village pub is more likely to be a princess-watching photographer than a ploughman or even a pesticide expert.

It's been going on a long time. Romans, wool barons, rural architects, craft revivalists, crime writers, folklorists, royals, gold or silver handshake-clutchers, the immigrants have taken over in successive waves.

And yet, by the strangest of paradoxes, it's a stretch of country comparatively little known to the tourists. The new natives are cunning. Having discovered it they keep it to themselves. They give misleading reports, wrong directions, false telephone numbers if necessary.

They are helped by the way these small towns and villages mostly keep off main roads, tucking themselves away in the folds of undramatic but tricky hills. The grander tourist cars could hardly get down these lanes if they tried.

Yet within a few miles of the Cirencester–Stroud axis is a paradigm of England, its geography and history, its industrious past and resting present, even maybe its specialist future, and it all began early. The Romans built some of their glossiest villas here, equipped in some cases with a central heating system that drip-nosed English squires and farmers had to wait fifteen centuries to emulate.

Our industrial revolution came early, too. Watermills were busy here a thousand years ago, and after centuries of dis-

52

tinguished hand-weaving and clothmakers, craft-proud as any Fleet Street printers and no more eager to rush into the arms of a new technology, fought the power looms and went down with, so to say, all bobbins flying. A few up-market specialities survived – cassocks for the top clergy, pink for the better hunts, scarlet for guards, tennis ball covers, baize for casinos and important billiard halls.

And when they first began discussing a Channel Tunnel the speculators were also contemplating another and equally bold tunnelling project – the one burrowing through the Cotswold escarpment to link the Thames and the Severn by canal. An obvious difference between these two great enterprises was that in the case of the Thames–Severn canal they went ahead and built it.

The first boat went through the tunnel in 1789 and somebody ought to be thinking up a bicentenary celebration – perhaps involving the diligent bargees who had to push on the tunnel roof with their feet to propel their barges through those black two miles. It lasted through the following century but not much longer. The canal is now the most romantic of derelicts, a kind of elongated nature park like an Amazonian jungle, with the crumbling tunnel entrance at Sapperton a ceremonious ruin, a mini-Mycenae. That roof the bargees trod is now collapsed. The last person to go through the tunnel is dead. Shout into that dark throat and it's small wonder if you get strange answers.

Cirencester and Stroud, the two modestly sizeable towns in this Little England, are unmistakably Cotswold yet entirely different in mood and style. Cirencester (pronounced that way: the battle for the old and proper Ciceter is sadly lost) fancies itself more than a little, as befits the biggest ex-Roman town outside London. It's sitting on an achaeological fortune, all buried there in orderly Roman fashion under the living streets; so near, so unapproachable.

It has an Oxford Minor air; give the place a few spires, indeed, and it would dream modern Oxford right off the map. Its parish church, massively towered, would be another town's cathedral. The atmosphere is gentlemanly but ladies, you feel, are not discouraged as long as they wear sensible shoes. Polo is close at hand, so is the Agricultural College. When chaps in the bars mention Jane or Sal you can't always be sure whether it's a girl or a horse; best listen a bit before venturing to join in.

Prosperous but not ostentatiously so, Cirencester extends a welcoming hand to the tourists without actually waving. Stroud is different. Stroud, you feel, would jump up and down to bring them in but doesn't seem to have much in the way of expectations. It looks less well-heeled than its neighbour. Stroud could do with a morale-boosting publicity campaign starting with that great and unrivalled asset, its grand perch overlooking the Severn estuary.

Cirencester is flat-footed in comparison. Capital of the Cotswolds they may call it, but the town has practically slipped off the hills altogether and is in no position to look down on what once, riding so high and so splendidly against a surging sky, used to be called Strutting Stroud. I hope it will live to crow again.

Between the two, jigsawing one's way through switchback lanes to the north of the main road, is a tangled cluster of villages unexcelled even in the Cotswolds. They don't depend on charm for their appeal though they have it in abundance. They just look right – as if they'd always been there, as if they'd grown. An old man living in a fold of the hills near Sapperton once told me he'd found an axe-head in his garden, which confirmed his belief that there'd always been a human habitation there. I tactfully refrained from asking whether it had been embedded in a skull; in any case the hill folk are more hospitable now.

A great thing about this countryside is that you can walk almost anywhere; there's a wonderful freedom of footpath and parkland. So no snags, no grouses to report? Well, I'm not too fond of the way many ex-local pubs are being suburbanized in a bid for the family-outing trade, with carpets desecrating fine stone floors and a liability to be warned about mud on your boots. Walking may be OK by landowners and even farmers but some innkeepers tend to regard it as uncivilized.

And a grouse, just one, about the churches. They're wonderful, rich in fonts and carvings and Norman arches, yet human with it; but too often they're overwhelmed by shady Victorian glass. (Why on earth did they do it; why was it ever thought devout to grope your way to grace?)

They also go in for visitors' books and some of the comments, if you can read them in the gloom, suggest that for better or worse we lack a language of reverential awe. Nice, they record when confronted with medieval masterpieces of oak or stone. Really nice, restful. At Fairford, where the famous old west window depicts the tortures of the damned with a gusto too much for some stomachs, the commentators are unthrown. Beautiful, they find this visual nasty; delightful, gorgeous, stunning. And nice, really nice.

Another celebrated spot I wouldn't include in my list of personal favourites is Bibury, where shoals of trout in and out of trout farms and shoals of cars in and out of car parks confront each other helplessly. As a modern west window might well depict, it is hell to be on the main road.

My own top village is Chalford, teetering on its hillside where cars can't (or shouldn't) reach, old packhorse territory only suitable in our day for donkeys or for people prepared to spend their lives treading on each other's rooftops.

Runner-up, Bisley – not the shooting one but the handsome, hidden Gloucestershire Bisley, still looking much as it must have done when the Tudor legend of the Bisley Boy was born. This is a tale of renewed fascination now that royalty is showing such interest in this neck of the wolds. The story is that Henry, not best pleased at seeing the late Anne Boleyn's infant daughter around the court, sent the little Elizabeth for an indefinite stay at a house called Overcourt at Bisley – suitably located, from Henry's point of view, at the far edge of the known world. The child took ill and died, which her hosts naturally feared would be seen by the king as going too far. Desperately they hunted for a stand-in princess but no suitable girl was to be found. The only likely substitute was a bright red-headed boy, who was accordingly trained for the crucial part and played it for life with (give or take a few embarrassments like baldness and marriage phobia) resounding success.

Finally, Minchinhampton, looking so authentic that you keep expecting characters to walk on in Restoration wigs. They have forgotten to take down a notice saying that you can park your horses for two old pence or hire the town crier for sixpence. Mrs Siddons played in the theatre where the local dramatic society's jubilee show is called, pointedly, Three Score Years and Then?

A good question, many woldsters must be thinking. One answer may be found in a village bistro not far away. Will they at last be using those snails – a large, distinctively striped, local strain – said to have been introduced by the Romans for culinary purposes? A bit hard, perhaps, but the creatures have been living on us for the past fifteen centuries.

26 July, 1986   **Norman Shrapnel**

A very English trouble maker

On Tuesday, a small but distinguished contingent from a legion of friends and admirers will gather in an upstairs room in that unique festive temple of the British Left, the Gay Hussar restaurant in Soho, to honour the eightieth birthday of our most famous living historian, A. J. P. Taylor.

In the chair will be the former Labour leader, Michael Foot, who in a spirited tribute in a book* to be published to mark the occasion, says of Alan Taylor: 'No one ever knew better how to spur the excitement of history.'

He has published some thirty books, mostly histories, though three years ago there was his autobiography, *A Personal History*, a book full of unexpected joys. His grandfather, for instance, a Lancashire exporter, who hearing that war was imminent, angrily complained: 'Can't they see as every time they kills a German, they kills a customer' – the true voice, Taylor says, of old Free Trade Lancashire.

In *A Personal History* there is a picture of a book-case in his home in North London with his works filling the shelves. Some are translations, quite a few Japanese. One is in Serbo-Croat.

* *Warfare, Diplomacy and Politics. Essays in Honour of A. J. P. Taylor*, edited by Chris Wrigley, is published by Hamish Hamilton.

The author's name is translated on the spine because of the deficiencies of that language, as A. Dz. P. Taylor, rather than the familiar AJP.

He handles these books with some reverence. Each is a work of art. Even his indexes, which he does himself, are famous for their invention.

For instance:

Hailsham, Lord, only Lord Chancellor not at a university, 236; suggests agreement to differ, 330; pushes Sankey off Woolsack, 378.

Or even:

New Statesman, cannibalistic practice of, 310.

His favourite, still, is *The Troublemakers*: a book of turbulent radicals from the English provinces, Bright, Fox, and E. D. Morel, much in the mould of Taylor himself. His life of Beaverbrook – to whom, like Michael Foot, he was, despite all differences of background and political cast, devoted – pleases him also. 'I think I did him full justice, without doing him too much.' The autobiography he speaks of as if of a favourite child, born unexpectedly late in life.

Looking back, at eighty, he would not alter very much. Some of his judgments have changed. Lloyd George, whom he made a heroic figure in earlier books, seems less so now. 'Considerable ability . . . a remarkable career . . . certainly I regarded him as a hero and in *World War One* (his book on the first world war) I presented him in that way. But compared with Churchill, he was in many ways inferior.'

He had a mild admiration for Lansbury, the Labour leader of the early thirties, but that has faded now. And Attlee? 'Probably the best Labour leader we ever had. There was a simpleness about him. He was probably the only good Labour prime minister. I had a poor opinion of Bevin . . . I admired the way Attlee stood up to him.'

And Wilson? A severe disappointment. 'I even wrote a letter of congratulation when he became leader of the party,' Taylor recalls in *A Personal History*. 'One of the few shameful acts of my career.' A more memorable letter, sent when a lecturer at Manchester in 1938, congratulated Duff Cooper for resigning from the Chamberlain government after the Munich agreement.

No formal honours have rewarded his achievement. There is no knighthood, no Order of Merit – not that he would have taken them, of course. To a radical Socialist such as he, such things are preposterous, appropriate for major-generals perhaps, but not for him. No Oxbridge college offered him a headship (thank God, he would probably say). No university chair has come his way.

There was a visiting professorship at Bristol, late in life, thanks to the lately beleagured John Vincent. But Oxford, which might have sent for him, settled instead for safer, more conformist men.

But the world has given him recognition, in the most practical of ways. It listened to what he said. It read and bought his books. His *English History*, the twentieth-century volume completing the sequence of fifteen of the Oxford History of England, was an instant and continuing bestseller in paperback. People who, before, might have regarded history as too arid, too remote, decided, having tasted Taylor, that perhaps it was for them after all.

The style is unmistakable. Terse, peremptory, each short urgent sentence pushing on to the next. 'The continuance of the war was never formally debated. It was taken for granted. On 28 May Churchill met all ministers of Cabinet rank and after surveying the situation, remarked casually: "Of course, whatever happens at Dunkirk, we shall fight on." Ministers shouted, "Well done, Prime Minister." Some burst into tears. Others slapped Churchill on the back.'

When at last he permits himself a more expansive sentence, there is a delicious sense of self-indulgence about it, like a feast at the end of Lent. Some say this has to do with a long exposure to journalism: the *Guardian* under Crozier and Wadsworth; the more machinegun-like conventions of the Beaverbrook *Express*. Taylor doubts it.

The comparison he prizes is with Macaulay. Michael Foot, in the newly-published Festschrift, quotes Taylor at seventy-five: 'I have just read Macaulay's *History*, all five volumes of it. I am sometimes hailed as his successor. I only wish I were. In my opinion he was the best narrative historian there has ever been, and I am proud to follow in his footsteps.'

There is Macaulay too, in his vigour, his sense of occasion, his setting of the context in which great events occur. Taylor wishes what he writes to flow as freely as a novel. Staider historians have frowned on such ambitions. But this shameless popularizer did not even stop at that. He opened up a second front on television.

The conventions of today's television histories were eschewed. There were no visual aids, no notes, no denim-clad presenter striding meaningfully through a sequence of exotic locations, no treasures from the archives, no clips, even, from British Movietone News.

The style was precisely that of the lectures which had packed the Schools in Oxford week by week, while equally eminent colleagues mustered only a dedicated few. He spoke as simply as he wrote. His level gaze engaged the audience at home; after an hour's enthralment, he released it.

Taylor is the supreme exponent of history as accident. Where others see vast and cunningly-constructed edifices, the gradual fruition of great plans, the inexorable working out of deep subterranean forces, Taylor often sees principally chance.

'It is the fashion nowadays to seek profound causes for great events. But perhaps the war which broke out in 1914 had no profound causes. For thirty years past, international diplomacy, the balance of power, the alliances, and the accumulations of armed might produced peace. Suddenly the situation was turned round, and the very forces which had produced the long peace now produced a great war. In much the same way, a motorist who for thirty years has been doing the right thing to avoid accidents makes a mistake one day and has a crash. In July 1914 things went wrong. The only safe explanation is that things happen because they happen.'

Taylor believes that chance dominates history; his own life has been dominated by chance (the only safe explanation is that things have happened because they have happened). He did not set out to become a historian. His First at Oxford still bewilders him: 'I was not well-taught. I had no contacts with the kind of thing I was examined in.'

When he left university, he took work as an articled clerk in the office of his uncle, a solicitor. 'From the first day,' he writes in the autobiography, 'I realized that I had made a ghastly mistake. The work, such as it was, bored me and I spent most of the day in a corner of the office reading Dickens and books from the Times Book Club.'

Release came 'in an unexpected way' through a series of unplanned events which led through research to Vienna to his first serious historical work – and so on, with the usual heavy engagement of chance, to an assistant lectureship at Manchester University.

The pattern of his books is curious and accidental too – for a radical Socialist, so much of war, so little of the heroes of the Left. He has written a book on Bismarck, but no full life of Cobden or Bright. When that's put to him, he seems surprised, but accepts that it is so. Perhaps, he says, there are few great heroes of the Left. Often his books have occurred because someone else wanted them, or because some course of lectures evolved naturally into a book.

Even the television lectures were something of an accident. Taylor had been a regular performer in the combative, sometimes cantankerous group which launched the first great exercise in topical TV discussion. First on BBC, as *In the News*, and then on the independent channels as *Free Speech*.

It ran for years and kept the nation talking in the pubs till the television hierarchy found it an embarrassment and killed it. Too much trouble-making perhaps? 'I certainly hope so,' says Taylor gleefully.

But before the axe fell Taylor had been invited to deliver the Ford Lectures. 'One day,' he now recalls, 'I said to John Irwin (his producer), "I stand up and lecture without notes. Why don't you put that on TV?"

'He said, "That's quite impossible," so when I was giving the lectures, I said, "Come down and hear one." He came down and was entranced. He said, "Name half a dozen lectures and we can start next week." '

Taylor has been married three times. His first wife's infatuations with Dylan Thomas and Robert Kee are recounted with vivid anguish in the autobiography; his second wife, on her insistence, does not appear in the book at all. Now he is married to a Hungarian historian, Eva Haraszti. They live in what he calls 'a nearly perfect house' nestling between Tufnell Park and Hampstead Heath, for him as for Michael Foot, always a ready lure in his walking days, terminated now by the onset of Parkinson's disease.

His portrait of Eva is perhaps the most endearing sequence of the autobiography. How she was assigned during a conference of historians to guide him round Budapest; how he recognized her instantly (he was now in his middle fifties) as the love of his life; how they parted, and (with the characteristic intervention of Tayloresque chance) were reunited and eventually married.

They were in Hungary last Christmas, but he fears that with his infirmity his travelling life is over. His wanderings decorate his pages. He was in Russia as a young man, formed a close acquaintance with Czechoslovakia and Hungary, and became, he says, something of a hero in Yugoslavia, for his steady assertion of that nation's rights to Trieste.

As the war ended, he advised the Yugoslavs in their negotiations on the issue. 'The one time I ventured into practical politics,' he says. 'Nothing was achieved.'

Later in life he developed, again like Michael Foot, a passion for Venice. Still later, he took his grandchildren there 'in batches'. What puzzled him was that they left him in the evenings for an undisclosed attraction. What had brought him to Venice, when approaching sixty, was the Carpaccio exhibition of 1963. His grandchildren had found their own equivalent attraction: a hall full of slot machines, the finest, in their judgment, in the world.

But he has never been to America. He saw it once across a bay, while walking with Beaverbrook in Canada. Was that enough? 'More than enough. I can't think of anything else I would have wanted to see.'

The early books, reflecting his wanderings, are continental histories: *The Italian Problem in European Diplomacy*; *The Course of German History*; *The Habsburgs*; *Europe from Napoleon to Stalin*; *The Struggle for Mastery in Europe, Bismarck*. Only then comes a book called *Englishmen and Others*, with *The Troublemakers* close behind it.

Yet Taylor is the most essentially English of historians, born of that tradition of provincial English radicalism which *The Troublemakers* commemorates. That he has revelled in his role of public iconoclast, he would certainly not deny. But if so, as in his famous revision of accepted truths about Hitler and about Germany, which made *The Origins of the Second World War* so shocking and affronting to some – that was not out of a deliberate taste for causing trouble, but simply because he found that the facts were pushing him that way and he felt bound to follow.

Such are the joys and perils of an incurable non-conformity. As he wrote in his most cherished book: 'Conformity may give you a quiet life. It may bring you a university chair, but all change in history, all advance comes from non-conformity. If there had been no troublemakers, no dissenters, we should still be living in caves.'

22 March, 1986   **David McKie and Chris Cook**

Signing off

Security men gave a whole new meaning to the GLC signing-off after the farewell ceremonies at London's County Hall. Barely had the council's flag been lowered – with some difficulty, as it appeared to be stuck, requiring some last-minute jerks to release it (no offence meant, chaps) – and the crowd drifted away, than the removal of detachable GLC sign boards began. At two o'clock in the morning.

2 April, 1986   **Andrew Moncur**

Heseltine's hopes in the wilderness

Striking grandly into the wilderness, Michael Heseltine took no step backwards yesterday. He has two historic models before his eyes. The pedigree of each is dangerously flawed. But both match the scale of what he is attempting, which is now, as it was not a week ago, the destruction of Thatcherism and the maiming of its leader.

The first model is Heath. Michael Heseltine is Ted Heath with children and a pretty wife. He embraces all the policies Heath held dearest, and he has never been diverted from them in the decade during which they have been so unceremoniously buried. What Heath stood for, he has always believed, was effaced by the merest chance that the first 1974 election was held three weeks late. Heathism has never been proved wrong.

What Mr Heseltine means by this is three things. First, he has an overarching vision of a Europe which, if not quite a political entity of the kind Mr Heath has worked for, is an industrial collective equipped to fend off the Americans and the Japanese. This was one of his salient preoccupations at the Ministry of Defence. It is also why the job he would most like to have had is probably that of his pathetically crippled antagonist at Trade and Industry, Leon Brittan.

Secondly, and most Heath-like, he passionately believes in the duty of government to intervene directly in industry: in investment, in making choices, in backing winners, in representing a corporate national interest. He reckons that anyone who does not see this is suffering from a species of insanity. Six years ago, when I ventured to suggest to him that Mrs Thatcher was a radical, he was utterly dismissive. She was a 'reactionary', gripped by the ridiculous idea that intervention is bad.

To judge from inside stories of his activities in government since then, his opinion has only grown stronger with the years. It has taken a durable act of self-denial – plus the compensation of a kind of reverse interventionism, achieved by importing management disciplines into Whitehall departments – for him to live alongside these lunatics without blowing up much earlier.

The third limb of his belief in recrudescent Heathism is connected to the second and consists of heavy support for large increases in public spending on capital projects. He thinks the record here is a scandal. Additionally, he has seen 'one-nation' possibilities, another very Heathish concept, growing out of a grand coalition between a job-creating government and job-saving trade unions.

63

This programme has always had costs. It did in 1980, when I first heard him enunciate it. It has barely changed. He despised the slowness of the government's already unpopular approach to the forcible industrial shakeout. He wanted more unemployment, short-term. It should all have been done much more brutally, to make way for much swifter industrial regeneration.

At the present time, he has continued to favour cuts in current spending. In all the recent arguments about this, he has been on the side of the hawks without always bringing himself to say so. Since he would cut current spending, and not cut defence spending, he would have to cut welfare.

The Heseltine compassion may resound through a Conservative party conference, especially when the beneficiaries are black or belong to a city like Liverpool which he has taken under his wing. But the ferocity of his belief in the industrial priority ranges him against the wets. He always scorned them as people who just wanted everything done more slowly. Now, in the critical decisions about social security, the logic of his position was to have wanted the Fowler screw tightened not, as the Thatcherites eventually agreed, loosened. Here he parts company with Heath as well.

There is a further parallel, however. Like Heath, Heseltine is an unsupple politician. He wants to be prime minister, and there are colleagues who think he could be a good one. But he does not care for politicians and their ways. It is wholly characteristic that throughout these last weeks, almost all his energies were directed to contacts with bankers and businessmen, hardly any to making common cause with other ministers.

Still, it is with this model, warts and all, that Heseltine is stuck. The Heath reversion is what he seeks to inherit and prove it to be a living thing. For if he does not, another examplar beckons.

Heath is the relevant political ancestor but the psychic parallel is with Enoch Powell. Heseltine and Powell stand for quite different things, and the old Powellites will be the first to savage his ambition to restore a world they thought they had destroyed for ever. Yet the space he occupies, depending on how the government recovers, would be the same.

His campaign cannot but be very personal. Having some

14 February, 1986

devoted admirers but no body of well-cultivated support, he will make a virtue of being a loner. Like Powell he lacks all political modesty. Fuelled by the enormity of what he half-accidentally did last Thursday, his certainty that he is right, not merely about Westland or the timing of meetings but about the destiny of Britain, provides the combustion for a messianic progress.

This is the authentic Powell-like role. In the aftermath of resignation, his personal popularity is attested in all the opinion polls. The mailbag, a faithful Powell standby, is making its appearance in the rhetoric. We'll hear more of that, with its thousands of letters of support. The more unpopular Mrs Thatcher becomes, the more readily this solitary figure will put on the hero's plumes.

What for the moment can be said about his epic challenge is that it has a grandeur appropriate to the level of what is at stake. I do not here mean the fight for Mrs Thatcher's job, a large and speculative venture. Nor is this really a contest about how she runs the government. How could anyone take that seriously who knows that prime minister Heseltine would be at least as overbearing?

No, what has been joined is the battle for the mind and soul of the Conservative Party. For a long time this has been prosecuted not by bangs but whimpers. Mrs Thatcher has routed her enemies from the field. Either they have quietly turned coat, or their corpses utter no more than a few squeals of pain. A revolution has been achieved, with no counter-revolution in sight.

That prospect Mr Heseltine has now altered. It has happened by carelessness and inadvertence, as so many political earthquakes so often start. Seeking the throne of Heath, he risks the fate of Powell. This is the more likely outcome, in my opinion, after a destructive campaign that has claimed Leon Brittan's scalp but may leave its perpetrator marginalized, declaiming righteously on the fringe of a party that deeply disapproves of what he has done.

No one, however, can deny that Mrs Thatcher has at last met an opponent she has always mistrusted, of mettle similar to her own.

16 January, 1986   **Hugo Young**

Moral? Poof!

Margaret Thatcher, it turns out, is not entirely without first-hand experience of South Africa. She went there once, as Secretary of State for Education and Science, to open an observatory. She does not make too much of this distant episode, but it has left a vivid impression and remains in the present tense. Could she say, I asked her yesterday, after she had sent Sir Geoffrey on his way, that she had seen apartheid in operation?

'You have to be very careful in saying that just becuase you've been to a country, you've seen it,' she replied. 'But I've seen the operation of apartheid in a number of respects. The first thing you see when you get off at Johannesburg airport is that you go into a hotel which is totally non-colour-conscious. You go into a dining-room and there's all colours and backgrounds. So your first impression of South Africa is rather different from what you've been led to believe.'

Soon, however, you came across other things, which were different from Britain. Mrs Thatcher had not been to Soweto or any other township. But she had seen both sides of South Africa, including the part where apartheid apparently did not exist. 'I've seen it on occasions where there's no apartheid, and I've seen it when there is apartheid. And I don't like apartheid. It's wrong.

'Let me make that clear, apartheid is wrong. It has to go, and it is going.'

The question is how to speed its departure. Despite the events of recent weeks and months, the Prime Minister is an unswerving believer in the virtues of contact, dialogue, persuasion. She had made a start, she reminded me, when she had received President Botha at Chequers last year and told him that forced removals of black communities were 'totally and utterly and particularly repugnant to us'.

Their meeting and subsequent correspondence had been fruitful. 'Those have been stopped now. Things are coming in the right direction. Naturally one wishes them to come faster.'

I suggested that this process might now have come to a halt. 'What leverage do we have through mere persuasion, particularly when the main characters in the drama won't even see our Foreign Secretary?'

Mrs Thatcher deployed the quiet voice of incredulous affront. 'I'm sorry, that's absolute nonsense. President Botha's seeing the Foreign Secretary. He was always going to see the Foreign Secretary.'

'But Sir Geoffrey had wanted to see him this week.'

'You have to try and arrange a date. I run eight, nine, sometimes twelve engagements a day. I can't just fit people in. Let's look on the positive side, and not try to make every single difficulty in this country, difficulties which don't exist. Mr Botha will see Sir Geoffrey Howe. Course he will. The question is arranging a date which is mutually convenient.'

'But wasn't it a bit humiliating that the trip was set up so publicly and then Botha said he wouldn't be available?'

Mrs Thatcher said it might have been better if they could have arranged the whole thing more quietly. But there would certainly be a meeting, and we should meanwhile look on the positive side, which consisted of fulfilling the terms of the last EEC communiqué outlining the need to get negotiations started between the South African government and black political leaders. Negotiation, not sanctions – the Rhodesian way.

'But Rhodesia survived sanctions only because it had South African support. Surely there is no South Africa to support South Africa?'

'South Africa has colossal internal resources. A colossal coast-line. And whatever sanctions were put on, materials would get in and get out. There's no way you can blockade the whole South African coastline. No way.'

So, I asked, was there no economic pressure which, in the Prime Minister's view, would have any effect?

The banks, she thought, who had pressed for repayment of the South African debt last year, had had some effect. But the main influence came from people inside South Africa who were fighting against apartheid. And who were these? Above all, industry, 'and some of the political parties'.

'But the question is whether governments, your government, can and should add to that pressure?'

'You're talking about economic pressure,' said Mrs Thatcher. 'I'm talking about how to bring about negotiations.' And here she launched into an attack on past policies. South Africa should never have been isolated by the world. 'I think we should have had more contact. We would have influenced her more. She would have been able to see that multi-racial societies do work in other countries. They do, of course, have certain problems. We've seen the problems in Kenya and Uganda. But South Africa would have been much more influenced to come our way.'

As it was, even the moderates, black and white, would respond badly if they saw the West just hitting out at their country.

'So are you saying there is no form of hostile pressure which is appropriate?'

'Let me say what I'm saying,' she responded, in a voice which had now long assumed the deliberate and emphatic timbre familiar at prime minister's question time. 'There is no case in history that I know of where punitive, general economic sanctions have been effective to bring about internal change.

'That is what I believe. That is what the Labour Party in power believed. That is what most of Europe believes. That is what most western industrialized countries believe. If that is what they believe, there is no point in trying to follow that route.'

So sanctions, first of all, would not achieve the desired effect. But that was only the beginning of the case against them.

We now approached the central thrust of the prime ministerial argument, that part of it which elicited her most withering scorn. But there was a moment of calm before the storm, even a brief, flickering line of self-doubt, concerning a point over which 'people, if I might say so, seem to me confused – although they might make the same allegations about myself'.

The matter in question was the *moral* case for sanctions. 'I must tell you I find nothing *moral* about people who come to me, worried about unemployment in this country, or about people who come to us to say we must do more to help Africa – particularly black Africans.

'I find nothing *moral* about them, sitting in comfortable circumstances, with good salaries, inflation-proof pensions, good jobs, saying that we, as a matter of *morality*, will put x hundred thousand black people out of work, knowing that this could lead to starvation, poverty and unemployment, and even greater violence.'

I tried to intervene. 'So the black leaders who . . .'

But Mrs Thatcher was thumping the table. 'That to me is *immoral*. I find it repugnant. We had it at the Community meeting. Nice conference centre. Nice hotels. Good jobs. And you really tell me you'll move people around as if they're pawns on a checkerboard, and say that's *moral*. To me it's *immoral*.'

'So how do you read the motives of the black leaders in South

Africa, Bishop Tutu and many others, who are actually in favour of economic sanctions?'

'I don't have to read them. I can tell you there are many, many people in South Africa, black South Africans, who hope to goodness that economic sanctions will not be put on.'

'How do you know that?'

'Huh. You've heard Chief Buthelezi say that. He said it in this room.'

'That's one.'

'But seven million Zulus. He said it on the doorstep of Downing Street. I've heard it, too, from some of my . . . from some other people, here in this room. Here in this room.'

'All right. But Tutu, Mandela, the ANC, the UDF, also represent a large segment of opinion – which you reject.'

'I totally reject it. Because I find it very difficult to know how they can turn round and say "Put our people into acute difficulty. They've got good jobs. They're looking after their children. But pursue a policy which can lead to children being hungry." I find it very difficult indeed.'

So sanctions, far from being moral, were positively immoral; and, as we have already seen, they would be ineffective. A third objection could also be made, and here one suddenly became aware of scores, nay hundreds, of unseen visitors who have passed through Mrs Thatcher's drawing-room and had some of the elementary facts of life explained to them, particularly the dire occasions for retaliatory action which are afforded by the geography of southern Africa.

'I sometimes get the map out and say look at it. Have you looked at how goods are going to get in and out of Zambia and Zimbabwe. Close Beit Bridge and how are you going to do it? That's the maize route. When there was drought, that's the route through which maize went to keep people alive.

'I ask them, have you looked at it? Have you looked at the poverty and hunger and starvation – just when we're after all trying to give things *to* Africa, to see she doesn't suffer in this way?'

The voice was shaking now, at this spectacle of a continent which displayed such inexplicable moral inconsistencies. 'I find it astonishing, utterly astonishing, that on the one hand we're doing everything to help Ethiopia, everything to relieve poverty and starvation, everything to get the right seeds, the right husbandry. And at the same time we're suggesting that you turn people who are in work, out of work. And add to the problems you've already got. When people call that moral, I just *gasp*.'

Nor would the retaliation stop with the impoverishment of black Africa. There was also the West's strategic interest in certain raw materials – and here too the moral issue kept breaking through.

'Platinum comes in quantity from only two places, South Africa and the Soviet Union. Are people who say there's a moral question suggesting that the world supply of platinum should be put in charge of the Soviet Union? And there are other things. Your chemical chrome, your vanadium, and of course gold and diamonds. They would have a fantastic effect on the economy of the Soviet Union.

'To me it is absolutely absurd that people should be prepared to put increasing power into the hands of the Soviet Union on the grounds that they disapprove of apartheid in South Africa.'

These lectures have evidently borne fruit. 'I go through these things with some people, and they say: no one told us, no one explained this to us.'

The rest of the world, however, would seem to be looking for deeper and different explanations. Particularly the Commonwealth. There was, as the Prime Minister had early in our conversation conceded, a desire at least for some mark of disapproval of apartheid to be made. 'Signs and gestures,' she called them.

This was why Britain had agreed to the EEC package last year. But this hadn't been enough. 'The Commonwealth wanted more. So we did krugerrands. And we put the extra gold coins in. And we've done no promotion of tourism. And various other things. But I don't know anyone in power in the western world who is suggesting punitive sanctions.'

'But they are suggesting bigger gestures, aren't they?'

Indeed they were, she said. But I had lit the blue touchpaper again. 'All right. Supposing you start with fruit and vegetables.

That would be 95,000 people, blacks and their families, out of work. *Moral?* Poof! *Moral?* No social security. *Moral?*

'Up would go the prices here. Some of it would be sold out of the coastline, through third countries, remarked, and perhaps come in at a higher price. And the retaliation we could have to things we export to South Africa! What is *moral* about that?'

This raised a question even about the gestures we had already taken part in. Insofar as they were designed, in a minor way, to inconvenience South Africa, they were surely open to objection from the Thatcherite point of view.

'We've gone along with the gestures and signals,' she said, 'because I recognize that people want to do something more than words.'

'But you don't really believe in them?'

'I don't believe that punitive economic sanctions will bring about internal change.'

'But even the gestures you're not keen on?'

(Pause.) 'I don't think the gestures are very effective. We withdrew our military attaché from South Africa. That means we don't get as much information as we should otherwise. Often you argue against the big things, the really damaging things that would cause unemployment. So you accept much smaller things, as we did.'

A few weeks ago, in the early stages of the sanctions crisis, the Prime Minister had formulated what struck me as a classic Thatcherite utterance, when she said: 'If I were the odd one out and I were right, it wouldn't matter, would it?' I now reminded her of this, and asked whether she was really so indifferent to the opinions of allies, Commonwealth colleagues, and so forth.

She said this had all been a familiar experience for her. There were many times when she had been the one to put arguments that no one else actually liked to put. She won some, she lost some, but the times on which she lost it was, it seemed, invariably because her antagonists were moved more by emotion than by reason. 'If you're alone, you only operate really by persuading. Your only way of persuading is by argument.'

So was she now winning the argument, from this lonely

eminence? Apparently she had more allies than we could know about.

'Look, in the world in which I live, sometimes you make the argument and sometimes people do not express their own views, knowing you will express yours. And they hope to goodness that you'll win your argument. Many people.

'In the world where I live, sometimes there's a public view and a private view.' This wasn't, of course, her own problem. 'So often my own converge,' she chortled, with legitimate pride. But she understood other people's difficulties and took comfort from their tacit backing.

Standing on her own high ground of unshakeable consistency, Mrs Thatcher is especially contemptuous of her political opponents – 'people who took the same view as we do when they were in power, and voted in the United Nations the same way we did.'

I suggested, in Labour's defence, that the internal situation had drastically changed since Denis Healey was in power and Dick Crossman was composing his diaries. Political upheaval had hugely escalated, and the government was weaker.

'And apartheid has been reduced,' Mrs Thatcher snapped back. 'There's practically no apartheid left in sport.'

'Due to a boycott,' I replied.

'Well.' Short pause. 'Due to a boycott. Due partly to a boycott. Not economic sanctions. A political thing.'

The prohibition against mixed marriages had also gone. 'As a matter of fact, I think it's the thing that signals the end of apartheid.' The pass laws were also going. And enforced removals. And job reservation. Even the Group Areas Act, Mrs Thatcher claimed, was 'starting to go'.

There were now 'many black people with professional qualifications and of considerable substance'. Their only problem was that they couldn't live where they wanted, and couldn't take a proper part in government. 'Those are the things to which you've got to address your minds and your action. I think we've done quite well by persuasion, particularly in the last eighteen months. But by *non-economic* ways. And we should go on that way.'

The next test is the mini-Commonwealth conference in early

August. By then Sir Geoffrey will have made his rendezvous with Botha, and Mrs Thatcher hopes that Bishop Tutu will follow. After all, she had opened the door to the bishop in London. 'He asked to see me. Of course I saw him. I don't just refuse to see people. I very much enjoyed talking to him.'

Even though she didn't agree with him? 'We got just a little bit more understanding between us, and if we went on talking I think we would again.'

She gave me a foretaste of how her emollient self would greet the Commonwealth. 'Emotions will be running high,' she predicted. 'And when that happens, you just have to let them run high and keep very calm yourself. Because it doesn't help if you let your own emotions run high, even though they feel as though they're running high.'

Her job would be steadfastly to remind her seething interlocutors of some of the facts. 'How many of you have states of emergency? How long have you had them? How many of you detain people without trial? How many have had censorship? How many of you have excluded people on racial grounds?'

I wondered whether they might not get irritated if she started talking to them like that. Wouldn't it be a little patronizing?

'It's not patronizing. That's just putting facts to them. Patronizing? What's patronizing about putting the facts? The Commonwealth's been strong enough to survive all those things. It's not for me to be patronizing. I try not to be. Not for us to be patronizing to South Africa either. We don't live there.'

So the Commonwealth is duly warned. There was an impassioned calmness about Mrs Thatcher yesterday. She appears to be ready, as ever, to attack.

'We can still get through, if we will,' she said at the end. 'We can still help to get negotiations started.' But to this end she did not sound like a politician preparing to agree to a single thing that much of the world expects of her.

9 July, 1986   **Hugo Young**

A nation bound for Nuremberg

Dear State President,

In this country torn apart by violence, your white minority regime and its agents (in one line I have already used three phrases proscribed by the emergency regulations in South Africa) have, through their arrogance, intransigence and organized campaigns of terror against the oppressed, created the circumstances you required for the declaration of a state of emergency.

Annoyed, no doubt, by the courts, by interference from concerned bodies and individuals, parliamentary investigators, enterprising journalists and others who persisted to bring to light the truths about your embattled regime, you have now succeeded in establishing a deadly silence surrounding yourselves; now no one can report on what you are planning or doing, no one can expose your lies and evils, no one can speak up for those oppressed, hounded, turned out of their burning homes, tortured or killed by the latest incarnations of the Gestapo. Not even the names of those who are 'disappearing' around us daily may be divulged.

You assure us that you have good reason. 'I have the facts,' you have been shouting since last August when, believing you could walk on water, you first tried to cross the Rubicon, and floundered. You require us to take your word, no matter how many times your regime has lied to us in the past.

We have seen the quality of your 'facts' exposed before. Your Minister of Police offered the world your facts at the time your courageous and beleaguered police tamed a violent mob at Uitenhage last year: when public pressure forced you to institute a judicial commission of inquiry, we learned that men, women, children and babies in a peaceful procession had been shot in the back.

Is that why you have been so adamant in refusing to institute another inquiry into what an Afrikaans commentator has called, 'in terms of human suffering and deprivation . . . the greatest disaster that has struck us this century' (Willem Steenkamp in *The Cape Times*, June 17), involving at least 50,000 people left homeless through violence in which, to say the least, your 'security forces' (*sic*) appeared to have played a dubious role?

Numerous affidavits by priests, medical doctors and others suggest that your own agents took part in the violence and the burning in Crossroads and the KTC squatter camp, to the point of allegedly firing at refugees and burning their shelters in order to 'persuade' them to move to a place you had previously designated for their resettlement.

If you deny such allegations, why do you refuse to appoint a judge to investigate what 'really' happened? You cannot blame me, and innumerable others, for believing the worst: we have only your record to go by, since the time you had a hand in laying waste District Six, the traditional home of generations of Coloured people in Cape Town.

You try to convince gullible Western leaders like Reagan and Thatcher that you are in fact a Great Reformer. So you scrap the Mixed Marriages Act, but then refuse to allow married people from different races to live together where they choose. You end forced removals; then fortunate coincidences like Crossroads happen to encourage the homeless to move voluntarily.

You abolish the pass laws, then set about arresting countless blacks for 'trespassing'. You bring a handful of Coloured and Indian people into parliament and offer them an illusion of powersharing, but the moment they hesitate to co-operate in passing some of the most draconian legislation this country has ever seen, you treat them like schoolboys – and press ahead with the legislation regardless.

You announce that you will discuss constitutional reform with black leaders, while ensuring that the true leaders of the people are kept in gaol or detention. You assure the world that this is a free country, yet since long before the state of emergency the meekest peaceful protests have been brutally broken up. You tell us you are a Christian, yet you send in your forces to fire tear-gas at funeral processions forcing the mourners to drop their coffins in the road. And when we profess

Actually this is quite promising –
I still have my foot in the door!

8 July, 1986

we cannot believe you, you try to end all criticism by imposing the Big Silence.

Where do I stand as a writer in this state of emergency? I know very well where I stand; the very act of committing to paper this open letter to you, is a crime. I can be arrested for this.

And if it happens, you may do your best to ensure that people in South Africa will not even know that I am among those innumerable nameless ones who disappear every day. But I also know that I cannot submit to being silenced forcibly as long as I have a conscience to live with, and as long as I have breath enough, not just to say: 'J'accuse!' but to plead: 'For God's sake, let this end before it is too late.'

I have no illusions about what a writer can do, physically. But neither should you have illusions about a writer's impotence.

You are confident that you have finally reduced us to silence.

But you have not. There may be some temporary silence in the land: the silence of prison walls so thick that you cannot see the blood on the insides or hear the muffled screams. But that blood, those screams, have a way of filtering through into the pens of writers.

I appeal to the writers of my land to bear witness. We shall not be silent forever. We have history on our side. We have truth on our side.

You have muzzled journalists. The 'facts' may not be reported, except in the bland or mutilated forms of your choice. But *fiction* has a way of recording a truth deeper than fact. What cannot be stated directly, we must record in other ways: that is what makes us writers. And if we are not allowed to publish, we must find other ways to disseminate what conscience impels us to write. If need be, we must now emulate our Russian colleagues and resort to zamizdat.

You may well fly into another of your rages at the thought of our following Russian examples. But how many times has your own regime allowed itself to be inspired by the Kremlin? In your state control of the economy, in your interference with production and marketing, in your restrictions on free expression, in your police-state methods?

Recently, in Argentina, a commission of inquiry reported on the atrocities of the previous military regime in its attempts to stay in power. The report makes chilling reading, especially in South Africa, where one recognizes so many signs of heading in the same direction.

The Argentinian report is titled *Nunca mas*: 'Never again'. What a sad and terrible plea, in this broken world. But there may be some small solace, too, in knowing that certain historical patterns do recur. Not only the darknesses, but the light as well. Nuremberg may indeed come round again. *Sieg heil!*

Yours,
André Brink

27 June, 1986

Coppers' mite

The Metropolitan Police are about to hand over £800 of public money to Anti-Apartheid. Not voluntarily, of course – the money is the compensation they've agreed to pay to two councillors from the London Borough of Camden who were unlawfully arrested while demonstrating peacefully outside the South African Embassy eighteen months ago. Robert Latham, a barrister, and Jenny Willmot, who chairs the borough's police committee, were offered the money when they had exhausted the complaints procedure and threatened civil action: they plan to hand it over to AA outside the offending embassy today. They reckon that if all 150 people arrested in similar circumstances took the same path, total police liability would be £60,000.

18 March, 1986   **Stephen Cook**

Some viceroy, some neck

Lord Mountbatten: The Last Viceroy (Central) has just begun. A couple of chaps are picking their way through sleeping Indians and talking nostalgically of strawberry jam when, without warning, a bunch of thugs rush in with large clubs and loud yells. They crush skulls, thump stomachs, slit a throat or two and vanish as quickly as they appeared, leaving wall-to-wall corpses. Could this unsavoury band, one wonders, trembling a bit, be the critics?

Clement Attlee and a taller man whom the eye of faith takes to be Stafford Cripps are talking the way cabinet ministers will when they know there are millions of people out there who have never heard of Lord Mountbatten. 'I suppose,' says Mr Attlee, 'Mountbatten is the man for the Viceroy's job? Many people in England are worried about his film star profile, his

79

dash, the playboy image.' 'Surely,' said Cripps soothingly, 'his success as supreme commander would settle all that. Victorious leader. Member of the Royal family. Man who accepted the Japanese surrender at Singapore.' 'Yes,' says Attlee, brightening up a bit. 'And for all he's an aristocrat, he does have the common touch.'

The door opens and Lord Mountbatten enters with no neck. It says a great deal for the natural courtesy of the working man that neither of them mentions that Mountbatten's head now sits on his collar like a boiled egg on an eggcup. Perhaps they think it is a war wound.

Mountbatten hurries to the Palace to see George VI. 'Good to see you, Dickie,' says the King. 'Where's your neck?' No he doesn't, for he has a kind heart as well as a coronet. He just says, 'Good to see you Dickie.' 'I've had a meeting with the prime minister, Bertie. He wants me to take over as Viceroy,' says Mountbatten. 'Yes, he told me,' says the King mildly.

Nicol Williamson was chosen to play Mountbatten for the best reason. He is a good actor. But what Mountbatten actually looked like was a bad actor or, if you prefer, a film star. What you saw was what you got: a powerful charm, endless energy and enthusiasm, bronzed bossiness. Williamson does not have the look of the man and his attempt to dig for something deeper is leading only to a nervous broodiness, like a man waiting for his neck to grow and worrying about it.

Lady Mountbatten when I saw her must have been close to death. She shone like a strong lamp with its bulb broken, a brilliant filament. Janet Suzman plays her with quite a bit of that nervous radiance and Ian Richardson has considerable power and presence as Nehru. Which leaves me to think that the story they should have been filming is Lady Mountbatten and Nehru, a touching love story and surely not an untouchable one. If they had, I guarantee that TV Times would not then have put Cannon and Ball on their front cover.

28 April, 1986   **Nancy Banks-Smith**

A bleak royal ritual

'Miss Warfield, the Duchess,' as the only wreath from a survivor of her American family called her in tender defiance, was laid to rest yesterday at Windsor with the barest human, royal and Christian ceremony after more than fifty years of vexing a throne.

Wallis, first and almost certainly last Duchess of Windsor, widow of the abdicated King Edward VIII, formerly Mrs Simpson, formerly Mrs Earl Spencer and before that Bessie Wallis Warfield of Baltimore, was buried without even a funeral address – the homage paid to less vaulting mortals by any parish church in her husband's land or in the United States.

Her name was not mentioned once at a thirty-five minute service attended by the Queen, the Queen Mother, sixteen leading members of the Royal Family and the Prime Minister at St George's Chapel, Windsor.

One of the chief honours given to her, a short blessing by the Archbishop of Canterbury, Dr Robert Runcie, was inaudible to most of her British friends in the congregation because of a malfunction in the chapel's loudspeaker system.

So was the psalm chosen for the Duchess, who died aged eighty-nine. It was Psalm 90, which says that 'though men be so strong that they come to four-score years, yet is their strength then but labour and sorrow.'

So was the only hymn, 'Lead Us Heavenly Father', promising 'love with every passion blending pleasure that can never cloy'.

The Duchess, who called herself 'Wallis-in-Wonderland' when the then Prince of Wales and his circle took her up in 1931, had come at last in death to what she quickly realized in life was the arctic heartland of that wonderland.

After dancing with the prince, she wrote – in words exclusively published in the *Daily Mail*'s current serialization of their love letters – of her feeling that 'all this graciousness and pageantry were but the glittering tip of an iceberg'.

When, over fifty years later, she returned to Paris after her husband's funeral in the same chapel where her coffin stood yesterday, she told friends that the royal family had acted kindly to her 'but they are cold'.

Her sparse funeral service resulted from the royal family's decision to abide strictly by the letter of an agreement reached with the couple before the Duke's death in exchange for their burial on English soil.

A Buckingham Palace spokesman said of the absence of a funeral address: 'I think you will find that the whole service – including that point – was agreed with them before they died.'

The only exceptions to this rule were the Queen's single wreath of white, orange and yellow lilies on the coffin and the wealth of individual wreaths on display in the chapel cloisters.

Among the inscriptions were: 'lots of love from the Hawkes family'; 'to a gracious lady, from Mrs Alan-Betts, Exmouth'; 'with deep sorrow, from Her Majesty's Cabinet'; 'affectionately, from Marie Bismarck'; 'reunited at last with your beloved David'; and 'with respect and admiration'. The flowers from 'Edward J. Warfield', her family name, stood among these.

In the main chapel, there was no such informality. But royal ceremonial tried to pay her its own austere salute at the end, as the coffin was carried out of the royal family's secluded choir stalls to the west door.

To the music of Elgar's Nimrod variation, a thirty-three-strong procession led by the Constable of Windsor Castle and backed up by the Queen, the Duke of Edinburgh, the Queen Mother and the Prince and Princess of Wales accompanied the coffin down the aisle.

However, the familiar funeral theme was played so slowly that the party could only walk some four inches at a step if they were to keep in time. They found themselves noticeably mincing down the aisle and took several minutes to cover the short distance.

It was magnificent in intention and dedication; but it was not, in its execution, effective royal ritual, any more than the Charge of the Light Brigade was effective warfare.

On the sunlit chapel steps, the royals posed in black for the historic press and TV pictures, the first time they were seen in public yesterday.

The Queen Mother, whose husband was forced on to the throne by the Duke of Windsor's wayward abdication, did not accompany the others to the burial at Frogmore. Buckingham Palace said the Queen had decided this.

And so the family had made its point about the fifty years of disruption, grief and redoubled rectitude enforced on them by the Duke and his divorcee commoner bride from Baltimore.

But no spirit – much less so one with the Duchess's sense of humour – could rest entirely unquiet in Frogmore after that slow, mincing march, which had been endured in the chapel in tribute to her by her old enemies.

30 April, 1986   **John Ezard**

Crown Prince of the Fleet Street rat pack

Early on the morning of The Engagement, James Whitaker is out on the prowl, dialling numbers on his car telephone, trying to get a fix on Sarah's whereabouts. 'We'll take a turn round KP, have a look-see, and on to BP to see if there's any action,' he said, shooting off through the rush-hour traffic.

At KP (Kensington Palace) a cold group of photographers and royal fanatics has been waiting in the dank grey light since five a.m. for some sign that Sarah is in there being groomed by Diana.

Whitaker, the *Mirror*'s ace royal reporter, jumps out and pats the *Sun*'s photographer on the back, 'Kenny, my old boy!' The photographers, however, are looking at him somewhat aggrieved, for the *Mirror*'s Kent Gavin has just managed to get one of the only four prized rota places to take pictures of the royal couple in Buckingham Palace later in the morning.

'A fix! It's bent,' they mutter. Whitaker beams at them. 'His delight is your despair! He'll be like a dog with two dicks about this!' They look sour.

Back in the car he gets Kent Gavin on the telephone. 'Gav,

you jammy bastard, fantastic! Oh, Gavs, I'm so happy for you! Now when you're in there, you fucking keep your ears open. Any little word they say, and jot it down at once! Amazing what you forget.'

Whitaker is the star of the hard core of the royal press corps. He it was who crept for two and a half terrible hours through impenetrable jungle, braving insects, snakes and dead goats to snatch pictures of Princess Diana, pregnant in a bikini, on a private holiday in the Bahamas. This was no mean feat, for Whitaker is no dapper young beginner, but a portly and dignified forty-five-year-old, his ample frame customarily attired in a bold buttoned blazer, silk handkerchief flowing out of his top pocket.

The Palace, the Queen herself, was outraged, the other scooped tabloids feigned profound shock. But his then editor on the *Star* declared stoutly that the British people had the right to know and be reasonably assured that their beloved Princess was indeed healthy and fit during her pregnancy.

'I'll be remembered forever for that story,' Whitaker chortles. 'We did have the profile shots of her, looking very pregnant, but we only used decent frontals, hardly looked pregnant at all. Charming.'

And, of course, it was he who broke the Princess-Michael-of-Kent's-father-in-SS-shock-horror.

He has spent a large part of his journalistic career in bushes. 'I love it! The thrill of the chase, the stalking, the hunting, especially in the Highlands in tweeds and country clothes,' he says. For five months he followed Diana without a break, before her engagement was announced.

'I discovered Diana,' he says. 'September 6, 1980. You can check. I had the story of them together first. Dempster rubbished it, called me a mendacious minion, as usual. And I can tell you, quite definitely that Prince Charles was not in love with Diana when they were engaged. He only fell in love with her later. You could see it in his eyes.'

For eighteen hours a day, every day, he chased Diana, and he says he had her private number and used to talk regularly to her. 'I put her on to homeopathy when she had a dreadful cold.'

And it was he, he says, who first got the Diana anorexia story. 'I think the press did her a service there. She was on the verge of anorexia, and we caught it in time, put a stop to it.'

He remembers Charles's bachelor days with a sigh of nostalgia. 'Such fun. Once I stalked him all day in Scotland and he never had the slightest idea that my photographer and I were there in the bracken. He was with a girlfriend. Very raunchy. We watched as he spread out a rug on the banks of the Dee, and they were at it in no time.'

Really? 'Well, not actually screwing, but he was just about to. My conscience got the better of me. We both stood up and waved. You should have seen him run! He belted into the bushes, the girl trailing after. We had all the pictures, but we decided not to give them to the editor. He might have used them.'

His least favourite Royal is Princess Anne. 'She behaves like a pig. She is awful, always was, always will be. Don't believe all that nonsense about how nice she's become lately. I started that. I got bored to tears with writing what a bitch she was, so I made a change and wrote about how wonderful she is instead. I changed her image overnight, and the other papers all followed on behind me.'

But he sometimes makes mistakes. 'It's a very high risk business, royal reporting. Highest risk reporting in the world. I did a big front page announcing Di pregnant again, when she wasn't. A pregnancy story catches up with you, because in a few months it's going to be obvious, one way or the other. It wasn't a story from a contact of mine, but you do lose credibility. My editor was very understanding.'

A car comes bowling down the drive from KP and he leaps out to see what is happening, the photographer's cameras cocked for the Sarah picture of the day.

'Only Prince Michael going to work!' Whitaker announces loudly, and the cameras are lowered.

Back in his car he telephones the office, and is told a hairdresser has just gone into BP (Buckingham Palace). 'Who was it? Charles Martin? No, nothing doing, he's the Queen's. Got the mother yet in the Argentine? I'm the only one who knows the real flight Ron Ferguson's taking today. No, don't tell the airport agency unless you want the whole world to know. He's going to Singapore and they all think he's going to Australia. Look, I don't want any crap about him toasting his daughter in champagne. He drinks Perrier, right?

'Someone collected that exclusive pic of Andrew and Sarah together as kids? Yes, yes, I know the engagement's ridiculously quick. They're telling you she's pregnant? Don't be appalling! Even if it were true I wouldn't fucking write it!'

He slams down the telephone and leaps out of the car as another Rover comes gliding down the drive. 'Diana!' he shouts, and they all jump up. But Diana keeps her head well down between the front seats and sweeps away without a wave or a smile. 'Playing silly-buggers again,' one photographer says crossly.

Back in the car Whitaker gives his office the number of Paddy McNally in Geneva, Sarah's old racing driver lover, then sits back for a long wait, and contemplates the engagement.

'I'm so *worried* for them,' he says, shaking his head sadly. 'I just don't feel they've had *time*. They've been rushed into this. He's hardly had any shore-leave in the last two years. She's so sophisticated, and of course, she engineered it. Wanted to be a princess. I doubt if he knows what's hit him.

He talks about her past in the raciest of London society. 'She's Dai Llewellyn's child's godmother. What more can I say? Nigel Politzer is a friend. Paddy McNally frequently reduced her to tears. She was going to be one of Diana's ladies in waiting, but wasn't thought quite suitable. Well, she didn't know the protocol.'

Vicki Hodge, the *Mirror*'s model who told all about her gambols with Prince Andrew, told James Whitaker a lot that was unfit to print. 'Hopeless! She said she could do nothing with him. But Koo Stark put him right, taught him a lot of tricks.'

He ran a story the other day about Sarah Ferguson getting herself a pedicure at Leonards the hairdressers. 'I pricked up my ears at that. I heard Andrew likes feet. And then I linked it in with the story about the butler who resigned his job after he once caught the Duke of Windsor painting Mrs Simpson's toe nails beside a swimming pool. Does it run in the family? I got it from someone who sat next to Sarah in the hairdressers, but Sarah was so angry she didn't go back to Leonards after that.'

He was, of course, the first to get the Sarah story. 'I discovered her, too. June 20, 1985. You check it, my dear. Of course Dempster rubbished me. Kept on saying she was McNally's girl, but I knew better.'

Who are his contacts, where does he get it all? He waves his hands in the air extravagantly. 'Lots, move in the right circles. Give a lot of dinner parties myself. I just know people.' He pauses before adding: 'Trouble is you have a good contact one day, you kick them in the teeth the next day and then you have to get a new contact. Keep finding new ones.'

He paid £350 to a girl he sat next to at dinner who gave him the front page Andrew-and-Sarah-Really-in-Love story. 'Mostly I don't pay. They aren't the types that tell you for money. They tell you for fun. Everyone loves to tell something no one else knows.'

He has worked for all the tabloids at one time or another. He is a funny, absurd and delightful man, a caricature of a gossip, a Beau Brummel of extravagant manner who loves every moment of his life and work. He lives with his wife in a modern suburban house in Chiswick, was born in Cheltenham, son of the chairman of Sperry Rand, went to Cheltenham College, and took to journalism after failing his hated chartered accountancy exams.

His relationship with the royal family is bizarre, for he plainly loves them, admires them (or most of them), is dazzled by their aura and genuinely fascinated by every tiny detail he can glean about them. And yet he hounds and hunts them mercilessly and they would indeed be magnanimous if they loved him.

Clearly by now there is nothing doing at KP so he steers the car off towards BP, where he drives up alongside the crowds at the gate. His car is greeted gladly by a phalanx of friendly photographers, some wanting to borrow his telephone. What does he know? What's going on?

Is Sarah already in there? Has she, poor girl, spent a night at Clarence House with the Queen Mother, like Diana did? The photographers are all toting official royal tour heavy gear, aluminium ladders, with umbrellas attached, ready to erect at a moment's notice to see over the heads of the crowds.

But there is nothing doing here either, so it's back to the office to write a double page spread Royal Engagement Souvenir Special.

24 March, 1986   **Polly Toynbee**

Oleggo, you beasts

Spy stories are, of course, jolly exciting. But they are also a lurid old bundle of candyfloss. Almost everyone involved – including politicians who would normally have to offer a checkable approximation to fact – lies or seems to lie with blithe impunity. Worse, they seem to enjoy it. Take the twenty-four hours of Oleg Gordievsky. Mr Malcolm Rifkind of the FO beaming disinformationally across television screens like a lad in a bowl of toffee. Wise men hailing a tremendous coup for the West. Other wise men pointing out that the coup was getting Gordievsky to spy in the first place – and that losing his services is, in fact, a disaster. Danes claiming to have brought home the bacon first. Whitehall denizens claiming that the fact Oleg chose us is a tremendous boost for Britain. Some saying he scarpered because of Tiedge: others saying he defected long before that. Americans professing horror at the alleged extent of Soviet activity, and then coughing when told about the files Gordievsky had supposedly been pumping to Nato for fourteen years. Pokerfaced Soviet officials denying everything. Downing Street shock and horror over the booted twenty-five. No shock and horror, on the other hand, because we've known about them all along. Who can guess what is possibly true? And who – looking back over those fourteen years – can put his finger on a single obvious event where any of it actually made a difference?

14 September, 1985   **Leader**

22 November, 1985

The Garden of Eden at Wapping

The new dawn of the newspaper industry began in appropriately brisk mid-Atlantic fashion. Journalists arriving for work were handed out plastic security ID cards identifying them simply as 'Consultant'.

'But I'm not a consultant,' complained a member of the City staff. 'I'm a reporter.' Lips were pursed. Arguments were entered into. Senior executives were called for. It was finally agreed that reporters could be called reporters.

It was a small point. Just as, for most journalists, being seen to arrive on foot or by car rather than in one of Mr Murdoch's buses was a small matter of principle.

The journalists are a bit touchy on the score of principle. There has been much talk of pistols and heads over a weekend in which they were offered more money – or the sack: 'We had to choose there and then. It was like being held in a police cell without being allowed to phone your solicitor,' said one reporter. But, in the end, the editorial staff took the £2000 and the free BUPA health insurance cover and said they would go to Wapping.

And what a world awaited them. When they had left work on Friday night they had left behind them a slightly seedy office – paper-strewn, dog-eared desks with ageing typewriters and half-drunk cups of coffee. And there on Monday morning was a gleaming dust-free open-plan room. A clinic more than an office. The whole of it was bathed in soothing computer-compatible light. For there in front of them stood row upon row of gleaming dust-free computers.

Almost none of them knew how to work the computers, but there were assorted clutches of Australians and Americans at hand if they had trouble reading the manual. One of them was Alan Howe, production editor of the *Australian*. He had a familiar face. That's right. He was the chap knocking round the office last year.

Some tentatively tapped at their screens. Some tried the phones, which didn't work very well. Some searched for phone books. Yes, there were a few. Some sauntered off to the new 'restaurant' where, Japanese-style, staff and big-wigs sit side by side. Some set back for the old office in Gray's Inn Road to scrape together some belongings. If they had crossed into the *Sunday Times* building they would have stumbled across the editor, Mr Andrew Neil, and his senior executives, clearing out various desks and filing cabinets. When out of the office Mr Neil is currently accompanied by a very large man who looks discouragingly at anyone who approaches too close.

For *Sunday Times* journalists the day began with Mr Neil addressing them at the Mount Pleasant hotel in Clerkenwell. 'He tried to persuade us that a Garden of Eden awaited us, with glorious working conditions and computers,' said one at the meeting. 'We tried to tell him that newspapers couldn't just be uprooted and dumped behind a barbed wire cordon – that it was to do with roots and access to the public. He didn't seem to grasp the point.'

'Quite frankly, we've been bullied. They'll get us to go because we've got mortgages to pay. But a lot will try to leave as soon as they can. A newspaper is supposed to be about truth, and here we are working for a management that has consistently lied to us.'

There is no doubt that the full plan for the move to Wapping was a secret shared by only a handful of executives – if that – until early last week. Journalists on *The Times* business news were told by their department head only last Friday that they would be asked to report to Wapping this week. *Sunday Times* copy was sent for setting in the Gray's Inn works last week – but one of three top executives took photocopies of copy and page layouts and sent them off to Wapping to be set again. Most departmental heads appear to have been kept in the dark and most of the planning was done by Mr Neil, his deputy, Ivan Fallon, and his defence correspondent, James Adams.

The Times editor, Mr Charles Wilson, told his staff of the terms they would be required to submit to at 7.30 on Friday night. 'He was very nervous and was shaking,' observed one journalist. 'He was clearly under great strain.' The journalists took hurried legal advice from a solicitor, Mr Lawrence Lever, and a barrister, Mr Alexander Irvine, and discovered that they would be on thin ground if they refused to go to Wapping, but would have a good cause for unfair dismissal by invoking the grievance procedure once there.

The journalists decided to go but about nine reporters – including the three-man labour staff – reported for work at Gray's Inn Road yesterday, thereby courting instant dismissal. 'It wasn't out of any great sentimental sympathy for the print unions,' said one yesterday. 'In fact there is almost no sympathy for the NGA and for the old Natsopa jobs. No, it was just a feeling that we'd been mugged by Mr Murdoch despite the fact that the journalists have always been the most compliant part of the workforce.' Those who refuse to go to Wapping have been offered £150 a week by the NUJ.

Sunday Times journalists last night followed suit with a 68-60 vote to go to Wapping. But those who refuse to go may present a larger problem for Mr Murdoch including, as they may, such key executives as the Features Editor, Mr Don Berry.

Staff on both papers say that even those happy about working at Wapping – and even those who despaired at Fleet Street working practices – were dismayed at the tactics used by Mr Murdoch. 'I think he will be quite surprised at the level of bad feeling there is amongst the journalists. A lot of them are shocked and appalled.'

None of this would necessarily cut much ice with Mr Murdoch's Sogat and NGA former employees huddled over braziers at the back of the old Gray's Inn Road plant yesterday. 'The price used to be thirty pieces of silver; now it's £2000,' said a former machine minder.

'We had lots of proud promises that they were right behind us and now, over a weekend, they've all ratted. I tell you, if there's no amiable settlement to this it will go on as long as Northern Ireland.'

The sacked men have established a twenty-four-hour picket of both the Gray's Inn Road office and the Wapping plant and have set up quarters nearby in the NGA offices in Doughty Street. They took some comfort at the evident inexperience of the electricians who replaced them in order to produce last week's *Sunday Times*. 'Bloody jokers. They even left the bloody date off the front page.'

Less cheering for them was the sight of a considerable number of Sogat members crossing their own picket lines to work in some areas of the Murdoch organization that are still functioning from Gray's Inn Road, several librarians amongst them.

Journalists who have moved to Wapping have the practical details to sort out immediately – a switchboard that can barely cope; a complete lack of familiarity with the technology they are now required to work with and, at least for the time being, the lack of access to any library. They insist that very low down their list of grievances is the distance of Wapping from what they might think of as the centre of London – and from the sort of restaurant in which they are accustomed to lunch their contacts. 'Obviously there are more agreeable areas to work in – but it really wasn't a factor,' said one who did make the move.

But perhaps the longest face yesterday was on the landlord of the Blue Lion, bang opposite the Murdoch buildings in Gray's Inn Road. 'I should think about 70 per cent of our trade comes from across the road,' he said yesterday. 'We'd just closed down for redevelopment and enlargement. It's a bit grim, isn't it?'

29 January, 1986   **Alan Rusbridger**

Reflections

It is possible that the award-winning journalist John Pilger doesn't know it yet, but he's leaving the *Daily Mirror*. He's in his native Australia at the moment and may not have received his redundancy notice from Robert ('Mad Max') Maxwell. Adding insult, the canteen at the Mirror Group's London office has been handed over to Trust House Forte and tea comes twice as expensive in plastic rather than china. As Max announced that he wanted it 'to come up to the standards of motorway restaurants', a cardboard box beside him rustled

mysteriously. It was found to contain two live lobsters for the
large tycoon's supper.
7 January, 1986   **Stephen Cook**

Rights of passage

You don't have to be partisan in the dispute between Mr Rupert
Murdoch and his printers to see that there are some pretty
disturbing things for civil liberties happening down at Wapping. Since late January, a little corner of London dockland
has become almost a British East Berlin. Particularly on Satur-
days, but at a lot of other times as well, local Wappingites are
unable to walk or drive down their own streets and into or out
of their own area without becoming objects of police attention.
When they are stopped, as they often are, Wapping residents
have to produce identification and have a hard time persuading
the officers manning the checkpoints to let them pass. People's
cars are moved by the police, without consultation, to let Mr
Murdoch's lorries zoom through, frequently at illegal speeds.
Heavy vehicle regulations might as well not exist. All this means
not only delay and irritation but restrictions on local life. Shops
and pubs have lost trade, while buses and taxis are kept out.
It's Passport to Wapping time, courtesy of Sir Kenneth New-
man and the lads.

All these points are made in a polite but powerful report
this week by the National Council for Civil Liberties. Some
know-alls will say that all this shows is what everyone should
know in any case – that the capitalist class and the state machine
are hand in glove. Well, up to a point, Arthur. What the
policing of Wapping does show is that if police think they can
get away with unlawful but handy practice, then they will.
Over the past two years, police have decided that 'intercept'
roadblocks are a very useful way of harassing drivers and
pedestrians. During the miners' dispute, when public opinion
mistrusted the legitimacy of the strike and courts were scared,
the intercepts were widely used and rarely challenged. The fact

94

remains, though, that they are almost certainly unlawful. Since then police have used them against CND supporters and at Stonehenge. And now here they are again, as unlawful as ever, but routinely used for more than two months, in the nation's capital city, to control a celebrated but in other respects not terribly important industrial dispute. Does anybody care that it is no longer possible to travel freely around this country, even around the bit you live in, except by permission of the police? Evidently not.

"Well, I really do think you ought to give him an obituary. After all, he was run down by a lorry racing to deliver the Times."

28 January, 1986

Most people will probably accept that the police have to balance conflicting demands upon their support and resources. At Wapping, these include ensuring the free passage of Mr

95

Murdoch's workforce and lorries, ensuring the free passage of local residents and ensuring the rights (such as they are) of the strikers and their supporters. It is clear that, at Wapping, only one of those demands – Mr Murdoch's – counts for much with the police and that all other considerations are peripheral to that central, and largely self-determined (though, as it happens, supported by the Government) police priority. But it is also evidence of something much more deep-grained in British law and policing – the extraordinary primacy given to the 'right' of wheeled vehicles to travel without interruption and the overriding importance which police attach to enforcing it. For years, police have argued that civic normality and the peace which the force must uphold are synonymous with the free flow of wheeled traffic – around which other human activity must adjust itself as best it can. Oh motor car! Oh lorry! what crimes against liberty are committed in thy name!

8 April, 1986   **Leader**

What the papers said

The leader columns of the three more right-wing tabloid national dailies, the *Daily Express*, the *Daily Mail* and the *Sun*, all agreed with the Home Secretary, Mr Douglas Hurd, that the rioting in Handsworth should be treated as a criminal, rather than a social or economic matter.

In a number of articles they took the argument a stage further: the criminals were black West Indians (although a very high proportion of the rioters had almost certainly been born in Birmingham, not Barbados) and, it was obliquely or more directly stated, this particular minority is inherently more likely to commit these crimes.

A notable example of this kind of juxtaposition occurred at page length in the middle of the riot coverage in Wednesday's *Sun*. Illustrated by a map of Britain, the first paragraph of the story stated that there are now 2.2 million 'immigrants' in the country. The article went on to say exactly where they lived, and in what numbers. It continued with a rundown of riots since 1980 in those inner city 'hot-spots' where the 'immigrants' were also to be found.

The *Daily Mail*'s leader column on the same day said: 'So was this a race riot? No it was not . . . if we have to pin a one word label on this predominantly black riot, it would be "tribal".'

The single-word headline over a piece in the *Sun* bore the same message: 'Barbarians!' (This latter piece, in which Mr Jeff Rooker, Labour MP for Perry Barr, which includes part of Handsworth, was quoted, caused Mr Rooker some awkward moments later in the day when he visited a black community centre – his defence that the word he had used was 'barbarous' and applied to crimes, not people, did not go down well.)

Coverage in Wednesday's *Express* took its tone from the front page, which accompanied a picture of a black youth carrying a bottle with the following: 'He walks with a chilling swagger, a petrol bomb in his hand and hate burning in his heart . . . chief constable Geoffrey Dear said that 400 young blacks "driven on by bloodlust" started the riot.'

The *Express* described the booing of Mr Hurd when he visited the area as a 'Zulu-style war cry' and continued the South African allusion with an article by Sir Eldon Griffiths, who blamed TV pictures of the townships for inspiring the riot's 'leaders'. Above this piece was a cartoon by Cummings depicting Mrs Thatcher, Mr Hurd and the Foreign Secretary, Sir Geoffrey Howe, cowering from a hail of missiles with the caption: 'We mustn't call it a state of emergency or the Americans will declare sanctions on us!' The missiles were being thrown by five caricatures of blacks looking like angry golliwogs, jam-jar style. The anti-racialist magazine *Searchlight* said yesterday that it had received several complaints about this cartoon, and it is understood that black organizations are considering whether it breaches the Race Relations Act.

These racialist overtones of aspects of the papers' treatment of the riots were given greater impact by the ritual hyperbole of their reporting. *Express* reporter Eileen MacDonald had a trying time during the brief 'mini-riot' that followed Mr Hurd's visit and was forced to hide among terrified screaming budgies

97

in a pet shop. She had run from 'chanting West Indians' and the pet shop owner presented her with a puppy, begging her to 'please take it home, it will die of fright in here.'

The purplest prose came from the pen of Mr Brian James, who in the *Mail* was 'Face to face with the fear and fury of Lozells Road.' He began his piece: 'Then I knew. When they overturned and set fire to the police transit vans behind which I had been hiding ten minutes before, then I knew. When I ran, tripping over a fence as bottles smashed onto the wall above my head and heard someone whispering, "Oh Christ" and recognized it as my own voice, then I knew. When I ran down Carpenter Street and ahead of me every door was slammed shut and there was nowhere to hide – then I knew about the fear of the night that Handsworth had just lived through.'

Like Ms Macdonald, Mr James had missed the worst violence that previous night, and was describing events well into the afternoon. From my own vantage point very nearby, the afternoon missile-throwing – though not car-burning – appeared to last a very short time, during Mr Hurd's five-minute tour, and henceforth was directed sporadically at police.

But possibly the Handsworth blacks had somehow gauged Mr James's feelings about them. There was an earlier time, his piece went on, when Britons had 'mingled in the streets needing company as if for confirmation that they were still alive – back in the blitz.'

The next paragraph was set in italics for emphasis: 'But then they were united by the fact that the enemy came from outside. This thing that had turned a decaying suburb into a pastiche of Beirut had been done by their own.'

No social phenomena for Mr James and the *Mail*: 'In the action centre, plastered with all the graffiti of the left, fierce young blacks spout figures about unemployment and local housing . . . those who have died, those who have lost all they lived to build up, they are the only oppressed minority we should plead for today.'

The hardest line of all belonged to the *Daily Express*. Criticizing Mr Kinnock's comment that unemployment, poverty and idleness had contributed to the riot, its Wednesday leader described this as 'kneejerk gobbledegook'. The article ended with a call for punishment, and for 'those champions of permissiveness who invent excuses' to examine their consciences and 'repent'.

16 September, 1985   **David Rose**

Bull about Kabul

Most British correspondents covering the Falklands war were indignant at the way the Ministry of Defence fed them selected and one-sided reports of the fighting. Supported by colleagues from other countries, they vowed they would never be 'used' this way in a war again.

This proud stand differs, regrettably, from the way things operate in the much longer, and more difficult war in Afghanistan. For six years now, before the Falklands war and since, British, American and other reporters have been attending one-sided briefings on the Afghan war, and usually transmitting the stories without any checking.

The weekly briefings at the American and British embassies in Delhi and Islamabad are known to those who take part as the 'Tuesday Follies'. But in the competitive climate of Western journalism they are taken seriously enough for few reporters to risk boycotting them.

Led by the wire services where pressures for a 'good story' and a 'strong lead' frequently outweigh natural scepticism and sound judgment, the stories flash to receptive news desks. When no Western forces are directly involved and the 'enemy' is the Soviet Union, distinctions between hard news, soft news, and outright propaganda seem to lose all validity.

At a recent US briefing in Islamabad I was astonished to hear that the town of Paghman, just outside the Afghan capital, Kabul, 'appears to remain firmly in the hands of the resistance despite repeated regime and Soviet efforts to assert military control over the area'. Eight days earlier I had been taken to Paghman by Afghan government officials whom I had challenged to prove that what the Western embassies were saying was wrong. From my observation the Afghan government was right.

It is not hard to understand why the briefings are accident-prone when one realizes that diplomats in Kabul, who compile the weekly reports and cable them to India and Pakistan, are not permitted to go out of Kabul by the Afghan authorities.

The briefings contain two categories of military information. One is a laundry list of sights and sounds of Kabul, consisting of aircraft and troop movements, and night-time gun and rocket noise. (The Americans have a man on their embassy roof all night.) This type of information is broadly accurate even though its significance is often vague. Where were the helicopters going? Who in the night time was shooting at whom and what happened?

Then there are events beyond Kabul. Their accuracy depends entirely on the reliability of the source. Is it bazaar gossip, rumour picked up by embassy cooks and nightwatchmen, or word filtered back from the conscript son or cousins of diplomats' servants? The briefings never make this clear.

True or false, the stories were all one-sided. 'Any mujaheddin casualties?' the hard-bitten Voice of America correspondent, Don Larrimore, asked after the embassy briefers recounted a clash in which 'seven officers and scores of Soviet and Afghan government soldiers were killed or wounded.'

'I don't see any mention of any,' said the briefer scanning his cable. 'There hardly ever is,' Alex Brodie of the *Guardian* and BBC explained afterwards. 'It's one triumph after another.'

Wire-service reporters at that briefing included a Pakistani representative of the Associated Press (who also writes for the *Daily Telegraph*), and others from Agence France Presse, the West German DPA, and the Saudi news agency. There was a man from the Japanese 'moonie' paper, *Sekai-Nippo*, a man who doubles for Radio Free Europe and another 'moonie' paper, the *Washington Times*, and a US freelancer.

At the British embassy the briefing was better because it included non-military items, such as political and economic developments and a selection of 'regime claims' which went some way to balancing the list of mujaheddin successes.

The accuracy of the military information was open to the

same caveats as that provided by the US briefing. 'All villages within forty kilometres of Jalalabad have been destroyed,' said one situation report in the very week that I was visiting thriving villages in that area.

Whether the tone of the briefings is gung-ho or modest, exaggerated or cautious depends on the style of the diplomat who writes it. An embassy which wanted to slip in deliberately false 'disinformation' obviously had the perfect outlet. The system would not work if journalists did not go along with it. In the context of a war in which the Afghan and Soviet side never show independent journalists the fighting, some argue that the Western briefings are better than nothing. Others claim the briefings are only one source among others, and provide raw material for checking.

The speed with which the stories appear on the international wires suggests that little or no checking is done. Reporters who attend the Islamabad briefings say they sometimes bounce the tales from Kabul on to their mujaheddin contacts as a check, but the reporters who go to the Delhi briefings have no such contacts. They file anyway. Some reporters complain that, even when they disbelieve the briefing and do not file, their newspapers sometimes print a news agency version because it sounds good or just to fill a space. The *Guardian* has succumbed to this temptation.

The result is that week after week the Western world is being fed a story of mujaheddin success and Soviet discomfiture which may be far from the truth. The only beneficiaries, at least in the short term, are the mujaheddin and their political and military backers. Later on, the bubble may burst.

10 March, 1986   **Jonathan Steele**

Melodrama in a global village

It was the manner of Ferdinand Marcos's political demise – rather than the mere, inexorable fact of it – that gripped the world day by day. When he lost the election, whatever the tardy results alleged, and when the extent of that scandal undermined his Washington sponsors, then the effective end of two decades of Philippine history was clear and signalled. But, hour after hour, what a remarkable end. Street theatre from the crowds of People Power for dozens of satellite-linked television crews. The leaders of the coup – and the failing President himself – locked into global breakfast TV, chatting to an American Selina lookalike. The grim departure for exile. And, perhaps most hauntingly of all, the symbolic moments of a change of power: the moment when Mrs Aquino's forces seized the Channel Television Four television stage, cut off Marcos in midstream and supplanted him with a couple of beaming News at Ten revolutionaries; the moment, soon after, when the last loyal TV station fell. This was a coup played out across the world on a billion flickering screens. Instant televised history, where it was often difficult not to feel that television itself was an integral part of the history-making.

That is by no means a damaging observation. On the contrary, in at least one sense, the presence of the cameras almost certainly saved hundreds of lives. Without them (who can say?) General Ver might have won the amazing TV debate with his master and gained permission to save the regime by shooting to kill. But Marcos, to his credit, did not give that desperate order. His troops, posing for the watching crews, simply fired in the air. The battle for hearts and minds – American hearts, American minds, American coffers – was conducted on the open line, and conditioned the way that all participants behaved. If it was a relatively bloodless drama, then television must take a deal of the credit. It was a dud election in this remote part of the global village that put the skids under Marcos. It was the global village that dictated the means of his fall. In the final, hectic minutes of his rule, throngs danced and performed for the cameras, turning people power into video power.

There is, of course, another and more difficult dimension to this unique experience. One the whole world (and the third world in particular) may ponder. For a new element has been added to the apparatus of superpower influence. The harbingers of change now are ABC, NBC and CBS, as well as the CIA. Cynically, perhaps, we don't suppose that the Central Intelligence Agency has gone out of business these past few days. No sooner, indeed, was the chief in the Oval Office in the most embarrassing and hapless of jams than, far away in Manila, many slightly surprising democrats threw their weight behind Cory Aquino. But the power of the networks to send politicians scurrying in their wake has never been more positively demonstrated. We've seen the negative power of TV before: the blood and bodies of Vietnam sapping resolve in Peoria. But we have never seen the characters on the spot dancing so energetically to a distant tune.

Remember how swiftly such a tune may change. For the minute Mrs Aquino – untried, gauche, uncharismatic – is the heroine. Genuinely, and exultantly, she is the spirit of the future. But she has inherited the most appalling of economic situations, not to mention guerrilla war rumbling in the hills. Twenty years ago, Ferdinand Marcos was the people's popularly elected hero. Over the years he basked in American approval. Only when – for the first time in his life – he failed the imported test of holding an election which was manifestly free and manifestly fair was the rug pulled out. Mrs Aquino, in his stead, will have to use the troops he commanded against guerrilla fighters. Mrs Aquino will have to take her own decisions about Clark air force base and Subic Bay. Mrs Aquino will have to respond to people power – the milling crowds hailing democracy – by becoming her own woman, an independent, a nationalist. She has won her freedom: now she must use it. And what will the networks make of her then? Mr Marcos was toppled, at the close, because he was not an image of leadership that the American voter or the American Congress could defend. But can we of the West construct not just policies and alliances, but images for the rest of the world which they are required to live by?

26 February, 1986   **Leader**

The shattering message on the wall

It might almost be the Almighty's idea of a sick joke: the most earthquake-prone capital city in the world, surrounded by volcanoes and built on a dried-out river bed that wobbles like jelly at the slightest tremor, has made one great contribution to the art of our century. It has provided the finance and the inspiration for an amazing outbreak of public mural painting. But what price painting on walls which every few years bend and buckle like a saw-blade waved at the wind?

The Mexican muralists were many. Most came from the intellectual suburbs, a few were foreign moths, from America, France, Spain, attracted by the glow of the post-revolutionary furnace. Some had unlikely origins reflected in unlikely names. How did Juan O'Gorman come to paint the outside of the Mexico University Library in 1949? Or Pablo O'Higgins to decorate the Emiliano Zapata school in 1933? Only the god of revolutionary serendipity knows.

In that first great wave of post-revolutionary euphoria the Mexican authorities turned over the walls of their schools and municipal offices, works buildings and factories to their artists. Later they added cinemas, hotels and theatres and for twenty years Mexico experienced an orgy of public painting on a scale which the world had not seen since the Italian Renaissance.

The reports of the September earthquake which reached us here said nothing on the subject of these great mural schemes. How badly had they been damaged? The Mexican Embassy in London had no idea. From Mexico itself the tales were always of football and hotels.

To make the situation even more poignant 1986 is the centenary of the birth of the greatest of all the Mexican muralists, Diego Rivera. Most of Rivera's best work is concentrated in the downtown area of Mexico City, the old Spanish colonial centre which starts under the dome of the cathedral and unfolds into a labyrinth of street markets and arcades cloven at intervals by imposing public buildings. This was the area most severely affected by the earthquake.

The Tate has a huge work by Rivera but never shows it. There are no plans to celebrate his 100th birthday with any exhibitions. You will not be following his truly fascinating life story on Arena or Omnibus or the South Bank Show. As the Pan-Am in-flight magazine puts it in a short preview of a Rivera exhibition in Detroit, 'the focus on Rivera's easel paintings works to his advantage because stripped of the bombast and propaganda that mar his frescoes they call attention to his overall aesthetic accomplishments'.

In fact the whole of Mexico City calls attention to Rivera's aesthetic accomplishments. The streets are full of the chiseled Indian faces he gave to his painted peons. The shops are full of clothes that come in Rivera colours, a red as thrilling as a field of poppies, a yellow as dusty and hot as the Mexican desert.

Even the thirties architecture in which Mexico City is, or was, so rich, seems somehow like a modern version of the glorious Aztec city which he painted in such evocative detail on the walls of the Palacio Nacional. The headlines in the papers continue to seem Rivera-like.

'Oaxaca teachers stage protest at Ministry of Education,' blares out the *Mexico City News*. As I strode through downtown in search of one of Rivera's earliest mural cycles I found not just the front door of the Ministry blocked off by Oaxaca's striking teachers but the entire district which they had turned into a giant tent-city. The teachers had walked from Oaxaca to live and sleep and eat and argue and sing and demonstrate in the surrounding streets. Their huge banners and fluttering posters spelled out the message with River-like directness.

To find the murals hidden deep inside the Ministry of Public Education you must blunder through a maze of corridors before finally emerging, blinking, into a large sunlit courtyard. The images seem to lurk under the arches: moustachioed revolution-aries riding across hot desert landscapes, huddles of women making bread, huddles of men gathering corn. At the far end of the courtyard a painted crowd supports a sea of red banners just like the real crowd outside. *Tierra y Libertad*, they proclaim, Land and Liberty.

According to the man from the Ministry the building shook itself like a stretching cat on that morning of September 19. Like everyone else in Mexico City he thanks God it was 7 o'clock in the morning, no one was yet at work, no children yet at school, no one in the theatres that fell down, no one in the ruined cinemas, not many in the cathedral when the giant gold ceiling medallions dropped to the floor from 200 feet.

But the Rivera murals were not tucked away in bed in the low-lying suburbs. They were there, attached to acres of Ministry walls by little more than the natural cohesion of water. The extent of the damage takes a while to become apparent. A huge white crack, six inches wide, zig zags from top to bottom of the famous scene in which Zapata and his soldiers sit around a camp fire singing revolutionary songs. Many of the arches can only stand with the help of scaffolding. A quarter of the murals seem to have suffered some kind of cracking and are being repaired. But the damage looks containable. And like a much-patched old violin, the noble Ministry building wears its scars well.

For three days I had tried to contact the government department charged with the upkeep of the murals, to ascertain the extent of the damage throughout the city. When I gave up telephoning I tried writing. But a combination of Mexico's notoriously bad lines of communication and what is clearly an official desire to say nothing on the subject made progress impossible.

The thought crossed my mind that if this had been Florence or Venice or Urbino thousands of frantic art historians, architectural enthusiasts, student volunteers and charity workers would now be sifting through the rubble. As it is you sometimes come across an old workman with a brush dabbing away at yet another cracked fresco.

My primary objective had been to visit the Hotel del Prado. Every great city seems to have an hotel at which writers and artists and film stars and actors like to congregate. In New York it is the Algonquin. In London it is Browns. In Mexico

106

City it had been the Hotel del Prado, a splendid piece of thirties hope and chrome and elegance. It was here, late in 1948, that Rivera completed one of his last great works.

It was entitled 'Dream of a Sunday Afternoon in the Alameda Park'. Rivera still had ten years to live and some fine murals to paint but in the Sunday Afternoon Dream it was as if the whole of the Mexican nation had flashed before his eyes in seconds, policemen, prostitutes, husbands, beggars, street sellers, children with balloons, Zapata, Diaz, Villa, the entire cast had turned out on a sunny afternoon to pose for the painter. In the crowd you see a familiar face, round, boyish, as smooth-skinned as an early Picasso head, Rivera himself.

The Hotel del Prado is now a ruin, one of the most badly damaged buildings on Alameda Park, singled out for special attention by this most fickle earthquake. High wooden fences keep out the public while hard-hatted workmen slowly go about its demolition.

With all official channels blocked there was nothing for it but to trust to the power of the dollar bill. In the event five were enough to persuade two young Charons with yellow hats and torches to lead me into Hades.

The once glorious hotel seemed as if it had been savaged by a giant dog. The floor was full of gaping holes, pillars jutted out at eerie angles. The light of the torches only just penetrated the thick darkness. It felt dangerous underfoot and dangerous overhead, and walking through it was one of the most claustrophobic experiences of my life. Eventually we reached a wooden partition with a door in it.

Inside hung a huge dust curtain. We lifted it and shone our torches at the wall – hundreds of fierce black Mexican eyes stared back at us, soldiers, priests, dictators, revolutionaries, painters, poets and children. As the torch moved from face to face and my eager guides argued about the identity of its owner, it gradually became clear that the wall on which Rivera had painted his masterpiece was almost the only one inside the Hotel del Prado to have remained intact. One lonely crack descended through the picture, just to the side of Rivera's portrait of himself.

The Mexicans I spoke to found nothing uncanny about the

way that their murals have by and large survived the earthquake. Art always survives, they replied with a shrug.

But the earthquake's damage may yet prove insidiously far-reaching. Back on the hotel telephone I eventually broke through to the relevant Ministry's conservation department. It seems that the Hotel del Prado mural is to be transferred to the Palacio de Bellas Artes, moved out of the mainstream of Mexican life and into a museum. That too is another kind of death.

12 April, 1986   **Waldemar Januszczak**

Mach 2 to Miami

It is ten years since Concorde made its first commercial flight. I flew on her the other day from London to Washington and then down to Miami, the second sector in the cockpit, and this is the story of that flight. It touches in places on the Wright Brothers, on a scholar called Dionysius Lardner, and on another and earlier aeroplane, the Douglas DC3. I write about aeroplanes *con amore*. My father was an engineer, and some things stay in the blood, and Concorde is an utterly beautiful machine.

At 1300 hours, BA 189 was ready to go, but Atlantic control would not let her. I have never seen such deep unhappiness over a delay. My version is that some damned Air France Concorde out of Paris had perfidiously wangled permission to take off first, and, since British Airways shared the same supersonic channel over the Atlantic, we had to wait. It was an international incident. We were ready to go on time and Air France was late, so we had priority. Air France was only a charter anyway. And priority to the Frenchmen had been given by Shannon and Prestwick control, known as Shanwick – Irishmen and Scotsmen putting their heads together. An hour's delay was threatened. Protesting telephone calls were made by top management, which reduced the wait to thirty-five minutes, which we later made up. This, as I say, is my own informal version, but there was no mistaking the restrained fury in the voices of the crew as they gave the passengers the bare facts.

In fifteen minutes we were over Cardiff, in twenty-eight minutes doing 1000 mph, and after forty-four minutes cruising at Mach 2, twice the speed of sound. We were into lunch – slices of smoked goose breast garnished with spiced fruits, and champagne Cuvée de René Lalou, Mumm's finest.

Now this is a splendid way to eat and drink, and anyone who declines such stuff on principle is paying a high price for his radical conscience, but Mumm's is not essentially what Concorde is about. Into his second glass, my American neighbour turned to me and volunteered the information that he worked for Short Brothers, an English company, which, he said, had built the Wright Brothers' early machines for them, because they couldn't get it done in America. That was only eighty years ago, and look what has happened since then. That is what it is about.

I first flew on Concorde in 1976, to Bahrain. I wrote then that in twenty years everyone would be flying long distances that way, and that the Americans would in ten years have built their own supersonic airliner. I was wrong. They have not, and when I look back at what I wrote then I detect a belief in an almost nineteenty-century idea of progress. This innocent belief has not survived intact in me. How could it in anyone who has seen the way the world has gone in the last ten years? But I still believe that Concorde has history on her side.

Because, in all forms of transport, speed has always won. The railways killed the stage coaches and canals, and amazed everyone by how quickly they did it. The steamship killed the sailing packet in twenty years between 1840 and 1860. Who would take thirty-five days from Liverpool to New York when he could do it in ten? And the jet killed the propeller aeroplane in five years, because it was twice as fast. Who would go on the cheapest package holiday today in a plane with propellers and straight wings?

But back to the Washington flight. At this point in my reflections I asked for lamb chops, pink, and the man in front of me had asked for lamb chops, well done, and I reckoned that if Concorde could do that it could do anything. By then we were cruising, against a strong head wind, at 1250 mph.

And yet, this is a time when ordinary subsonic jets are in fact cruising more slowly than they did twenty years ago. An average transatlantic flight in a Boeing 707 twenty years ago was faster than an average flight in a 747 today. Some new planes are even built to be slower. An Airbus 310 cruises 100 mph slower than the ancient Caravelle.

This is a plateau, not to say a decline, previously unknown in the history of modern transport. All history and instinct is against its continuance. I remember meeting Tex Boullioun, head of Boeing Commercial, the most successful planemaker in the world, and his whole generous instinct was to praise the aeroplanes built since the war which had used whole new technologies, and which all happened to be English or Anglo-French – the jet-prop Viscount, the pure jet Comet, and what he called the brilliant Concorde. 'Fifteen years ahead of its time.' He would love to have built the Boeing SST, which was cancelled.

And for the United States, of all nations, to have cancelled that plane, and on account of timidity, is extraordinary. Of course, so daring a thing as Concorde costs money it will not recoup. But neither did the great ocean liners of the 1930s. Before the war neither the *Queen Mary* nor the French *Normandie* ever made money. Neither could be afforded. Both were built out of national pride. In my patriotic moments, I tell myself that Concorde is the last great gift of the British and the French empires to the world. That's hyperbole, and I stand by it.

At this point we were in mid-Atlantic, at 58,000 feet, and the ozone layer, so far as one could detect, seemed not noticeably to have deteriorated. This brought triumphantly to mind the objections of the Friends of the Earth, the Wilderness Society, and Dr Dionysius Lardner (1793-1859).

It was the Wilderness Society which ten years ago was confidently predicting that supersonic aircraft would cause a significant increase in cirrus clouds, and that passengers on such planes would suffer physical, physiological, and psychological stresses in the hostile environment of Mach 2.

How close all that was to the life's mutterings of Dionysius Lardner of Trinity College, Dublin, who mathematically calculated that if a train entered Box Tunnel on the Great Western Railway at 40 mph it would emerge, there being a slight gradient in that tunnel, at a speed which would have killed all the passengers. He was a clergyman as well as a Fellow of the Royal Society, and great attention was paid to him even after passengers emerged alive in Bristol from the hostile environment of the GWR's carriages, having passed unscathed through that tunnel. He continued to devote his life to the condemnation of the steam engine, the steam locomotive, and the steamship – until in the end he eloped to Paris with the wife of a director of the London and Brighton Railway, crossing the Channel by steamship.

By this time, on its transatlantic crossing, Concorde was coming up to scenes of great astonishment. You do not see them from the cruising altitude of ordinary planes. From 58,000 feet the whole spoon-shaped peninsula of Cape Cod was set out like a map come alive. I could pick out not only towns and beaches I knew but also, because it is at the narrowest part of the island, the site of a house I have stayed at. Then Long Island, and then, in a lovely understatement by the captain, 'a very large inlet', which was New York Bay. Manhattan stretched out below. Central Park stood out, and there on the North River, on a pier at about 42nd Street, a light flashed. That was the Cunard pier.

And so on, over the frozen Susquehanna river, over the meandering Potomac, into Dulles International at Washington, where the space shuttle Enterprise was parked, as a sort of trophy, by one of the taxiways. I sat in the plane as the Washington passengers disembarked and reflected that if I were very rich, and had 100 friends to whom I wanted to show something they would always remember, I might take up an offer made to me by British Airways the day before. Almost a seventh of their Concorde revenue now comes from charters. A charter round the Scillies and back was proposed to me. No, I said, to Cannes, the long way round over the Bay of Biscay so that we could go supersonic, and then back. How much? I was quoted sixty thousand pounds. But, I said, I would want to stay overnight before coming back. That, then, would make it seventy thousand.

That quotation was given to me by Captain Brian Walpole, who is general manager of British Airways Concorde division but who still flies the aeroplane a lot to keep his hand in. He is a contemporary of Norman Tebbit, when he was a pilot, and flew with him on 707s for ten years, often sharing a flightdeck. The other day, at dinner at No. 10, he offered to charter Concorde to Mrs Thatcher at cost for her next overseas tour, pointing out that she had never flown Concorde though the Queen had. Mrs Thatcher declined with thanks, which is reasonable, since I suppose the RAF flies her for nothing, though not on Concorde.

Concorde captains are the *crème de la crème*. Captain Norman Britten, who was in command of the flight I made to Washington and Miami, looks and speaks just as I imagine the archetypal Cunard captain would have done. Really, he looks more like a Cunard captain than any Cunard captain I ever saw, because he is fully bearded and speaks with a West Country brogue that could have come out of Robert Louis Stevenson but comes in fact from Piddletrenthide, Dorset. I come from Poole, so we were brought up within a few miles of each other, but his art, that of flying this aeroplane, is as far beyond my understanding as higher physics is from simple arithmetic.

Out of Washington, I sat in the cockpit with the captain, first officer, and engineer. 'Speedbird 189 Heavy. Ready?' asked Dulles flight control. 'Ready. Ma'am.' And so on, out on to the taxiway and then the runway. Air traffic control at Dulles, having such light traffic (because internal flights go to National, which is much closer in to the city) have the reputation of being more pedantic than even Sydney.

Now when you sit in a passenger seat, there is less sense of flying in Concorde than in any other plane I know. This is not so on the flight deck, when you can see ahead of you the runway down which you are throwing yourself at about 250 mph, and see the sky and the clouds into which you are climbing at 8000 feet a minute. She flies like a fighter.

'This aeroplane leaves a Lightning standing,' said the captain, and then, while his first officer and engineer flew the plane, he carried on a running commentary, uttered with the greatest passion, urging me to lean closer, over his seat, so that

I could hear better. At the beginning of the flight, at Heathrow, he had mentioned over the intercom that this was the finest plane in the world, but you can hear American airline pilots say as much of their 747s. But inside his cockpit, which resembles nothing so much as the inside of an immense computer, he spoke with the complete conviction of a man doing what he does best.

'I know I rabbit on about my aeroplane,' he said, 'but there are only two fighters who are faster.'

Which? He said the American F15 and the Russian Foxbat, but then, they could only do Mach 2 for fifteen minutes and then they were out of fuel. Perhaps a Tomcat could catch Concorde, but they'd give him a hard time. Fifteen minutes and a fighter was out of fuel, but they could go out over the Atlantic and back at Mach 2. Nothing else could. He recounted conversations with fighter pilots in which they had given Concorde best.

We went through Mach 1 and Mach 2. I asked where we were. 'We never know where we are,' he said, 'only where we were,' and calculated where we had been at that moment.

Was he saying, then, that an aeroplane designed in the 1950s and 1960s was still in some respects superior to modern fighters? He said indeed he was. There was nothing else like it.

Then we were coming in through thick cloud, known in the trade as 'rubbish', and were into a rain-sodden Miami, having taken only one hour and twenty minutes from Washington. Captain and co-pilot were as cool as if they had been driving a well-behaved BMW on an empty motorway at a steady 50. I was exhausted.

I muttered something about having once met Keith Granville when he was chairman of BOAC and he had said he began his airline service clearing goats off runways in the Middle East. Then we taxied in next to an ancient DC3, which was standing turning its propellers over. Fifty years ago, and a bit more, it was the Concorde of its day, an aluminium monoplane, faster than any fighter of its time. 'Lovely thing,' said Captain Britten.

What of the future? Concorde will last until past the year 2000, and is at present unapproached. No one is even trying to approach. But where from there? I had put this question to

Captain Britten about half-way from Washington to Miami. He said you needed a Mach 2 plane, made of aluminium like Concorde, not titanium, which would get you to Mach 3, but was tricky, and you needed a plane that would take, say, 200 passengers, and have the range to fly London-Los Angeles.

'It needs,' said the man from Piddletrenthide, 'it needs the Americans to pluck up the political courage to build it.' Only the Americans could make such a new plane now, but it would be an Anglo-American aeroplane. The technology was there already, pretty well, with Concorde.

18 January, 1986   **Terry Coleman**

A warning for the global village

It has already become the great logo in the sky: a huge white hand-shaped cloud with two long clutching fingers of vapour. As an image of an American tragedy it straight away took its place alongside that of Jackie Kennedy crouching, ungainly, on the boot of the speeding car in Dallas. We saw them both over and over again, long into Tuesday night and yesterday morning. Nothing is ever likely to erase them.

Live television has had some extraordinary moments in the past year or so. Tebbit is rescued from the wreckage of the Brighton hotel; the Bradford stand becomes a pyre, the Heysel stadium a charnel house. However calamitous, they were not beamed instantly round the world, they remained essentially domestic. There have been events of world import like Live Aid, but they were staged.

The Challenger disaster is the first world-scale story brought to British audiences live through the Cable News Network and its twenty-four-hour satellite coverage. Yet in prospect it was a story where there should have been no news. The news in the event was that there was no story. The explosion had written that lethal full-stop, eight miles up. So what exactly did this massive media event bring to us?

It brought us news of a horrible accident that killed seven –

fewer than a bad motorway pile-up. It cast doubt on the future of manned space vehicles, and on the already shaky credibility of the Star Wars strategy. It was an appalling experience for relatives and friends watching, for Christa McAuliffe's pupils. But the scale of the reaction was determined not by the suffering of people who knew the seven who died, but by the fact that it had been turned into a spectator event.

The millions who watched were planned, they were the reason. After all those successful launches, this one should have been routine, scarcely worth covering. It was the public relations idea of the 'first ordinary citizen', the teacher who would give lessons about space from space, and it was the satellite technology that could turn the PR into an international boost for American astro-politics that changed the nature of the event.

The same things then turned it into what could be presented as a human tragedy shared by the whole planet. And where television goes, newspapers follow.

But does that media picture match the events? I don't believe it does. But I believe that the selling of the idea that it does has disturbing implications for the ways in which round-the-clock, round-the-world live coverage might be manipulated.

Sometimes what we saw had the quality of an instant scratch video. ITN broke the news on screen first by interrupting scheduled programmes at 5 o'clock, some minutes ahead of the BBC, and was able to use Reagan's solemn address to the nation more or less live on *News at Ten*. I say more or less, because a technical fault meant for about the first half minute of Reagan's speech, voice and lip movements were well out of sync.

It was an eerie effect. The presidential face was heavily and crudely made up, and his message was coming to us like a badly dubbed Italian movie. No cunning scratch video artist could have undermined Reagan's words more effectively or more simply, or made him sound more bogus as he mouthed the quote comparing the astronauts to adventurers who had 'slipped the surly bonds of earth to touch the face of God'.

Channel 4's series about video art, *Ghosts in the Machine*, is a brutal reminder of the effects of stored images – especially when coupled to alien sounds. Last night, Susan Hiller's *Bel-*

shazzar's Feast was just a blurred picture of a fire beginning, slowly blazing up and dying away. The soundtrack whispered reports of strange images seen by viewers on blank screens after transmissions have ended. Arty-farty stuff with no resonance, until you thought of what might be done with that white cloud image now printed on our minds as the edge of life on earth.

Tuesday night's programme in the series had a more chilling example. In this video, *The Eternal Frame*, actors had recreated that famous Kennedy drive through Dallas. Over and over we saw Jackie apparently climbing out on to the boot to haul that desperate secret service man on board after the fatal shots rang out. And we saw how those Dallas worthies (it was made in 1975) reacted as this loathsome piece of street theatre was played out among them.

'I'm glad we were here,' said one bystanding woman, wiping away a tear. 'It was too beautiful.' The most interesting thing, said one of the actors, 'was watching people enjoy it so much.'

'I think that is what television was meant to do,' said a male watcher, 'bring the truth to the American people.' I'm not sure if he had realized that the actor playing Jackie in that ghoulish re-enactment was a man.

30 January, 1986   **Hugh Hebert**

Arrival at Terminal Bore

The sound of Heathrow terminal four as it lurched through its second working day yesterday was that of booming apologies on the public address system. 'British Airways regrets to announce that passengers on flight BA409 from Amsterdam are still awaiting their baggage.' The flight had landed at 1 p.m.; it was now 2.30.

'British Airways regret that passengers on flight BA409, 072 and 174 have been delayed and are still awaiting their baggage.' It is now 3 p.m.

The other sound was that of rows of cursing chauffeurs, holding boards with businessmen's names on them. Mr Michael

Poat, of BCH Chauffeur Services, laments: 'I've been here two hours. What a mess. And have you seen the toilets? I think they must have let the vandals in before the passengers.'

Terminal four does not hold back on provisions for the ego of the executive man of the skies. There are 'super clubs' and 'speedlinks' to 'super shuttles', there are American-style courtesy mini-buses to hotels and car hire depots, administered by girls with heavy lipstick, wavy blonde hair and toothy smiles. There are no high street banks, only 'the Travelex Corporation' at which to change money (commission 1½ per cent).

But the breezy efficiency of Europe's other spanking new airports, like Paris or Frankfurt, seems to have eluded terminal four. 'It's the biggest cock-up ever,' seethes Mr Don Harper of Erith, Kent, back from Los Angeles, after a ninety-minute wait for his baggage. Those in officialdom prefer to talk about 'teething troubles'. That was the catchphrase of the afternoon – 'just teething trouble, sir.'

After following signs reading 'Terminal four 1½' for three miles, one is ready to negotiate the 'short-term park' – a maze of ramps and lanes apparently modelled on a micro-chip circuit. A family is confused in the lift to the main terminal by the fact that each floor is labelled 'departures' and 'arrivals'. A porter helps out. 'Terminal bore, we're calling it,' he says cheerfully.

The cramped arrivals hall is built in a grey material which, when tapped, produces a sound like that from the insubstantial plastic dashboards of new cars. It is lit by a sickly, sulphurish glare.

The lavatories, if they can be found, are not appreciated. Mr Harper says: 'We've been round the world – Delhi, Tahiti, the lot – and these were the worst we've seen. The wife says the ladies' was blocked. The men's was like a cesspool.'

The gents' in the arrival and departure lounges seem better, but the 'Cannon Top-dri' (*sic*) air drier remains stubbornly silent after the button is pressed.

Both card phones in the arrivals hall refuse to permit a call, simply rejecting a card. Six out of twelve coin phones tested accept a 10p piece but only four obtain the number.

On the 'catering level', the 'Euroelectrics WMF Programmat 2' coffee machine has a sign on it reading, 'Out of order – coffee across the aisle.' There the 'WMF Filtromat' is working at 35p a small cup.

Dr Mervyn Carse, from Detroit, has finally got his baggage after waiting one and a half hours. 'Something caught in the conveyor, I think. It's an absolute disaster in there.'

Mr John Archer, a BBC producer from Hammersmith, got off with a light one hour and ten minutes in the baggage hall after his arrival from Los Angeles. 'I was travelling club class so I was lucky. It was a shambles. Mind you, they were good on giving us information about how the computer had broken down. I decided to have a read but the light was too awful.'

The chauffeurs are getting distraught. 'BA292 from Miami – 12 o'clock it touched down, it's now 2.23,' fumes Mr Derek Barkham of Ace Cars, Chessington. 'It affects us because you can't offer other people a car.' Another driver had waited two hours on Saturday for a Karachi flight to unload, and was only ten minutes away from beating that yesterday.

Why? That's what everybody wants to know from Mr Jeremy Watts at the information desk. 'Well, we really don't know why, but it is affecting all flights,' he says. 'It could be teething troubles.'

'It's the airline's problem,' insists Ms Margaret Nettle of the security staff. 'Ask desk 25,' grunts a woman at the British Airways ticket desk. At desk 25 – 'customer service' – Mr Paul Scott says: 'Problems? I didn't know we had problems. Must be teething problems.' 'Definitely teething problems,' adds a police officer.

When the multi-storey car park is reached, the payment booth is shut. A boy in a red 'Euro Car Parks' blazer explains: 'I'm afraid the machine's packed up and my intercom has broken. You'll have to drive over there to pay. It's not our fault, sir.'

14 April, 1986   **Edward Vulliamy**

A country diary: Keswick

Sound can do strange things in quiet November weather. A thick mist along the valley can deaden everything but given a clear valley and a low cloud layer it can travel far. A friend who lived all her life on a farm near Thirlmere used to say that she could sometimes hear the bells of Crosthwaite church clearly – six miles away and in the next valley. It seems that their voices can rise, hit the cloud layer and echo southwards. The ring is an old one. In 1699 the churchwarden's accounts record four shillings and sixpence a year for the four ringers and five shillings for a new bell rope. In 1706 it was sixteen shillings with ale for Thanksgiving Days and November the Fifth. By 1714 the Great Bell needed attention so it was taken down, sent by cart to Whitehaven and by ship to Dublin to be re-cast. Those accounts have almost forty items varying from 'one shilling the night the bell was cast' to 'one pound and sixteen for our diet, lodging and washing our linen'. The grand total – belfry to belfry – was just over £37 and the bells rang for the King's Coronation in 1715. Six bells were hung in 1775 and with that change-ringing began. A Yorkshire man arrived in Keswick with a small travelling circus and, a shoemaker by trade, he stayed on to follow it and to teach the art of change-ringing in the belfry. Ringers had discipline. A board still in the church adjures a man to have an upright heart and there are fines for wrong-doing – eightpence for ringing with spur or hat or for overturning a bell. Times and bells may have changed but most of the names of those old ringers can still be met in the flesh in a Keswick street.

2 December, 1985   **Enid J. Wilson**

Gaudeamus igitur . . . post jucundum juventutem

On Monday morning I noticed that two of my colleagues were wearing slightly stunned expressions, as doubtless I myself was. All three of us had spent the weekend at college reunions. At Oxford they are called gaudies. Cambridge has no special word for these lavish occasions – at which the intake of three or four consecutive years are invited back as guests of the college, free of charge, given a room for the night, a sumptuous feast and oceans of wine and spirits.

Doubtless the alcohol contributed to our stunned expressions, but only in part. Returning after quarter of a century to the place where you spent three years of your youth is a salutary experience. Meeting old acquaintances from time to time, I sometimes think, 'He's aged a lot.' But it's a very different matter meeting your contemporaries, two hundred of them at once. The truth is no longer escapable. It's middle age you're looking at. Your own.

Cambridge last weekend was lovelier than I've ever seen it. It looked splendid in 1958, but now all the stone and brickwork has been cleaned, everything is freshly painted, the weather vanes are gilded, the grass manicured, the flower-beds ablaze with colour. Clearly there's at least one part of the educational system that's doing very nicely, thank you, under Sir Keith Joseph.

In my day, eating in Hall was not a great gastronomic experience, but the dinner last Saturday was quite the best large-scale catering I have encountered. Galantine of Pheasant, Paté Turbot Andalouse, Roast Loin of Veal with lemon and thyme stuffing. Salsify, Calabrese and Parmentier potatoes; Pears Dijonnaise (superb ice cream), fruit, and then coffee, cigars with the 1955 port or 1966 claret, which had been preceded by 1978 Hermitage, 1976 Côte Rotie, and a 1975 Riesling. The college's huge collection of silver was on display, and the chapel choir sang glees to us, and then there were speeches. The Provost, Bernard Williams, made a speech saying what a fine college King's is, was, and ever more shall be so.

I think it was this speech that brought home to many of us what an orgy of complacent self-congratulation we were all involved in. Even as undergraduates we were aware that Cambridge was a privileged, cloistered place, far removed from what even then we called 'the real world' into which we were about to be banished after eating the fruit of the tree of knowledge. Now we had all come back to reaffirm our collegiate identity. My neighbour at dinner had come all the way from Australia. ('Over the North Pole,' he said more than once.) Another old friend had made the trip from Jerusalem.

It so happens that King's has a fine record as a tolerant, liberal, humanistic institution, greatly distinguished both in science and the arts. In that respect the Provost was justified in the self-indulgence of the college patting itself on the back. But, but . . . What about the real world, where the educational system of the whole country is falling about our ears?

Suppose we accept the conceited boast that we (and graduates of other Oxbridge colleges) are the cream of the cream, product of the finest educational institutions in the country. What have we got to show for it?

Most of my contemporaries I spoke to have followed careers that are enjoyable, interesting and mostly lucrative, but hardly essential. Many, like me, are in the media (a word hardly known in 1958). Others are lawyers, bankers, academics. One is a parish priest. One is a top cardiac surgeon (and that's pretty useful). One has been unemployed for nine years. And one works in textiles in Bradford. Out of the whole lot of us, he was the only one I met that could be called a primary producer, contributing in real terms to the economy of the country.

After the meal, whisky flowed, the talk was scintillating, reminiscences were exchanged, the laughter was loud. We had a very good time.

In the small hours I was sitting outside in Webb's Court. It was a lovely night, the kind that Cambridge uniquely and only rarely produces, with a slight mist that is somehow warm and cool at the same time. The atmosphere was like that of

Belmont at the end of *The Merchant of Venice*. On such a night . . .

I was talking to someone I had not seen for twenty years. While he was telling me his interesting and rather moving history, two drunken men in dinner jackets joined us. They were talking noisily, and we politely pointed out to them that it was 2.30 in the morning and we were sitting below the windows of people who were probably trying to sleep.

One of them (he's in the wine trade) then pissed into a flower bed. The other (a film producer) then proceeded to make guffawing comments about the size of his friend's penis. These were not undergraduates but men who will soon be fifty. I had had enough and went to bed.

Breakfast in the morning was excellent. Then we packed our bags and stood around shaking hands and saying why don't we meet for lunch sometime? A last loving look at the Banks and the chapel, and then out into King's Parade to buy a Sunday newspaper. Brixton was in flames.

2 October, 1985   **Richard Boston**

A lesson for everybody . . .

Little harmony comes from the third form music lesson. For this is a class proud of the anarchic reputation it has won – in a school where discipline is never easy. Many kids play truant, an indication of their belief that education, for them, is almost wholly pointless.

Each child has an instrument. One boy draws up a chair to the Yamaha electric keyboard claiming his legs are tired. He blasts out chords with his chin. The bass guitarist pretends to be one of the Shadows, and one boy and girl can be observed dismantling a xylophone. The music master's attempts to get silence, while they are supposed to be watching him demonstrate the part to be played on the bass guitar, are brazenly ignored. But he is patient. Only occasionally, in the continual struggle to make himself heard, does he sound irritated.

Eventually, near the end of the lesson, they do actually all play the tune – together. He praises them to the skies, and for the first time there is quiet. 'They're smashing to teach,' he says afterwards. 'When they eventually hear themselves doing it properly, they're really proud.'

The science lesson at least looks orderly – this is the top band of fifteen-year-olds – but inspiration is in short supply. Twenty boys and girls stare at the blackboard in blank silence as Richard Clayton explains radio isotopes. His voice is clear and commanding and he asks questions to force participation. He gets a muttered reply the second or third time. A touch of humour – 'You've got an even chance of getting this one right' – and then he runs a video, with a question sheet for each pupil to fill in.

They gather round, dragging their stools. Some write, others look at each other. Five minutes before the bell, Mr Clayton tells them to go, to avoid the stampede.

He's preparing them for a combined sciences mode three CSE, a syllabus the teachers write and assess themselves. Over 150 out of the 1240-strong year will take it, and most will get it, he says. How does he persuade them a science CSE is a worthwhile thing to do, when none of them will get jobs as scientists?

'I tell them it will make them more aware of what's going on. Some accept it, some don't. Yes, I tell them they could build on it, but I don't pretend they could become a nuclear physicist.' How many are really enthusiastic? 'Oh, one or two,' he says cheerfully.

History with a group of fourth years, mainly girls, looks as if there is a constant struggle to hold their attention and inspire some interest in the subject. This time it's the beginnings of the Welfare State. Their syllabus requires them to study a topic through time – they are looking at medicine. So Chris Gardiner, the teacher, tries to relate 1948 to the present National Health Service, of which they all have some experience.

Today he is having an uphill struggle. Julie, who can usually be roused to express strong opinions against compulsory inno-culations, won't be drawn. He appeals to all of them. 'What do you think about it? Is the NHS a good thing?' Every time he focuses attention on one child, the rest start to fidget, to giggle and chatter.

They would all rather write answers to exercise questions – half-copied from the textbook and half from their neighbour – than take part in discussion. But Chris refuses to give in. His last resort is to provoke them. 'Do you think you should all pay for treatment then?'

The bell rings. 'Now sit down. Don't you know it's the height of rudeness to put your coat on while we're still talking? Now Andrea. What do you think about private medicine?' He has won, at least as far as she and her neighbour are concerned. 'Some people might get treatment before others who might be more ill,' she volunteers.

It seems pretty thankless work but Chris, like most of the teachers, is proud of what his class achieves. 'They got talking at the end, didn't they? We'll probably have a good discussion next lesson. I felt it was an important topic.' He is not just teaching it for an eventual exam qualification. Most of the best and most enthusiastic teachers do not see exam results as the principal and only target. 'I feel the lesson was worthwhile in itself,' says Chris.

This school – the Middleton Park High School in south Leeds – where jostling sullen-faced boys and girls in motley bright coloured garments stampede screeching out of class whenever the lesson bell rings, is no more typical than any other, but it is at the sharp end of Britain's education system.

'Anyone who can teach here,' says Hugh Robinson, head of games, biology teacher and union rep, 'can teach anywhere.'

According to Ralph Clark, the head, 85 per cent of these kids are under-achievers. The school stands slap in the middle of an estate of homes built for the heroes of the 1914-18 war. It now houses their low wage or long-term unemployed descendants. Most of the building is brand new, built on the ashes of William Gascoigne girls' school, destroyed by arson six years ago. Judged by exam results, standards are low. Out of 120 taking 16-plus history this year, for instance, not more than ten are expected by their teacher to get an 'O' level pass. There are 720 pupils, but only just over twenty in the sixth form.

This is the sharp end, where the quality of education really matters – much more than for the top 20 per cent who will do well anyway. Even the Government agrees on this. It has recently floated vague plans for 'Crown schools', Government-funded, that would employ the 'best teachers' in inner-city areas to raise standards.

*"In our history lesson today
we shall trace the origins
of the teachers' strike."*

6 December, 1985

It's an exhausting and demanding job at the best of times, and the past year of industrial action has taken its toll. This school has slightly more members of the National Association of Schoolmasters/Union of Women Teachers than of the National Union of Teachers. Although the NAS/UWT nationally has advised a return to normal working, in this area (as in many) the teachers have redefined normal to match what they consider are still inadequate wages. In theory they refuse to carry out any management instruction – anything the head asks them to do – and will not work during lunch or after school.

Lunchtime is dead. The teachers are in the staff room eating sandwiches, and the kids, except for those who get free meals, are hanging about in the corridors or outside in the grounds or on the nearby council estate. There used to be clubs and activities – every teacher used to do something. Those days, says the head, are gone. They will never return.

That makes him sad, of course, and weary, and he's under some stress. Never before has he had to take sleeping pills.

'Life was simpler when I went into teaching,' he says. 'We knew what we were supposed to do. We were brought up with a sense of duty. We came into teaching because it was what we wanted to do and we recognized it was a way of sharing our enthusiasms with people. I have a love of English and philosophy and the great outdoors.'

Education to him is taking a party of scraggy, urban children from the relative security of the council estate to the breathtaking heights of the Lake District – opening their eyes and stretching their imaginations. His convictions are little different from those of his most committed staff, but he fears that society now wants something different of its future citizens.

'Expectations have risen. Materialism has become more important. It's not for me to judge. If you grant that this is a materialistic society then you are going to have to pay for the society you have created.'

Recognising this themselves, perhaps, the pupils and their parents on the estate do seem to think the only point of school is to prepare you for a job. The art master calls them 'pragmatic'. He has trouble getting children to take his subject as an option these days. They think it's not job-orientated.

The reverse is true in home economics. Half of those in the third year opting for cookery are boys, because a few boys from the school have done well in the catering trade.

But for the most part, Middleton Park children are likely to leave with a small clutch of low-grade CSEs and a very limited selection of job possibilities. Brian Seekins, head of community studies, thinks exams for them are a waste of time. He is hard on those teachers who will not adapt their ideas and teaching methods to what he sees as the particular needs of these children.

'Teachers con themselves that "I'm here to teach physics as if I was in grammar school or whatever". Then you get the argument that CSE is a nationally recognized qualification. The fact is that before the school burned down you could paper the walls with unrecognized CSE qualifications.'

He tries to encourage other teachers to help establish an alternative curriculum. Under the Northern Partnership for Records of Achievement scheme, children can take modules of four and five weeks – on two-year courses these children get bored. Staff would write the module – for instance, a study of a child or old person, building, gardening, computer studies or community service. The child gets a certificate for each one, recognized by examining boards. 'They will end up with a whole record of achievement. For years they have left with nothing.' What these children lack more than anything, he says, is self-confidence.

Hugh Robinson, the NAS/UWT representative, agrees with him. In spite of his union job, he is not afraid to agree with the Government for once on dead wood in the profession. 'I'd sack four or five teachers here and send another twenty on retraining courses. But the rest work like dogs.'

Such high standards are typical in what is undoubtedly a caring and hard-working school, up against the odds. But Hugh, like the others, could be earning far more in almost any other profession. It makes one wonder what heights education might reach if teachers were more highly valued.

12 May, 1986   **Sarah Boseley**

The looking-glass jaw

'Curiouser and curiouser,' said Alice. 'It seems the more that I learn about education policy the less that I understand it. Why, it appears almost to belong to the looking-glass world and not to the real world at all.'

The sheep said nothing, but continued with its knitting. 'What I mean,' Alice went on, 'is that where I go to school the Conservative Party favours the public, which is to say the private, school system. To take money from the Exchequer and to spend it upon education, without any local control, is considered Socialistic and Levelling and quite certainly wrong.'

'Idiot,' said the Blue Queen, tossing her head impatiently. 'Of course that's what it is. She must be a Libyan. Off with her head!'

'Nonsense!' said Alice very loudly and decidedly. 'Look at this speech by your minister, Mr Christopher Patten. On April 4 in Cardiff he said that central government might have to play a more direct role in the funding of schools, at the expense of the local authorities. Now he is saying that the Government must also take the funding of polytechnics out of local hands too. It stands to reason that that isn't Tory policy.'

'If it stands to reason, it can't be Tory policy,' chuckled a voice at her side. Alice looked and saw that the Welsh Rabbit had returned and was clutching a copy of Labour's ILEA manifesto.

'Hold your tongue!' said the Queen, turning purple. 'I never change my mind!' Then the procession moved off.

'You are no better, I'm afraid,' said Alice to the Welsh Rabbit, though she was glad to see him after the argument with the Queen. 'The way I was brought up, socialism was about ensuring equality of opportunity and that could only be done through a strong centralized state. You would think that when Mr Patten says these things Labour would welcome them. Instead, I now read that, far from endorsing these moves, you intend to abolish the county councils and devolve control still further. Where's the socialism in that?'

The Welsh Rabbit looked at his watch as though he was late for an appointment. 'Who mentioned socialism?' he muttered. 'I know I didn't.' And he gradually began to disappear in front of Alice's eyes until all that remained of him was a vague sense of well-being.

'Wait, wait!' cried Alice. 'Before you go. Four years ago, when you were Labour education spokesman, you proposed the setting of minimum national standards for under-fives provision, for school books, laboratory equipment, staffing levels and in-service training, all to be financed and enforced centrally. Am I right? Or is there nothing left?'

'I am right and left. Yet there is nothing right and nothing left,' replied the Rabbit enigmatically. And with a friendly cry of 'We're all realigned now' he disappeared so quickly that, a moment later, Alice had difficulty remembering what he had looked like.

Alice wandered on, talking to herself as she went, till, on turning a sharp corner, she came upon two little fat men. She was just saying, half out loud, 'How can people control something that they haven't got?' when one of the little men interrupted. 'Contrariwise, how can people get what they can't control? Answer that, eh?'

'Oh now I'm thoroughly confused,' said Alice. 'The Blue Queen says she's against the state, but she wants to centralize to protect the middle classes. The Welsh Rabbit is supposed to be against the market, but he wants to decentralize so as not to alarm them. What's a person to think?'

'You aren't supposed to think,' said Humpty Dumpty. 'You're just supposed to listen to the sound of the words.'

'The question is,' said Alice, 'whether you can make words mean so many different things.'

'The question is,' said Humpty Dumpty, 'which is to be master – that's all.'

17 April, 1986   **Leader**

Four men in a boat

The Fishing Party (40 Minutes, BBC-2) was a killing film, as funny as it was deadly. You could feel the bait taken and the line tighten as four fine fish – Guy and Henry and Robert and John – were tenderly played and tidily gaffed.

It was Guy Cheyney – you can see, thinking back, it would be Guy – who rang the BBC suggesting they should cover his attempt to catch a record skate, conservatively estimated at fifteen feet from fin to fin, or a halibut weighing 1000lb. Oh, well then, 200lb. In the event, they caught a conger eel, whose baleful eye as its head was levered open to extract the hook I found it hard to meet.

Fortunately the producer, Paul Watson, who made *The Family* about the working-class Wilkinses, was not relying on filming a hand-to-hand battle with a halibut. He was evidently fascinated by the fishermen themselves, all prime specimens of their kind: the young, rich, right-wing male. Three Hoorays or, if you like, three cheers. The fourth, who had not been to public school, was a rather different kettle of fish.

The little trawler plied to and fro across the Pentland Firth collecting lobster pots; they grew bored ('I can't think why there are no bloody fish here') and talk expanded to fill the forty minutes available.

The voice of Guy rose above the rest. If this were *Wind in the Willows* then Guy would go on as Toad without rehearsal and to ecstatic notices. He and John are commodity brokers. 'We sell something we haven't got in anticipation of buying it back cheaper.' In a good year they claim to make half a million.

Guy on capital punishment: 'It must be reintroduced. I don't know how many men have gone to the gallows that shouldn't have. Ninety per cent is good enough for me. The other thing is who will hang him? I can think of a dozen people straight away who would volunteer. I'd have no qualms whatsoever. If it ended up to be a mistake, well, it was a mistake. We all make mistakes in life.'

Guy on kindness to animals: 'I hate cats. I shoot cats. It takes a lot to kill a cat, you know. The vicar caught me going through the graveyard with a gun trying to shoot a cat.'

Guy on law and order: 'The bloody ambulance was there. The police were there. I was seven points over the limit. It was entirely the Kraut's fault. They were very understanding. She wasn't white, she wasn't English, so nobody really worried. The police said they were not going to pursue the prosecution. Bought myself a large drink and went for a drive. I thought, 'Thank God, there's still a decent law left in this country.'

Guy on a military coup: 'Many of our friends worry about the aggressive young men of the loony left. I think the Armed

Forces might be a bit concerned about the outcome of the next election. I don't think it would take very much for a military unit to take control of London, the country, the Government.'

Henry Carew would like to be an MP. He already has the essential requirement, a way of saying things three times. There have been Carews in Devon, admittedly usually submerged under heaps of dogs, since the eleventh century. His ancestor was in charge of the *Mary Rose* when she sank.

Henry on unemployment: 'The unemployed in many people's eyes represent a threat to security, to stability, to law and order. Perhaps we should go and ask the unemployed what they would like to do given the facts of life that there are no jobs available.' No, no, Henry. You go and ask the unemployed. I'll just stand here and hold your horse.

Robert Hutchinson hasn't got a job either but that's how he likes it. 'Work and myself do not get on with each other. I play a bit of backgammon but, unfortunately, that doesn't pay all the expenses.' Like the polo and the clubs: 'The RAC is very good for sports facilities. Brooks for backgammon, and the Turf Club has an excellent snooker table.'

Robert on patriotism: 'As Noel Coward said – "the English, the English, the English are best, So up with the English and down with the rest." I think that sums it up.' (As Donald Flanders said, actually).

It is a remarkable thing that none of the women said a word. 'Dogs are more bloody useful than women,' said Guy. 'There are two reasons for getting married,' said Robert. 'One is to have children and the other so your wives can drive you home when you get drunk.' A single-handed waitress was serving the fishing party to a running commentary from Guy: 'She's only one bloody table to do, hasn't she? If you want something ask for it. The acceptance of mediocrity is no good to anybody. Demand it.' A dog, of course, would have bitten him.

By now they had been drinking steadily and were shooting seagulls. Guy on the wheelhouse roof was pouring drink over Henry, who was throwing fish at him. The shattered wings of a seagull were sinking in the sea. The skipper came out and said: 'Come down before you bugger up the liferaft and the

131

radar.' On the BBC News the Home Secretary was congratulating the police on containing a criminal mob on a council estate.
28 February, 1986   **Nancy Banks-Smith**

Muffled by the Woolsack

Lord Hailsham is an old and brilliant man who has occupied the Woolsack for almost twice as long as anyone this century. He has been a jewel of our post-war politics, gleaming with untarnished quality beside the bankers and bootboys who have come and gone from the table he has occupied for much of his political life. It must be said, however, that at the end of his years Lord Hailsham has become deformed by a single obsession.

That obsession is with what he calls the independence of the judiciary, and it is, on the face of it, commendable. He has been repulsing the challenges to it for many years, on occasions which nobody who cares for the law would cavil at. In particular, when Labour politicians, Michael Foot among them, launched the most unjustified attacks on the integrity of the bench under the Heath Government, Hailsham retaliated with an eloquence that vanquished their odious insinuations.

Latterly, in his second term as Lord Chancellor, he has been just as vigilant. When MPs criticized particular sentences, he has pounced on them. He has railed against his predecessor, who denied preferment to Sir John Donaldson for a purely political reason. Altogether, he portrays the judiciary as men at bay, whose only protection, it appears, now lies in 'the courage, political experience and integrity of a man, and that man is the Lord Chancellor'.

An increasingly perfervid note has been creeping into these utterances in the last two years. And however much one values judicial independence, it is time to wonder whether its chief and only guardian is not now extending his remit so far as to eliminate the very quality he imagines himself to be upholding. This is revealed by an incident trifling in itself but resonant in its gross presumption. BBC Radio Four decided to make a programme about the bar and its present troubles, and approached a number of judges for contributions. There was nothing very novel about this, since senior judges had been interviewed about legal matters several times in the last decade.

The result this time was different. Almost all the judges approached said they could not appear. They consulted the Lord Chancellor first, and the Lord Chancellor said no. They were very apologetic, these eminent men, who have an unrivalled perspective on the bar from which they had all come, but Lord Hailsham could not be defied.

A conversation ensued between the BBC and the Lord Chancellor's office which disclosed that on today's Woolsack casuistry has become the first handmaiden of moral fervour. Any salaried judge, it was said, had to ask the Lord Chancellor before going on the air. This did not, however, amount to seeking his permission. A massive indignation overcame Lord Hailsham's senior official at the suggestion that the judges were being 'stopped' from broadcasting. They were not being stopped. They were merely consulting. On the other hand, there was no way, we were to infer (for I have written and presented the programme, which goes out tonight), that consultation would conclude with anything other than the Lord Chancellor stating that judges should not be interviewed.

Casuistry, you might think, could reach no more exquisite heights. But the cream of it is yet to come. For what is the general purpose underlying this position? The judges must not talk, it seems, because this is the only way 'to preserve their independence'.

Thus, the independence of the judiciary can apparently be protected only by removing the independence of individual judges. Several senior judges, among them past and present office-holders in the apparatus that invigilates the bar, wanted to contribute to a serious public airing of its problems. But, although they are free men of whom it is proudly claimed that they owe nothing to anyone, they were told not to do so.

A passing aspersion must be cast on these characters themselves. The Lord Chancellor runs their lives only because they let him. Ultimately they have no obligation to bow to the rulings of him and his officials – as a law lord, Lord Templeman, and a circuit judge, Quentin Edwards, well showed by agreeing to take part, come what may.

But the principal culprit is the Lord Chancellor himself, now fired up by the interesting idea that independence means its opposite. Judges must be free from political criticism, but not from administrative control. They are the incorruptible beacons of independent justice, yet they cannot be trusted to come down from the bench into the market-place without imperilling that great function.

This is an insult to them, and surely does the cause of the law no good. For what particle of their independence, of justice, of the esteem in which judges are properly held is endangered if they occasionally contribute their wisdom to a debate they are directly concerned in? It is not as if they are being asked to attack the law lords' judgment on Victoria Gillick, or second-guess the Cyprus secrets jury, or enter into a discussion on the merits of Thatcherism. These are cautious men, trained not to let themselves go – but with, perhaps, a greater sense than Lord Hailsham that the law and its functioning needs a better-educated public constituency which they, as the men at the top of the tree, could help create. For one accompaniment to the cloistering of the law, and the preservation of the judiciary as a priesthood that surpasseth understanding, has certainly not been the expansion of the law as a popular public service. The law needs to be better valued. Lawyers need to shed their public image as grasping and expensive procrastinators.

Judges can contribute to this necessary process. They could with benefit descend on occasion from their pedestals and demonstrate the truth: which is that many of them, far from being toffee-nosed reactionaries, are ordinary men of the world, with matchless experience, first-class minds, judicious habits of speech, and a certain sagacity which they could impart without inviting the charge that they had compromised their position.

The Lord Chancellor, faithfully echoing his department, will have none of this. It is as if the privacy which surrounds all its processes must now reach as far as humanly possible even into the public role of judges. All judicial appointments are made without reason given or public scrutiny allowed. Sir Derek Oulton, the Lord Chancellor's permanent secretary, holds more patronage in his capable hands than any other official in Whitehall, and divides the elect from the damned with no explanation.

It's a system which, judged by results, has worked well; there are remarkably few disastrous appointments. But it fathers a philosophy that is terrified of any breach with the myth that judges are bloodless mediators, untouchables, inhuman magic-men.

They are, in fact, people who could do a lot to make the law more valued and respected, and therefore perhaps more available: a task in which successive Lord Chancellors have dismally failed. Legal aid, the key to availability, has not kept pace with the minimum demand for it, as today's annual report on it yet again reminds us. Government after government has declined to give the law more resources. Hailsham after Hailsham has failed to persuade the cabinet that legal service deserves not to be bottom of the priorities. Declaiming about judges, they have fought a losing battle for law.

The Lord Chancellor may not agree that judges who went more public could help him to rescue the image of his profession. But he should at least not violate the language. Let him not pretend that it is for the good of their independence that he commands them to be silent.

23 January, 1986   **Hugo Young**

Doubts about Lloyd's

One sunny morning a couple of weeks ago Richard Rogers and his partner of twenty years, John Young, were standing on the crowded floor of 'the room' at the base of the soaring atrium of the new Lloyd's building. They were positioned only a few yards from the tall, columniated wooden frame that supports the Lutine Bell itself, now incongruously boasting a large colour TV monitor and a microphone as well as the dangling white rope attached to the clapper traditionally used to announce a shipwreck.

Among the milling throng of underwriters with their security badges the two stand out in their baggy pastel summer suits. It is not long before a middle-aged, pinstripe figure approaches.

'Excuse me, but are you Richard Rogers the architect?'

'Yes. I am.'

'My name is Stevens and I am an underwriter here. I was hoping that you were the architect because there is something that I want to tell you.'

'Go ahead.'

'Look, I don't care what you have done to this building on the outside, but some of us have to physically work inside here and let me tell you it really is bad news. All this concrete, it's like a car park, it's atrocious. Can't you paint it or something, surely it's not too late for that?'

Rogers, whose demeanour shows that he had expected praise from the tone of the initial inquiries only to suffer a nasty shock, replies at last: 'There is an underwriters' committee that has approved every step of the design . . . Perhaps you should . . .'

'The committee!' ejaculates Mr Stevens, sudden anger replacing the tone of pleading in his voice. 'I am appealing to you an as individual human being who has to work day after day in this monstrosity. Is there nothing you can do to make conditions here more tolerable?'

Before the plainly disconcerted Rogers can answer, another figure, this time much younger, detaches himself from the throng of underwriters milling round their strangely prep-school-looking wooden booths.

'I heard that, Mr Rogers, and I would just like to say that I completely dissociate myself from my colleague's remarks. I think this building is a work of genius. I work here every day too and I think the whole conception is brilliant! I would like to shake the hand of the man who designed this modern miracle.'

Rogers complies with a bewildered grin. The two underwriters smile confidently at one another, as experts in invisible exports should, whatever their opinions. After a few moments they both politely take their leave.

Since its opening two months ago the £180 million Lloyd's building with its most prominent façade on to Leadenhall Street opposite the Commercial Union Plaza in the City of London, has become the first high-profile symbol of high technology architecture in England. There have been high technology buildings before, and there are even more impressive ones overseas, but all previous English examples have been either too small, too cheap, or too provincial to arouse strong feelings.

Lloyd's is different. The people who hate it do so because they know it is the product of new and dangerous principles against which their own innate conservatism is as powerless as the helpless rage of Mr Stevens the underwriter.

To the surprise of the planning authorities who permitted it as a curiosity in 1978, Lloyd's has come to represent the real beginning of a new finite architecture. In the same way as the oil price crash and Chernobyl can be said to foreshadow the end of the last energy subsidy for the old traditions of English life, Lloyd's can now be seen as the first real harbinger of a traditionless future, sharing only the word 'architecture' with such infinite and eternal structures as Salisbury Cathedral, Blenheim Palace, and even James Stirling's brand new, but utterly obsolete, proposals for Mansion House Square.

The essentially pre-industrial role of buildings like these was to remain the same from generation to generation by way of eternal repair regardless of expense. But the new finite architecture is post-industrial, something designed to last for fifty years at the most; and that only if technological and market trends run as predicted.

No viewing of Lloyd's prior to its opening could prepare anyone for the amazing density of occupation of its underwriting floors, where more than 5000 people now gather in a space that under the Offices Shops and Factories Acts should only contain one-fifth that number.

Standing in what is intended to be the visitors' viewing gallery on the fourth floor (except that some underwriters are bidding for space already) and staring down into this gigantic pit, through three floors of criss-crossing transparent escalators,

137

is an unnerving experience. Directly below, the seething mass of underwriters is so dense it almost obscures the acres of blue carpet. To the side the streams of people on the escalators become invisible against the greyness of the concrete, the steelwork and the specially developed bubble-finish glass walls and only the whirling yellow bogey wheels inside the moving stairways catch the eye. The immense ground floor is like the cargo hold of a huge ship taken over by troops who have parked their kit in every available corner.

'Excuse me, sir, may I ask what are you doin' up 'ere?' A character from Dickens dressed in red and black forces open a plate-glass door and advances upon me.

'Let's see yer pass then.'

I show the Lloyd's man my pass and his manner changes. Even so he escorts me from my vantage point to somewhere less convenient. I ask him what he thinks of the new building.

'It's been . . . 'ot in 'ere the last two weeks, sir,' he begins, as I look at his thick woollen cloak, hat and leather boots – designed no doubt to be struck by lightning. 'And they don't like it at all.'

Alas, the new car-park style is even less classy than those pranksters who heave files across the void from one level to another imagine. For one of the most important calculations made as soon as Lloyd's accepted that the new building was to take the form of a vast multistorey cube with all its ancillary accommodation – 'the fifteen-year parts', as Rogers calls them – bolted on around the outside, was the precise number of lavatories needed to accommodate the distended bladders of the underwriters at 2.30 in the afternoon.

The answer came as close to giving the exterior of the car park its distinctive configuration as any other single feature – except perhaps for the escape stairs.

Richard Rogers is completely straightforward about this approach, as well he might be, in the knowledge that nothing else can remotely come to terms with the 20 per cent a year growth of the financial services industry, or the microtechnology boom that increased power consumption at Lloyd's by six times in as many years. He got the Lloyd's commission because the great insurance conglomerate was bursting at the seams and needed an architectural concept that would hold it together more than it needed a traditional corporate headquarters.

Standing in the Commercial Union Plaza, facing this shiny uncompromising structure, I asked Richard Rogers: 'If you put the fifth-year part on the inside – and the fifteen-year parts on the outside – where is the architecture?'

'It is like modern poetry,' he said. 'It doesn't rhyme like a limerick any more, but the beat is still there.'

When I first saw Lloyd's I was sure that Rogers had lost control of it; that the heating, cooling, power, lifts, escalators and ventilators were running riot round a vast empty core. Now I have seen how crowded the 'empty core' can get, and how extensively the service towers might be changed around without really altering the concept at all – I am not so sure.

30 June, 1986   **Martin Pawley**

Wimbledon, Inc.

Wimbledon's poignant moments repeat themselves each year – and I don't necessarily mean John Lloyd's moist-eyed impersonation of Kim Hughes as he handed in his badges after yet another first round calamity, or even Annbel Croft's ditto departure.

The poor lamb said afterwards she'd had a rotten headache all through the match, but her new agent from Mark McCormack's IMG was undaunted. 'It should be easy to find lots of sponsors for her because she is so attractive,' he said.

Wimbledon is a sponsors' beanfeast now. If Wimbledon didn't exist, no sponsor could have dared invent it, but seeing it's there, they are working on it. Oh boy, do they keep in the poignancy!

Though it easily could be arranged to sell a number of season tickets on a first-come-first-served basis to the general public for the fortnight, they do not do so because nothing is more poignant each day than to have the privileged corporate guests helicoptered and limousined past the bleary, blanketed, tennis-loving hoi polloi who have camped outside the gates all night.

This is one hippie army the establishment does not move on, for this lot proves the very point of their privilege.

That 12 o'clock rush by the dawn queue for any left-over standing room on the Centre Court used to be a touching thrill to be in on. Now it seems as seedy and forlorn as it was always unfair. For just across the way, out of sight, the smoked salmon and champagne is being guzzled by captains of industry, who can't tell a backhand pass from a tennis elbow, and their clients, who can tell even less.

The grandest parade at Wimbledon these days takes place long after play has begun, when the captains and their clients, cigars chomping at one hand, and a parasoled Poll at the other, hold sway. Every day this week they have stepped blinking and briefly into the real world of unshaded sunlight, sweaty armpits and concourse crush to make their way as quickly as possible to the reserved exclusive reservation of the Centre Court seating.

Wimbledon – quite simply the finest laager in the world. Wimbledon is now a corporate outing. A freebie for BP, ICI, BAT and all that lot, and the talk is not of sport but of deals and dollars. Wimbledon is big business – and business is business in Mrs Thatcher's brave new world of macho money men and their haughtily mournful mascaraed molls.

Of course Wimbledon and its oligarchic All England Club (membership less than 400, with three free tickets each day) was ripe for the plucking from the moment some years back when old Bagenal Harvey, the same London agent who persuaded Denis Compton to smarm his hair in Brylcreem, suggested that Wimbledon charge a little more for Robinson's Barley Water to put their product under the umpire's chair.

Now it is Coca-Cola, of course. You might not have actually seen any player this week with tell-tale brown stains smudging his lips after quaffing the revolting American fizz, but as long as the paper cup has Coke printed on it, that's good enough for the marketing men. Business is business, and business is booming.

They make strange bedfellows, but opposites attract. Big business does the deals while the All England keeps up appearances. At Wimbledon sweets are called bonbons. Alongside the

Centre Court there are a series of temporary crush bars where you can wash down a £1.50 hot dog on a paper plate with a £22 bottle of non-vintage champagne. Or perhaps sir would like ten soggy strawberries in a paper bowl at 10p per strawberry.

You stand with your paper plate on this acre of concrete surrounded by signs which read 'No glasses may be removed from the Lawn – By Order of the Committee.' Lawn? What lawn?

The committee bangs on: 'Spectators are requested NOT to take crockery or cutlery away from the catering area.' Crockery? Cutlery? What age are they living in?

The clock of St Mary's church strikes four – and the Royal Box rises at once and goes in for tea. If a match stood at two sets all, 5–4 and 40–30, they'd still go in on the stroke of four. And that's where the real crockery clinks.

Sarah Ferguson was there on Tuesday. She seemed to enjoy it. Martina was playing, but about fifty cameramen kept their lenses trained on Sarah throughout. The bonbons passed round the Royal Box like at a pantomime matinee. Sarah had more than most.

In front of the seat for the royal personage there is a miniature TV set. In black and white, of course. On Tuesday it went on the blink for a bit, but nobody bothered to tune it. Not a thing to do with white gloves.

A couple of years ago, John McEnroe's father asked if he could meet, at his convenience, the Wimbledon boss, Air Chief Marshal Sir Brian Burnett, to clear up a couple of matters relating to his son, the champion. 'Impossible' came back the withering message via a minion, 'Sir Brian is far too busy entertaining Royalty.' What a heck of a two-week job for the old boy.

Mind you, this week has been a bad one for the club. Stares are blank and upper lips twitch when you ask a member about the essays their former Supremo, Major David Mills, has been contributing to the *Sunday People*.

In his three-page spread last week the Major, sixteen years the club's secretary, unaccountably and luridly filled in the space under such headlines as 'Sex Scandal of the Women's Stars', 'Wimbledon's Sodom and Gomorrah', 'Perils of the

Women's Locker Room' and 'The Day I Nearly Spanked the Brat'.

This was the man who for so long called Royalty in for tea at 4 p.m. precisely. If he had stayed longer perhaps he would have flogged the Royal tea-time to the highest bidder.

Which is that company that uses chimps in their ads? Somebody did once say that if two such simians made it to the final the crowds would still throng in and clap. 'Quiet, please!'

Come to think of it, that command is one of the sharpest reminders of old imperial England that remains at Wimbledon. Quiet, please. You natives must stop being so restless.

Except tea-time, everything else has long been up for grabs at Wimbers. The small print in each day's official programme reads like an old theatre cast-list below which the producers thank such as 'Puma, who provide the footwear for ball-boys . . . Radio Chemicals for massage creams and other products used in the dressing rooms . . . Sunsilk for hairdressing services for lady competitors . . . and Slazenger sport toiletries for anti-perspirants.'

Soon after tea, the Royals have gone and so too, after a final few for the road, those in the chauffeured helicopters clatter up into the evening sky carrying the sozzled wheeler-dealers of industry and their still deadpan dolls.

Then the Sunsilked players come out to talk – Tim Mayotte, all-American Gatsby-type with eyes closer together than Borg's; Ivan Lendl, pouting distractedly as if programmed by some Ruritanian Karloff; the still bewildered Boris Becker who is learning fast, however; Mikael Pernfors, new man with old-time shorts and early Steve McQueen hairdo.

John Lloyd offers yet another sad farewell; Jimmy Connors, as game as ever, says he'll be back, you betcha. He had better be. Yet did old Wimbledon end the very day Connors first came?

Dusk and dust. Someone is sweeping the paper 'crockery' from the concrete lawns. And outside in the street the cheery, bleary little handful of sport-lovers puff up their sleeping bags in readiness for another long night with the pavement as their pillow. All very poignant, ain't it? Must keep that bit in.

28 June, 1986   **Frank Keating**

Tin pan alley end of The Wedge

There are four million young people who will be entitled to vote for the first time at the next election and every last one of them can understand the lyrics of pop songs.

This is a gift peculiar to the young. After a certain age you can't hear the cry of a passing bat, you can't understand the lyrics of a pop song and your toes don't curl upwards when your sole is stroked. Come to that, nobody wants to stroke your sole so that question doesn't arise. It's all very sad, but there it is. Personally, it suits me well enough. I can call my sole my own and pop lyrics do seem to lose something in translation.

To get the ear of the young, the Labour Party has adopted its own pop group, Red Wedge, *TV Eye* (Thames) reported in *Pop Into Politics*, prudently running the lyrics of the songs as subtitles for the benefit of the wrinkly vote.

Sellar and Yeatman said the Danes wrote a very defiant kind of clanking song ('What Cnut Cyng the witan wold enseoff Of infangthief and outfangthief') while the Anglo-Saxons wrote a sad, keening kind of song ('Sing a Song of Saxons in the Wapentake of Rye four and twenty eaoldermen too eaold to die'). It is very like that in Red Wedge.

Paul Weller of the Wedge writes a fierce crunching sort of song ('For liberty there is a cost – it's broken skulls and leather cosh.') Jimmy Somerville, on the other hand, sings a sweet, sad song in a crystal voice like a child who has been crying for a long time. ('Life goes down, down, down, down, down. Life goes down. Life goes down.')

It was Weller who said, grinding a tooth or two, 'Armed revolution isn't that easy to organize, you know. Not in this country' and Jimmy Somerville who said softly that he didn't want to be a millionaire. He didn't believe in it.

Gary Numan is also a pop star but he isn't in Red Wedge because he does want to be a millionaire and, for all I know, may be one already: 'I can't understand anybody that wouldn't want to be in the South of France on a great big yacht. It goes against anything I've ever thought. It amazes me.' In the recording studio he owns, a new group Ho Ho Kan were making their bid for riches with a confused-medical-student sort of song 'Where is your heart beat? Where is your heart beat?'

TV Eye evidently had some difficulty finding pop stars prepared to speak up for capitalism. All pop stars are rich but most look as if their last Giro had just bounced. 'Certain people', said Numan, 'are very, very good at pretending to belong to the working class and making an absolute fortune out of it.'

Bob Geldof, who always looks as if he is going to touch you for the price of a meal and, in fact, is, said, 'I've never had much of a thing going for missionaries. Pop music holds up a mirror. The best pop music articulates the common expression, what's already there. I'm not supporting any party whatsoever. I don't accept that's the way of doing it.'

The viewing figures for this programme should be instructive. The mere mention of pop will have cost it most of its normal audience. The producer's mother, faithful to a fault, has told him she won't be watching. If it even holds its viewing figures, then the young have been transfixed by the sound of Billy Bragg ('Which side are you on, boys, which side are you on?') coming at them strong and straightaway from the set. And that is the theory behind Red Wedge.

While we're on the subject of talking to the animals, that endearing programme *Discovering Animals* (BBC-2) was interpreting the song of the passing bat. Brought within the range of our hearing, it sounded something between a bird and a rubbed balloon. The bat, who, despite its name, is demonstrably all there, views belfries with distaste and selects for preference a nice, clean, centrally heated home on a modern housing estate. This is tough on the nice, clean centrally heated housewife who had 330 bats hanging up like hams in her attic, not counting the one in her daughter's bedroom. The bat is protected by law. Dr Stebbings (with bat net) showed her and two thrilled small boys points of interest about the bat's anatomy. The little thing's mouth was open in an inaudible

shriek of terror and resentment. So was the housewife's. She asked, hopefully, how long they lived. Thirty years, he said.
31 January, 1986   **Nancy Banks-Smith**

Skinheads put boot in Christmas

A company linked with the extreme right is offering a service to enliven Christmas office parties. For £30, it will send round a 'bootagram' to terrify the managing director, two massive tattooed skinheads skilled in the arts of debt-collecting and security work.

Skinhead Productions – 'by skins . . . 4 skins,' according to its calling card – is based in Hornchurch, Essex, and besides bootagrams, hires out skinheads for film work, security, promotions, publicity stunts, and what it terms soldiering and crowds. It can supply up to 150 skinheads at a time. It appears to be run jointly by Mr Peter Crain, who works from Hornchurch, and by Ms Lin Sargent, who takes bookings and recruits skinheads from the office of her other business, Lin Sargent (Travel Consultants) Ltd.

Mr Crain said that his skinheads carry out security work for the racialist rock band Skrewdriver, whose past hits, recorded on the White Noise label, include 'Smash the IRA' and 'White Power'. The band's leader, Ian Stewart, is a leading member of the National Front and his concerts are usually organized in secret by Rock Against Communism, a section of the Young National Front. Skinhead Productions has provided security and shepherded the group's fans from pre-arranged meeting places to the clandestine gigs.

Ms Sargent said that the boys she could provide were 'really threatening'. Most of them were unemployed. She had used them for debt-collecting, but there had never been any trouble. They all wore tattoos and some had to turn sideways to walk through doorways, they were so big. Mr Crain, she went on, had been in the Foreign Legion, 'but they threw him out because he was too heavy.'

Mr Crain explained the details of the special Christmas bootagram service. 'Generally a lot of people in the office gang up on their managing director. Usually they buy a Christmas pudding or something, so we come carrying a large bag, looking a bit conspicuous, and we go and give him the once-over like.

'We have a word with him. After a bit of chat usually the poor old managing director is terrified, and then we give him the Christmas pudding.'

The skinheads, he maintained, were 'proper stuff, no beating around the bush people like'. They included 'quite a few ex-army geezers,' which was why the card offered soldiering as an option. Currently he was hoping to find acting work for his lads on a film being made about the Vietnam war.

How far were his staff prepared to go? 'We're not into anything illegal,' he said, 'we're trying to keep within the law.' When the boys went debt-collecting, 'usually we do harassment tactics, not violent tactics.'

5 December, 1985   **David Rose**

Oil our yesterdays

In the pawnbroker's shop on the ragged edge of glittering downtown Houston the smart young man stands out among the housewives pawning jewellery and the young men examining racks of handguns and almost new stereos. Their former owners will not return. They have succumbed to the greatest 'oil bust' in living memory which has wiped out 150,000 jobs here in three years.

The young man, who bears a passing resemblance to Prince Andrew, plainly has not succumbed. He wears a dark blue suit and has arrived in a Jaguar XJ6. But he has come to redeem his watch. 'This is ridiculous,' he says. 'Last year I made $125,000 (£90,000) and here I am in a pawnshop.'

In Dallas 200 miles to the North a real-life J. R. Ewing would probably be a banker or defence contractor. Houston is actually the oil capital of the United States. With a population of three million it is smaller only than New York, Los Angeles and Chicago. Its clump of downtown skyscrapers rises above the Texas plain like a secular cathedral, a Chartres dedicated to mammon: megalopolis twinned with megalomania. Naturally the young man's gold and steel watch is a Rolex, 'the Texas Timex' as they are called locally, more sold here than in any other state. It cost him $2000 and he pawned it just a few days earlier to Shaw's jewellery for $900 cash.

The strapped young man, twenty-six and in real estate, is not typical of Houstonians in the fourth year of the oil slump. This week when West Texas Intermediate – the US bench-mark crude oil which touched $35 in 1981 – briefly followed Britain's Brent crude below the $10 mark, 9.6 per cent of his fellow citizens were out of work. At 8.4 per cent – it fell slightly yesterday – Texan unemployment is again above the national average (7.2) for the first time in fifteen years. Its wages – one-fifth of the young man's – are just below it, where they always used to be before the Opec-led boom of the seventies.

Yet that Rolex in Keith Shaw's pawnshop is an apt symbol of Houston's current dilemma. The young man needed ready cash. 'People are not paying their commissions promptly. I needed to pay my mortgage,' he explained. Shaw, who would have sold it for $1400 if he hadn't come back, didn't want it: he had thirteen Rolexes already and the other day an oil company executive rang to try to pawn his helicopter. 'I wouldn't take it. I never take things I can't store on these premises,' he said.

No one in Houston is unaffected by the oil bust. Keith Shaw's customers come increasingly from nearby River Oaks, the sprawling city's finest suburb (one of the few where planning was allowed to play a part). The local KPRC-TV station has just run a 'food drive' for the Houston food bank, raising 200,000 lbs of goods for the estimated 10 per cent of citizens who might need it. Unemployment pay has a modest $203 per week ceiling and a twenty-six-week limit. After that it's food stamps for those not too proud to ask.

Some of KPRC's viewers' parcels will end up at the 'food pantry' which Dona Schlitt runs at Fairhaven Methodist Church in suburban Springbranch. Before the recession they supported two or three families a week. Now forty to fifty families get a grocery bag of rice, beans, tinned macaroni and cheese, cornflakes and hotdogs. Chiefly, she and others say, the brunt is borne by the new middle class, people who found affluence and a home (mortgage foreclosures have reached a record 1700 a month), only to lose them. 'We have a few professional people, but mostly they are blue-collar and office people who worked directly or indirectly in oil.'

Neiman-Marcus, the Harrods of the nouveau-riche (reproduction terracota ming horses, a snip at $20,000), reports nothing more serious in the recession than a tendency towards better quality purchases by its customers. But the bust has affected the exclusive Petroleum Club whose members pay $5000 for the privilege of a fine view from the forty-third floor of the Exxon building and discreet dining (not a boot or stetson in sight: open-collared shirts at lunchtime being the only concession to flamboyance). Its waiting list is down from more than 2000 to fewer than 100.

Houston's First City Bank, the most over-stretched of the oil-lenders on the federal sick-list (it actually offered free Porsches recently to anyone who would deposit $1 million for five years) sacked some directors the other day. James Levoy, president of an ailing Betchel Corporation subsidiary, shot himself.

Mayor Kathy Whitmire, gets cross about crisis talks. At a bash for the Houston Festival on Thursday night she chided the *Wall Street Journal* for a headline. 'Oil recession plunges Houston into a state of mental depression.' Local columnists mock out-of-town reports about Houston dentists facing an epidemic of anxiety-riven teeth-grinding. They have a point: all recessions are relative and this is one for which many British cities would eagerly swop their own. 'It may be un-American to take the long-term view,' says a professor who came south eight years ago from frostbelt to sunbelt. 'But the long-term prospects here are very good. Everyone I know who has any money is buying up oil equipment cheap. It won't rust much and in a few years' time they will sell it at a huge profit.'

Harold Gross, an economist at Southern Methodist University (which is admittedly in rival Dallas), goes as far as to say that places like Houston 'are in many respects like developing nations with economies that, in the late twentieth century, are still basically resource-extractive with manufacturing that is dependent', by which he means petro-chemicals and steel which oil has spawned.

Even on an overcast spring day it manages to be both clammy and windy. Houston's downtown shops are sensibly to be found in a five-mile labyrinth underground. Street level is fit only for car parks. But the current buzz-word 'diversification' has been around for a generation or more since the elders of the state realized that agriculture (no comfort either in the present recession) and oil were not enough. Having LBJ in the White House helped, as the Johnson Space Centre here makes plain, and Texas advertises itself as an astronaut in cowboy boots. Actually medicine is the city's No. 2 employer.

But does Texas have the social and educational infrastructure to consolidate such diversification as took place in the affluent years, ask the likes of Harold Gross. Its public universities, funded by oil revenues, are still cheap and often excellent. But what about elementary and secondary education fit to turn rig workers into lab workers? This is a state which prides itself on having no local income tax to augment sales and oil taxes – and precious little sign that rich or macho poor actually want one any more than they want gun control.

So in the short term how will cities like Houston which has just discovered a $72 million hole in its budget, and the state itself, still dependent on oil for 14 per cent (once 25 per cent) of its tax revenue, cope with the calamitous drop in prices? A fall of $1 a barrel costs Texas an estimated $100 million in taxes, 25,000 jobs and $3 billion in total economic activity.

There are several delicious ironies in Texas's plight, ideological but also regional. At the height of the Opec-induced boom Texans told the frostbelt states to get stuffed. 'Let the bastards freeze in the dark' was a popular car bumper sticker of the period. Now the *schadenfreude* is on the other foot. Texan unemployment has risen to the point where Houston this week hosted a seminar to see what it could learn from high-tech Massachusetts which has weathered its own crisis and is even getting its own 'gone to Texas' citizens back again. Humiliation indeed. And of course, Texan politicians running for re-election this year, are crying, from Governor Mark White down, for Washington to intervene and save their ruggedly individualist way of life from the Arabs.

Actually free enterprise rhetoric has always gone hand in hand with pragmatic statism, import and production quotas, price controls and tax incentives. The difference today is that the White House is occupied by an administration which acts on the rhetoric. In Senator Phil Gramm, a Texas Democrat-turned-Republican, the state has a free market ideologue. The Texas delegation to Congress is split. So is the Petroleum Club and the industry at large. The independent producers and the little men whose small but important 'stripper' wells are most vulnerable to an Opec production war favour the popular panacea of an oil import tax. A Lawson-style gas tax on all producers has few takers here.

As Vice-President Bush's confusing signals before setting out for Saudi Arabia underline, the Administration is caught between what is good for the US (cheaper oil), good for Texas and Mr Bush, an adopted native son and an oilman who needs the state in '88, and good for national security. For the industry has wrapped itself in the flag. As companies cut their exploration budgets (two more did this week) they denounce a return to over-reliance on cheap foreign oil. The language is universal. It could be Iowa farmers or industrialists, British or American. A shake-out is fine, they say. But we are quite shaken out enough by now, thank you.

The rhinestone cowboys and the Houston doctors and lawyers who invested in oil when they expected it to soar to $85 ('85 in 85' was a saying) have retreated, the amateur gold rush types have gone home to Massachusetts. Give us a stable price, say $20 a barrel, and all will be well, say the pragmatists. Rock bottom viability is $15, say more public-spirited types. 'I can make money on $3', says the spirit of the Alamo.

5 April, 1986   **Michael White**

150

Over a barrel

It was an intermittent whistling noise which first alerted Sheikh Ahmed Zaki Yamani to the extent of superpower concern about the collapse in oil prices. Discreet inquiries established that the maddening whine in his eighteenth floor suite at the Geneva Intercontinental, which lasted throughout the last Opec conference, came from a badly-tuned parabolic listening device operated by the Russians from a nearby tower block.

Reliable information has always been hard to come by in the world's biggest business. Traders hire light aircraft to fly over the massive tanks which dot the landscape of the Antwerp-Rotterdam-Amsterdam ports complex to assess the level of company stocks.

Forecasting the price is a profession for failed kamikaze pilots and the analysts have had a particularly bad time of it of late. In Britain, the only one who has remained unrelentingly bearish as the cost of a barrel has slithered down through every floor predicted by his counterparts is Humphrey Harrison, the flamboyant Opec-watcher for the stockbrokers Fielding, Newson Smith.

Harrison is a fish out of water in the City – an exiled white South African, whose anti-apartheid activities during the period of the Soweto uprising earned him spells of detention in solitary confinement. His mother is the journalist, Nancy Harrison, whose biography of Winnie Mandela was published here last year. But Harrison's pro-Third World opinions, which raise eyebrows in the Square Mile, open doors in Opec.

The lesson that oil does not mix easily with conventional Western attitudes seems to have to be learnt again and again. People make fortunes in every generation by grasping that fact sooner than their rivals.

Dr Armand Hammer, the eighty-seven-year-old president of the Occidental Petroleum Corporation, is a case in point. His cordial relations with the Kremlin go back to his friendship with Lenin. Soon after the coup that brought Colonel Gadafy to power in 1969 he stepped in to do a deal with the Libyans which many have criticized but which even more have envied.

Circling the world in a corporate 727, with Oxy-1 painted on the fuselage, this commodity trader-turned-liquor magnate-turned oilman (after retirement) and part-time cattle-breeder and art connoisseur preaches a doctrine of peace through trade – a creed which, as one commentator pointed out, 'would, not coincidentally, be of no small benefit to Occidental Petroleum'.

It is altogether typical of Hammer that he should have chosen as his personal PR on this side of the Atlantic the explorer, Sir Ranulph Twisleton-Wykeham-Fiennes.

His assistant tells me he is currently on Ward Hunt Island, 475 miles from the North Pole, carrying out scientific research into – among other things – why the ice shelf up there is breaking up, sending massive chunks off to menace the rigs which are drilling for oil nearby.

That alone must qualify Sir Ranulph as an 'oily', which is what the people in the business in America, and increasingly elsewhere, call themselves.

No doubt, Sir Ranulph would not appreciate being told this right now, but wandering icebergs are the last thing on the minds of oil executives, with prices falling to figures not seen for a decade.

A good deal of interest centres on whether the quality of British government thought on the subject has changed since the days when a senior official philosophized that 'if the Arabs put the price of oil up then they can bring it down again.'

This trenchant insight is unlikely to be appreciated by the workers laid off last week in Great Yarmouth, or by the many more who are certain to lose their jobs elsewhere on the east coasts of England and Scotland if the slump continues much longer.

So far, however, only one British oil executive has explicitly challenged the Government's refusal to co-operate in efforts to solve the crisis. It was left to Dr Colin Phipps, the boss of Clyde Petroleum and a former Labour MP, to raise his voice in favour of cutting North Sea output by 10 per cent. An ex-Shell man with a most un-Shell-like background (Acton

County and Swansea Grammar schools), Dr Phipps lost his seat in 1979 and became a founder member of the SDP – not perhaps an altogether unfamiliar career structure.

The man who nudged prices into single figures last week – with a prediction that they could go as low as $5 a barrel – was the United Arab Emirates' Oil Minister, Mr Mana Saeed al-Otaiba. It was not the first time he had moved the markets – last year he sent prices plunging, and clipped a cent or two off the pound in the process, when he stormed out of an Opec conference claiming to have been insulted by the Nigerian representative.

But then poets are a mercurial lot, and Dr al-Otaiba is Opec's very own laureate. His muse is especially aroused by Opec meetings and a conference rarely passes without his suave London-based factotum, Mufid Merie, descending to the lobby with a pile of cyclostyled sheets bearing the minister's latest poem. My personal favourite, which dates from 1982 and is entitled 'My Worries with the Quota,' begins:

> *Oh quota, my worries over you*
> *Are in my inner depths engraved*
> *In all my meetings you appear*
> *As a bomb fitted with a time fuse.*

I'm told it sounds better in Arabic.

In spite of having to fend off a spirited challenge for the title of longest name in the oil business from Sir Ranulph Twisleton-Wykeham-Fiennes, Sheikh Abdul Aziz bin Khalifa al-Thani of Qatar has succeeded effortlessly in holding on to the record for shortest attendance at Opec conferences. Known as Lifo ('last in, first out' – an accounting term much used in the industry), Sheikh al-Thani's belated arrivals and early departures from session after session have more than once led hacks covering their first Opec to file stories predicting Qatar's imminent withdrawal from the organization.

His greatest achievement came last year. At the beginning of each conference the journalists are invited in to listen to the opening speeches and are then courteously shooed out by Opec's endlessly patient Nigerian press officer, James Audu. As the reporters, photographers and camera crews shuffled reluctantly along the corridor leading away from the chamber, they were disconcerted to find 'Lifo' ambling along amongst them.

7 April, 1986   **John Hooper**

Swinging Japan

On a brilliant morning near the centre of Tokyo, business at the Shiba Golf Driving Range was beginning to pick up. Many of the 155 boxes, stacked in three tiers around a wide arc, were empty but enough balls had been driven off to leave the overnight snow heavily pockmarked and looking as though the range had been invaded by a pack of the city's stray cats.

Nowhere outside the United States is golf bigger business than it is in Japan. And because there are nowhere near enough courses to accommodate the growing number of players the driving ranges have become not merely practice centres but surrogate clubs.

In summer the Shiba range stays open until eleven o'clock at night. Its facilities are luxurious – a pro shop that would not disgrace a department store and a spacious restaurant. Considering a player pays 500 yen (about £2) to hit twenty balls and 700 yen at the weekends perhaps this is not altogether surprising.

Not all of Tokyo's driving ranges are so well appointed. Shortage of land restricts the Korakuen Golf Range to just twenty-eight boxes from where the players hit balls out over a net. Underneath the net is the car park. Other mini-ranges have been constructed on the flat roofs of skyscrapers. In at least one respect Tokyo is a swinging city.

Which is hardly surprising when one considers the import-ance of golf to Japanese business life. A survey conducted among Tokyo's male golfers last year revealed that half of them played the game with clients or business partners. The average man spent the equivalent of £120 a month on the game.

Of course golf in Japan is apt to be much more expensive

than that. Memberships of the more popular clubs are regularly quoted on the Tokyo stock market and are reckoned to be a better investment than some gilt-edged securities. Golf even has its own index, compiled by Juchi Golf Inc., a brokerage dealing exclusively in club memberships and based on one hundred clubs in the Tokyo area.

To join the Koganei Country Club, which lies on the outskirts of Tokyo amid a maze of suburban streets, supermarkets and car showrooms not unlike the sprawl of Los Angeles, it is necessary to find 90 million yen (about £360,000). For this sum a golfer becomes a member for life and owns shares in the club. However, he must still pay just over £14 for a round and each guest is charged £72 which rises to £80 at weekends. Not that guests can just turn up with a member and expect to tee off. At the Koganei Country Club reservations have to be made three months ahead.

The male pronoun is not used loosely when describing life at Koganei. The club bars women from its membership, a policy which led to a controversy last spring when a leading female politician, Mayumi Moriyama, was prevented from taking part in a goodwill tournament for government officials and foreign diplomats.

The miffed minister declared that Koganei was 'following rules which might have been applicable in Scotland three hundred years ago but not in present-day Japan'. Several dignitaries, including a number of foreign ambassadors, boycotted the tournament as a protest – but Koganei still does not admit women members.

Hideo Hara, the urbane assistant manager, explains that they have nothing against women. Indeed they can play at the club if they are part of a member's family. 'It is just that among the rules laid down when the club was formed fifty years ago there is one which says that members can only be men with Japanese citizenship. True, there is a body of opinion which would like this rule changed but we do not feel any strong outside pressure to do so.'

An even stranger restriction is Koganei's lower-age limit of thirty-five. Presumably the logic of this is that anyone under thirty-five with time to play golf cannot be wholly serious about being sufficiently successful in business to afford to join.

Not that the club rejects young blood. According to Mr Hara, 'children of over twenty can play here if their father is a member.' However the vision of five hundred middle-aged handicaps – five hundred is the maximum membership – pottering round a course designed by Walter Hagen in 1937 is hard to dispel.

At least Koganei's hole-in-one premiums should remain fairly low. Yes, in Japan it is advisable to insure against holing out from the tee. This is because Japanese golfers who hole in one are expected to buy their partners dinner, be more than usually generous to the caddies and take home souvenirs of the occasion to give to friends.

It can cost a player more than £1500 which is a little different from buying a round in celebration of a hole in one on a British course. Thus more than twenty of the leading Japanese insurance companies offer hole-in-one cover. For about £15 a golfer can protect himself against £1200 of expenses incurred by the inspired driver.

The Taisho Marine and Fire Insurance Company gathered statistics from thirty golf courses in Japan to estimate the chances of holes-in-one occurring and reckoned that the likelihood of an average player holing his tee shot during a round of eighteen holes was 0.0002993 per cent.

In spite of this the companies have been steadily losing money on their hole-in-one policies and are now murmuring about false claims. But as a spokesman for the Fuji Fire and Marine Insurance Company says: 'If players submit documented proof authorized by a golf club we have no alternative but to accept the claim.'

The Koganei club requires from any avuncular claimants 'Not only the witness of partners but also that of caddies when we issue documented proof.' But even they confess that 'if all of them gang up to invent a story we have no choice but to believe them.'

Recently an official of the Japan Golf Association was quoted as saying that 'as the number of golfers has risen their morals have lowered.' This seems a harsh judgment on the 13 million people now playing the game regularly on the country's twelve hundred courses or simply swinging along on the ranges.

With an average of 8500 players to each course – a figure distorted by the restricted memberships of clubs like Koganei – Japan's golfing accommodation problem is not going to ease in the foreseeable future. Ninety new courses are under construction but these will make little impact on an ever-growing demand.

Japan's enthusiasm for the game has been reflected at tournament level by the successes of Isao Aoki, winner of the Hawaiian Open and the World Match play tournament at Wentworth, and Ayako Okamoto, who won the British Women's Open in 1984 and more recently the Elizabeth Arden tournament in Florida.

3 March, 1986   **David Lacey**

A Country Diary: Keswick

It was decided some years ago to try to let part of this garden go back to its original meadow state – what had been wild could, surely, become wild again? It seemed a good idea, it would save grass cutting except perhaps for a late summer scything and, anyhow, things had got too formal over the years. It needed a good shake-up and already there were old apple trees, a tall guelder rose buth, barberries and a hazel bush. Things do not, however, come about as easily as that and for the first two years it all looked simply neglected in spite of a mown grass-edge. Then the grass itself began to change, more varieties came in and moon daisies and columbines, red, white and purple (the easiest of colonizers), arrived. There began to be wild arums and ferns in the shadier places. I have just come home from a fortnight's enforced absence and begin to see, at last, the coming of that early hope. There are bigger patches of moon daisies with orange hawkweeds and tall buttercups. The apple trees are setting fruit, there is a blackbirds' nest with young and honey bees are hard at work. My cat, whose first real-garden summer it is, is home too and making the very best of it. He happily chases every passing butterfly and bee until he flops into the grass roots to cool off or sit, prick-ears and tiger mask, only visible when the wind bends the silvery fruiting grass tops over him and sends silver running along the green. Indeed, I think we are both a bit heady with warmth – and freedom.

30 June, 1986   **Enid J. Wilson**

Flagging out the Merchant Navy

High and dry in a seamen's hostel down East India Dock Road, Captain Pat Brannigan does not know when his next stint at sea will be. His last was taking a 600-ton tub, loaded with second-hand cars, from London to Dominique. The runs, plus a few short trips between other islands in the Carribean, meant a couple of months' work.

Any middle-aged mariner – Brannigan is fifty-six – has seen his vistas slam like shutters with the changes in world shipping. The Meat Run (to New Zealand/Australia) has almost gone. The Grain Run (East Europe to the Gulf), too. Passenger liners are rare as albatrosses across the Atlantic. And even the short North Sea Run is threatened: Archie Boyd has just left a Danish vessel ferrying oil from the Forties Field to ports in north-east Europe, knowing that a pipeline is soon to be laid.

Boyd is at the end of a month's leave. He was sacked four days before he was due to come ashore, in what he calls 'a long-running feud' with the second officer. There's no blemish on his discharge book, like in the old days. But where will his next job come from? He has been along to the Merchant Navy Recruitment Centre, which notifies men in the pool of registered labour, of vacancies.

In spite of high unemployment, the place was absolutely dead, he says. No need to go down again: the centre will ring if it has anything. Seamen have got used to long silences on the job front. Boyd isn't panicking. But then he and Brannigan are in a small minority who have been to sea recently: most of the 200 men at the hostel have not. Brannigan doesn't have any faith in the recruitment centre. He reads *Lloyd's List*: and relies on small pieces of luck. That's how the Dominique trip happened – 'a man came looking for me.'

The Queen Victoria Seamen's Rest is full of the casualties of vicissitudes in the shipping industry. Every week brings its toll of bad news for the merchant fleet. The constant gloom is that, on average, two ships a week are transferred from British to foreign registration, thereby reducing the employment chances of British seamen, and increasing the likelihood of lower pay and less security for crews serving on 'flags of convenience' vessels.

In fact, a third of all ships in British ownership have been 'flagged' out – mostly on Liberian or Panamanian registration – to cut costs by recruiting Third World crews, and to save on maintenance and legal costs. The fleet itself is shrinking almost faster than statistics can record the fact. Before the last war, 40 per cent of the world's merchant shipping was British. Now it is 4 per cent.

The decline has been rapid since 1975, when there were 1614 British owned and registered ships. Now there are 640. High costs, cut-price competition mostly from South Korea and Taiwan, and loss of government incentives via tax concessions to shipping lines have combined to have a parallel effect on manpower. At the start of World War Two, there were 159,000 merchant seamen. By 1978, there were 60,000. The current total is less than half: 14,700 officers; 19,000 ratings.

The shrinking of what they represent and belong to – the Merchant Navy – is shadowy compared with the well-documented damage to shipping, the major industry which ranked along with railways, coal and steel. There are few signs of the Merchant Navy. The London phone book, for instance yields a hotel, a welfare board and a pension fund. The seamen's missions in the East End died far more quietly than the docks.

Yet the Merchant Navy was once a visible and viable entity, a concept dating from World War One; civilian ships assisting the Royal Navy. In the last war, the merchant marine lost proportiontely more men than any of the three armed services.

The link last had real meaning during the Falklands War, when the Task Force included fifty-four ships flying the Red Ensign.

Both the Navy and the all-party Commons Select Committee on Defence have recently expressed concern that there would not be much of a merchant fleet to call on in the event of a similar conflict. Edward DuCann, chairman of the Commons Marine Affairs Group, has criticized government policies on the Merchant Navy as ambivalent and unco-ordinated. Of the few jobs going, the MoD is recruiting more merchant seamen than any other single British shipowner, for the Royal Fleet Auxiliary.

The Falklands has shown that such worries are more than the last jingle of patriotism. 'I don't think there'll be any more jobs unless we get a Labour government that's sympathetic to us,' reflects Archie Boyd, as he survives against the tide of redundancy. 'Or unless Thatcher starts another war.' There's a grain of truth in the joke.

That possibility must have occurred to BP Shipping, who have just announced that they are offering redundancy and early retirement terms to the 1690 seamen employed on thirty tankers. BP has lost £160 million on its shipping operation in the last five years. To cut costs, it's already 'flagged out' five tankers to the Bahama's Registry. But directors are worried about how easily they could transfer back to UK registration those same ships if the Navy needed their support. So future transfers will be to the Bermuda Registry – Bermuda is still a British Dependent Territory, so the switch back, in an emergency, should be simple.

Preserving the Merchant Navy's identity, which is being fogged by increasingly complicated international deals involving vessels and manpower which owners come up with, falls to the unions. There's scarcely an institution to cling to; the fight is to preserve the Merchant Navy as a job category. The implications of BP's package worry both the National Union of Seamen and the National Union of Marine, Aviation and Shipping Transport Officers.

Although the company talks of average pay-offs of £27,000, the proposals mean that BP itself would cease to be a direct employer of tanker crews and would instead hire them (with first chance given to present staff) from three manning agencies. In order to save costs, but maintain present levels of pay, the agencies would offer deals, under which, as men would be in effect employed abroad, they would not have to pay UK tax – if they stayed at sea for longer periods than they do now.

BP crews also would cease to contribute to the British social security system, and would lose benefits; any entitlement they have to state pensions would be frozen. And the unions fear that, with one-year contracts of employment, the agencies would be tempted to get rid of British seamen and replace them with Third World crews. Basically, the operation, designed to save BP £20 million a year, is to buy out jobs, as the unions see it.

Jim Slater, of the NUS, and Eric Nevin, of the officers' union, are angry at what they see as the deviousness of the proposals; and are particularly alarmed because the overseas agencies which BP is to use will not recognize British unions. Slater says: 'If BP thinks it can use manning agencies to do its dirty work, and cut pay and crew levels, then it's got a fight on its hands.'

In fact, the NUS has a whole fistful of fights. In the lobby of its offices in Clapham are bundles of stickers – in French – part of the maritime unions' campaign against the Channel Tunnel, and the consequent loss of jobs.

Slater is fighting also against the likely recognition of the flags of convenience system by the United Nations agency, UNCTAD, which seems about ready to signal its approval for this system to continue, laying down minimum standards on all aspects of practice. He himself has made several speeches in Geneva attacking the growing trend to 'flagging out', attacking what he calls 'the marine mafia' for exploitation and discrimination of seamen; and of piracy, fraud and breaking of sanctions against South Africa, which, he says, foreign registration makes easier.

Jim Slater gives the impression that most of the manpower problems could be put right if flags of convenience were outlawed. The shipowners, huddled under the General Council of British Shipping, disagree. Deputy director John Whitworth says that flagging out is here to stay, however much the unions rage against it.

The unions have not been making excessive wage demands recently, Whitworth says, but the emergence of 'a labour force of Third World seafarers, who have been trained to quite proper international standards, who are seeking rates of pay significantly below European standards, is a fact of life.'

Both unions and shipowners have tied themselves in knots in trying to mesh wildly different national payscales over the years. Red tape still ties up £35 million in a fund intended to compensate Indian seamen who were paid much lower rates than their British counterparts working on the same vessels. It is the accumulated conscience money of owners who have got a cheap deal from the Third World, and the unions, who, while crusading against exploitation, must protect the dwindling future of their members.

In fact Indian ratings are leaving the British fleet at the rate of about 1000 a year. But the internationalism of their work prods British seamen all the time. In port, too. There is, in the Queen Victoria Seamen's Rest, a large contingent of Somalis. Archie Boyd, who is a tough survivor after twenty-nine years at sea, says 'I don't resent anybody working, but I do resent the exploitation of Third World seamen.'

If Archie Boyd's views are typical, then at least the Merchant Navy's altruism is intact. Little else is. There's an air of depression in the Seamen's Rest, 'like gravediggers passing the time of day,' says one Welsh resident. There's cynicism at the NUS headquarters. Researcher Phil Heaton says: 'It's the Merchant Navy when the Government wants to send civilian ships to the Falklands. But it's the British shipping industry when they won't lift a finger to help it in difficulties.'

Seamen, who once had two identities, are in danger of losing both.

24 January, 1986   **John Cunningham**

Why the Cabinet heat should leave the voter cold

The funny thing about the current state of British politics – genuinely funny as well as funny-peculiar – is the extraordinary amount of heat generated by such matters as the Westland affair and the political opinions of the Queen, compared with the remarkable lack of heat associated with what Tony Benn would probably call 'the real ishoos'.

To say this is not to underrate the damaging significance of the revelations which emerged in the Commons last week about the 'disreputable' behaviour of ministers and civil servants in their handling of the battle for Westland Helicopters. Nor is it to ignore the potentially awesome constitutional implications of a political clash between the Sovereign and her Prime Minister.

But there is surely something odd about a situation in which, for example, many of our national newspapers virtually ignore the fact that our already record unemployment total is now rising again, and at a faster rate than at any time since the early years of the Thatcher government.

We cannot put this down entirely to the time-ism that the overwhelming majority of those newspapers are owned and run by pro-Thatcher proprietors; after all, those same proprietors have not been slow to beef up the alleged row between Downing Street and the Palace.

To be sure, some of them did not exactly bust a gut covering the Defence Committee report on the Westland affair. The *Daily Mail* did not get round to it until page nine, preferring to put a report of the Prime Minister's 'winning message to MPs' on page two.

But I somehow doubt if Mrs Thatcher feels any great sense of warmth or gratitude to the editor of Rupert Murdoch's *Sunday Times* for projecting her relationship with the Queen onto his front page for two weeks running. If it has damaged the Queen, it has damaged her more.

I say this in defiance of the views of a bizarre chorus of right-wing MPs and newspaper commentators who are suddenly denouncing the poor old Queen as if she and her family were Bolshevik agents out to undermine Old England on behalf of the Blacks. I was seriously assured last week by one such person that the Duke of Edinburgh is a committed Marxist – views he is said to have acquired from his left-wing kinsman, Lord Mountbatten.

The current theory among this group of well, shall we say right-wing eccentrics?, is that the Queen's alleged failure to observe strict constitutional convention has suddenly supplied Mrs Thatcher with the secret of eternal life. All she has to do is quit, call an election on the issue, and Bob's your uncle – Kinnock would be worsted and the Queen disarmed!

The whole thing, in other words, is getting out of hand. In that respect, the present fit of highly imaginative jitters reminds one of nothing so much as the final two years of the Macmillan government, when one grotesque scandal after another engulfed the Prime Minister until he finally quit in the belief that he was not well enough to cope with any more disasters.

Mr Macmillan's scandals were even less directly related to the aforementioned 'real issues' than Mrs Thatcher's. They included not only the glorious Profumo affair, with its superb cast of pimps, prostitutes and Russian diplomats, but the equally colourful Argyle divorce, the seedy Vassal spy case, and the genuinely alarming Pontecorvo defection.

But ministerial reputations, in one form or another, were directly involved in all of them. And the reputation which was most in question was Macmillan's good name as a competent, trustworthy, wide-awake Prime Minister. By the end of it, the Super-Mac image had been comprehensively shattered. What was left was the grouse moor and the ducal relatives.

It did for Macmillan, even if Sir Alec Douglas-Home almost succeeded in pulling the Government's fortunes back at the subsequent election. But it is worth pointing out that the future Lord Stockton's scandals, though infinitely more entertaining, were intrinsically far less serious than Mrs Thatcher's current crop.

For the implication of the Select Committee report on Westland is not just that a few officials broke the rules under the impression that they had ministerial clearance to do so, or even that the Prime Minister was prepared to mobilize the Whitehall machine to dish one of her own Cabinet colleagues. No doubt such things have happened before, and they will very likely happen again under future Prime Ministers. That's politics.

No, the smell that is left by the whole affair, and which seems certain to pollute the atmosphere surrounding Mrs Thatcher's remaining years at Downing Street, is rather different. It is that she is a Prime Minister who is prepared to play dirty when it suits her but is ready to let others take the blame when the plot goes wrong.

It is no good her defenders claiming (as the *Daily Telegraph* did in its headline last Friday) that the report had 'cleared' Mrs T. What it said was that, in the absence of any other evidence, the committee accepted her word. The real verdict was 'not proven' – a verdict which, as every Scot knows, is a long way from 'not guilty'.

It is against that background that I come back to the 'real issues' which were mentioned at the beginning of this column. For the atmosphere of dishonesty which increasingly surrounds this government is even more blatant in its handling of matters like the unemployment figures and the poverty figures.

The case of the poverty figures is the more immediate, since it happened only on Friday and what's more, it backfired. Hoping to avoid a public row, the DHSS sneaked out a written answer showing that the numbers living in poverty had increased from 11.5 million in 1979 to 16.3 million in 1983.

The reply was timed to reach MPs and journalists some hours after the Commons had risen for its three-month summer recess. But the ploy was so outrageous that Labour protests made major news stories next day. Indeed, the dishonesty may well have won the story more publicity than might otherwise have been the case.

But the history of the unemployment figures is even more scandalous, since it has been going on far longer. The facts are simple enough: that since 1979 the present government has made no fewer than sixteen changes in the formula for calculating the numbers out of work. All have reduced the figure.

165

If these changes had not been made, the present total of 3.22 million would have been nearly half a million higher. Moreover, pocket calculators have also been busy on the percentage figures, resulting in a cut in the rate of unemployment from 13.1 per cent to 11.7 per cent.

Yet even this deliberate campaign of deception (some might call it falsification) has failed to conceal the overriding fact that unemployment is now rising at a rate of 15,000 a month – five times faster than a year ago, and the fastest since 1983. Mrs Thatcher now has by far the worst record on unemployment in the industrial West, while her Chancellor continues to boast of his 'success'.

That should be the real issue when the country at last goes to the polls to settle the fate of Mrs Thatcher and her dreadful -ism. But if the Select Committee on Defence has helped to highlight the underlying dishonesty of her uniquely personal brand of 'conviction politics' it will not have been wasting its time.

28 July, 1986   **Ian Aitken**

Blue Grey is in the red

It has come as a much needed jolt to the misguided sociologists who thought that Dickensian poverty had been eliminated from London to hear of the sad case of Alexander Patrick Greysteil Hore-Ruthven which has stirred the conscience of a hitherto oblivious nation. Alexander Patrick, who also goes by the name of Lord Gowrie in another place, claims that he has been forced to live on £33,000, barely £1500 a month in take home pay which, he says, 'is not what people need for living in central London'. Not indeed. Some social workers believe that this is only the tip of the iceberg and that there are people in London living on still lower salaries further below the caviar line. If the noble Lord's courageous decision to 'come out' leads to others coming forward so the full depths of the problem can be revealed then it will not have been made in vain.

Who is to blame for this unfortunate case of self-privatization? Not Mrs Thatcher, surely. She has done more than any previous Prime Minister to enable people like Lord Gowrie to boost their living standards. Not only did she reduce the top marginal rate of taxation from 83 per cent to 60 per cent in 1979, thereby providing the biggest boost ever to the higher paid, but she also persevered with mortgage interest relief on houses, which offers far more in tax subsidies to richer people than to the poor. Despite all this and more the Minister for the Arts is down to his last Hockney. Who, pray, is to blame?

Part of the blame must go to Mr Ken Livingstone, Leader of the Greater London Council and self appointed protector of

"Isn't it romantic – now we can both go down to the Jobcentre until we're sixty-five."

3 April, 1986

minority rights for, inexcusably, overlooking the plight of impoverished monetarist poets in the Privy Council. Part of the blame must also go to the Low Paid Unit, which has become so obsessed with people earning under £50 to £100 a week and the unemployed that it has become blind to the upper-class poverty trap, the *anciens pauvres* with wife and two small homes to support.

Maybe Mrs Thatcher hasn't gone far enough. Her policy has been to increase considerably the rewards of the rich (to induce them to take risks and increase the size of the national cake) while at the same time reducing the rewards of the poor (to price them back into jobs and prevent them shirking). Maybe she should ask the poor for more sacrifices so that the likes of the noble Lord can be priced back into a job without increasing the public sector borrowing requirement. He, himself, being one of the Government's best-regarded communicators (and an outspoken advocate of the need to remove benefits from the 'workshy') would be better explaining the details of all this than we are. Tread softly, Lord Gowrie, for you tread on their dreams.

6 September, 1985   **Leader**

Back to front Minister

One of the skills which Paul Channon brings to the office of Secretary of State for the Department of Trade and Industry is that he can think and speak backwards. If he wants to leave a party early, he once explained, he whispers to his wife 'lufwa si siht, emoh og s'teL.' ('Let's go home, this is awful.') Wags have suggested that this remarkable facility springs from his family's connection with a dark, mysterious liquid of mind-enlarging properties – Guinness. His mother was a Guinness, as is his wife, who was formerly married to his cousin Jonathan Guinness. His liquidity includes Guinness shares which under-pin Kelvedon Hall in Essex and a Mustique villa.

His father was the colourful MP and political diarist Sir

Henry (Chips) Channon, friend of the famous. One such, Sir Terence Rattigan, dedicated *The Winslow Boy* – a tale of British hypocrisy with unspeakable undertones – to the infant Paul Channon 'in the hope that he may live to see a world in which this tale will point no moral.'

His new DTI seat has ejecting tendencies (Cecil Parkinson, Leon Brittan) but he has been able to intimately study the mechanism as the department's Number 2 since 1983. Far from leaving the party early, he will be eager to bolt himself into a job that crowns long years of caretaker roles. His ambition is to be Father of the House.

He strode from Eton, Christ Church and the Blues into politics at the age of twenty-three, when his father died. When he took the latter's seat at Southend West, known as Guinness-on-sea, his grandmother commented: 'I think you have done right by backing a colt when you know the stable he was trained in.'

As shadow arts spokesman he was wont to sport an ice-cream pink coat and dine off gold plate – a phase, he later acknowledged, when he sounded like 'a rich, feudal aristocrat'. But as minister of arts in 1980 he was soberly low-key, perhaps in deliberate contrast to his ejected predecessor, Norman St John Stevas. 'He was shrewd without being rigid or doctrinaire,' says an insider.

His unspectacular years at the DTI were relieved by a rare and outspoken attack on open government, which he said would create a 'massive' and 'horrific' increase in bureaucracy. Recent experience of open government suggests an urgent need for more minds that can think backwards. Ylkciuq.

28 January, 1986   **Stuart Wavell**

Dickens family drama

It would not abuse the privilege of this column to salute the stoicism of Tory MP Geoffrey Dickens, whose desire to name suspected perverts in the Commons has brought him only revilement. For 'Bunter' Dickens is a much misunderstood man.

The misunderstandings date almost from the moment the eighteen-stone MP began voting against his party upon entering Parliament in 1979. It slowly dawned that he was accidentally trundling into the wrong lobby. Once, when he was locked in with Labour, the enraged Tory whip Spencer Le Marchant waved a placard scrawled with an unparliamentary imprecation. They made it up by jointly purchasing a racehorse – a ruse, many thought, to calm an upstart dizzied by his rise from shopfloor to the board of an engineering firm.

But misunderstandings came thick and fast in 1981 during his war on paedophiles (which he thought was pronounced fidopiles). The amiable Dickens used parliamentary privilege to name a former diplomat as a subscriber to Paedophile Information Exchange. Then, as now, he was roundly chastised but, detecting obstruction from high Tories, he called a press conference to demand the Attorney-General's resignation. The assembled scribes were astonished when Dickens announced that he had 'a skeleton in the cupboard'. This turned out to be a by no means cadaverous divorcée whom he had met at a *thé dansant* which he frequented between parliamentary duties. He said he was leaving home 'for good'. Thoughtfully, he asked the press not to ring his wife until he had told her the news.

Then a second skeleton wiggled out of *thé dansant* – a forty-one-year-old brunette who claimed Dickens had ditched her after a passionate nine-month affair. Dickens felt she had misconstrued their friendship. 'I like to help people and I don't like disappointing them,' he declared reasonably. Two weeks later he was back home 'for good'. Some mistake, protested the jilted divorcée, with whom Dickens had just bought a new bed.

The 'Casanova' episode did not harm his prospects: he beat fifty-seven Tory applicants for the new Lancashire marginal of Littleborough and Saddleworth and won the 1983 election by 5000 votes, perhaps aided by the late deletion of his election pledge to nuclear deterrence 'until unilateral disarmament'.

If, as Ralph Waldo Emerson believed, to be great is to be

misunderstood, the magnitude of Dickens's eminence is almost beyond measure.

18 March, 1986   **Stuart Wavell**

Richardson's run rampage

Just in case you were wondering whatever happened to bats-manship, the West Indies – and Richie Richardson in particular – showed everyone yesterday as the Bridgetown Test inexorably headed, via a different route, to the same terminus as the first two.

This time the West Indians were obliged to bat first. They responded by scoring 269 for two on the first day. Richardson, who must now be accounted in the first rank of world batsmen, was 150 not out at the close after putting on 194 for the second wicket with Desmond Haynes. For England, it was yet another bloody day in paradise, dictated by disappointing bowling in the opening session, crucial dropped catches and utter West Indian superiority.

At least Gower won the toss, so the dreadful first-day pattern of Jamaica and Trinidad, could not be repeated. He inserted, as he said he would. It was primarily a defensive move, but still there was a reasonable expectation that England's seamers could to some extent exploit Bridgetown's traditional first-morning juice.

But in this series every theory comes unstuck against the harsh reality of West Indian power: 50 for one after 10 overs, 113 for one by lunch. Greenidge showed what he thought of the pitch by lofting the first ball back past Botham, and the pattern was established. And though there were some signs that batting could be made difficult, Thomas, Botham and Foster were neither zippy nor straight enough to do so with any consistency.

The Greenidge assault was mercifully short: 21 in 24 balls. It was ended in Foster's first over of the series, which began with Haynes striking one hard past second slip and stinging

Botham's hand. For a moment he looked like a kid who had just trapped his fingers in a car door; well, just about everything else has gone wrong for him out here. Then Foster caught the outside edge of Greenidge's bat as he drove, and Botham gratefully moved to his left and grabbed it.

There are more Union Jacks in Bridgetown this weekend than at any time since independence, and this was an excuse to wave them. But it only brought in Richardson, and it was back to polite, slightly bemused, applause.

In England two years ago, Richardson never looked happy. Out here he flourishes like the green mango tree. Having scored the first century of the series, he now scored the second; including the one-dayers, he has passed 50 in his last four games against England.

A few weeks ago one saw him mostly as Richards's protégé and clone. Now he is emerging as a West Indian powerhouse in his own right. Some old-timers say he reminds them most of Collie Smith, but some Richardson shots – like his hip-high offside force – are his own invention. There are already streets in Antigua named after Richards and Roberts, and I expect Richardson's turn will come.

Probably England's best chance against him is to get on both spinners quickly and bottle him up. Compared to most modern Test captains, Gower is spin-crazy; but even he finds it hard to contemplate Edmonds and Emburey bowling together on the first morning. By the time he had contemplated and done it, Richardson, as in Trinidad, had flown to 50 – this time in 54 minutes.

Even England's fielding, for a few years our pride and joy, has become ragged on this tour. Richardson was dropped twice in the covers: by Gooch on 55, and Emburey, a harder chance, on 85; Haynes was put down by Edmonds at square leg.

The ground announcer here adds to the erring fielder's misery by calling his name. But these were all full-blooded, misplaced shots; there were few edges, and there was not even an lbw appeal until, after 90 minutes, Thomas decided he had to say something.

But through the afternoon session West Indies were kept much quieter. Only 74 runs came, with a spinner on at one end throughout. Haynes was almost wholly subdued and took some stick from the home spectators clustered around the Official Local Character, King Dyal, who was holding court in his saffron suit and matching pipe.

Richardson also slowed up and went through some very nervous nineties against Botham's angrier second spell. When he did reach his 100, after 198 minutes, it came, with sad aptness, through a misfield.

Even after that, Richardson was kept in check. For 35 overs, in which time he moved from 83 to 127, he did not score a boundary; Botham got nowhere when he tried bowling round the wicket with two men back for the barbed hook, but that was largely because Richardson was going through a period of not making contact.

Emburey was proving hard to get away, Edmonds was making the odd ball turn and lift, and there might have been some encouragement for England provided they did not look at the scoreboard and, above all, the list of batsmen to come.

The tortoise Haynes, meanwhile, was showing some signs of gaining on his partner. He batted with great solidity for 84 runs and five hours until Foster came back. Then, once again, Foster persuaded an opener to drive and once again Botham was at slip to take the catch, this time judging it very astutely low down.

This was classic stuff: overseas batsmen struggling against English outswing. Unfortunately, four and a half hours of playing time had elapsed between the two dismissals.

Richardson's quiet time ceased after he was treated – by a smiling Botham as well as the official physio – for cramp. Immediately after that, he was back playing lovely whisking strokes past cover point. His 150 took just short of five and a half hours. Defeat No. 3 is now just a couple of batting collapses away.

22 March, 1986   **Matthew Engel**

Philip Larkin

Legend has it that once, at a dismally inept amateur boxing match in Hull, Philip Larkin turned to his neighbour with the words 'Only connect'. In its way, this is typical of Larkin. Not only that he should thus introduce a hallowed Forsterian nostrum into a coarse context, but also that he should yearn for aggression and directness.

Introducing Betjeman's work to American readers, he began with relish: 'The quickest way to start a punch-up between two British literary critics is to ask them what they think about the poems of Sir John Betjeman.' The nice thing about Larkin is that he was a reactionary. Or, put it another way, a counter-puncher. He enjoyed hitting back at received progressive opinion on Picasso, Pound, Charlie Parker and pulling out the troops.

His poetry, though we are used to it now, is full of explicit aggression against the idea of poetry itself. His first book, *The North Ship*, shows a young writer hypnotised by the example of Yeats, the old spell-binding tenor he was to repudiate with the help of Hardy: 'When I came to Hardy it was with the sense of relief that I didn't have to try to jack myself up to a concept of poetry that lay outside my own life – this is perhaps what I felt Yeats was trying to make me do.' After two novels, *Jill* and *A Girl in Winter*, Larkin returned to poetry with a voice of his own – a voice no longer straining for the top notes, but content with the middle range.

The note it strikes is apparent in the title, *The Less Deceived*, the authentic Larkin note of sceptical disenchantment. And a poem like 'I Remember, I Remember' takes the standard literary presentation of childhood, backs it into a corner and dishes out a tremendous pasting:

> Our garden, first: where I did not invent
> Blinding theologies of flowers and fruits,
> And wasn't spoken to by an old hat.

> *And here we have that splendid family*
> *I never ran to when I got depressed,*
> *The boys all biceps and the girls all chest . . .*

The negatives, the denials, are strung together like combination punches until the myth is counted out. 'Deprivation,' he once said, 'is for me what daffodils were for Wordsworth.'

Larkin had little time for poetic props and easy atmospherics. Groping back to bed after a piss, one poem begins, identifying the speaker with *l'homme moyen sensuel*, before going on to ridicule artistic treatments of the moon as 'Lozenge of love! Medallion of art!' Larkin's chosen analogue for his art was the camera:

> *But O! photography! as no art is,*
> *Faithful and disappointing! That records*
> *Dull days as dull, and hold-it smiles as frauds,*
> *And will not censor blemishes*
> *Like washing-lines, and Hall's distemper boards . . .*

Larkin censored nothing on the grounds that it was unpoetic. His verse, like Betjeman's, was 'resigned to swallowing anything', even 'Don't throw old blades into the WC' – a phrase taken from his review of *Summoned by Bells*.

A camera himself, rejoicing in disruptive accidents to compositional decorum, he once remarked to a photographer who was about to take his picture: 'I tell this to all photographers: I am not bald. I do not have a double chin. And this doesn't exist.'

'This' was his ample stomach. It wasn't vanity. It was a wry comment on vanity and its absurdity, followed by a rich guffaw. He included himself with the mass of humanity. And when Larkin praised writers it was always for this: his reservations about Tennyson ('vapid onomatopoeics') are balanced by praise for his 'gruff ability to hit the nail on the head in matters of common concern'. He likes Hardy because he is direct – a man speaking to men. He reveres Wilfred Owen: 'his secret lies in the retort he had already written when W. B. Yeats made his fatuous condemnation: "Passive suffering is not a theme for a poetry". "Above all, I am not concerned with poetry".'

Neither was Larkin. And yet, having disposed of it, having written it off, having disarmed us, he can touch us easily and directly with the real thing, without the capital P. Poetry, when it comes, is earned. It has to live in a world where people grope back to bed after a piss, where people fuck each other up, where boys puke their hearts out behind the gents. Then, and only then, can the moon be seen for what it is:

> *A reminder of the strength and pain*
> *of being young, that it can't come again,*
> *But it is for others undiminished somewhere.*

A mixed blessing is what one takes away from Larkin. But a blessing nevertheless. To return to E. M. Forster, his phrase applies in full to Philip Larkin: 'Only connect the prose and the passion, and both will be exalted, and human love will be seen at its height.'

In Larkin's poetry, the prose and the passion are not merely connected, they are inseparable, as they are for all of us.

3 December, 1985 **Craig Raine**

Geoffrey Grigson

I hope and trust that Geoffrey Grigson will not be remembered solely as a cantankerous and grumpy reviewer. He was more, much more than the scourge of art officials, professors of poetry and academic critics that readers of this newspaper associate with his name. He was a man of rare and wonderful enthusiasms, and it is that man who will ultimately endure.

In the meantime, there is the Grigson with the legendary billhook to put in perspective. Like his friend and mentor, Wyndham Lewis, he relished the role of devil's advocate. He enjoyed being the nay-sayer when all about him were saying yea.

He was the first person to cast doubt on the genius of Dylan Thomas, for example, and he never took Edith Sitwell at her own generous estimate: the booze-induced lyricism of the one and the High Priestess posturing of the other were repellent to him.

He refused to hitch himself to the Bloomsbury bandwagon, and was equally scornful towards Bloomsbury's fiercest opponent, F. R. Leavis. Both represented different kinds of literary respectability – and Geoffrey Grigson was, from the beginning to the end of his life, determinedly and consistently unrespectable. He even edited an anthology of *Unrespectable Verse*.

He had an enduring respect for those artists – poets, painters, novelists – who went their own sweet ways, who refused to kow-tow to Fashion, who functioned, as he believed they should, on the outside. The outside – far away from the passing Establishments, literary or otherwise – was the only decent place to be.

Cézanne and Pissarro, 'the grandest and humblest of landscape painters,' were among his heroes, along with Hopkins, John Clare, Samuel Palmer, Crabbe and Christopher Smart, about all of whom he wrote freshly and lovingly.

His book of 1947, *Samuel Palmer: The Visionary Years* is a major work of re-assessment of a misunderstood and misrepresented English genius: he was neither a follower of Blake nor an inspired amateur, to be cherished for his naiveté. 'His religion, his reading, his politics blend in his work, blend furiously with the clear-sighted unity between himself and nature.'

Grigson possessed that 'clear-sighted unity', too. His knowledge of the natural world was immense. He could put a name to each and every flower, bird or insect he saw. It was a duty and an honour for him to be able to do so, since it displayed a proper respect for the varied naturalness of all living things.

In that marvellous book of his old age, *The Private Art*, he tells the cautionary tale of the proof-reader on the *Odessa News* who remonstrated with the young Isaac Babel: 'And you dare to write! A man who doesn't live in nature, as a stone does or an animal, will never in all his life write two worthwhile lines.' Babel went away and learned the names of those trees and birds he had ignorantly called trees and birds.

I shall always regard my friend Geoffrey Grigson as a great rescuer and discoverer. You only have to look at his anthologies to be made aware of the depth and range of his reading. He

177

loved to grub in the Bodleian Library or the British Museum in the hope of rescuing some deserving poet (frequently the author of a solitary, deserving poem) from an ill-deserved obscurity. In his grubbing days, he chanced on William Diaper, George Daniel and Giles Fletcher ('Love no med'cine can appease/he burns the fishes in the seas') among many others.

Grigson the enthusiast is at his most beguiling in the collection of essays, *Poems and Poets*, in which he celebrates such wonders as Whitman's 'Memories of President Lincoln' and Smart's 'A Song to David' in language that is finely sensitive to what makes each poem peculiar and wonderful.

An observation like the following is a world away from the lit crit that is practised by the majority of Grigson's despised profs. He quotes these lines from the 52nd stanza of Smart's masterpiece:

> The grass the polyanthus cheques;
> And polish'd porphyry reflects;
> By the descending rill.

and then observes: 'Anyone who knows, by good luck, the limestone county of Raby, and of Staindrop Moor alongside, and Teesdale, will at once see the flower and the rock and the waterfall in a characteristic conjunction which Smart must have known in his Co. Durham days, the limestone so finely polished by centuries of the descending rill, protruding from grass chequered with the lilac umbels, by the thousand, of the Birdseye Primrose.'

Geoffrey Grigson is a good and honest poet, as his recent *Collected Poems* demonstrates. The quiet celebrator of the delights of living and loving is more to my taste than the sometimes heavy-handed satirist who takes a bash at Muggeridge, the Arts Council, and other subjects of marginal interest. The celebrator is, essentially, the man I knew in the last decade or so of his long life.

Geoffrey, whose beloved brothers were slaughtered in the Great War, was never ever 'half in love with easeful death'. Extinction was the nastiest of his enemies. He loved a letter by William Cowper, written in 1790, 'after madness and preliminaries of vengeance and hell': 'The consideration of my short continuance here, which was once grateful to me, now fills me with regret. I would like to live and live always.'

Well, he has gone now, and so has his grumpiness. His standards, his knowledge, his devotion to the genuine – these remain.

30 November, 1985 **Paul Bailey**

Billie's Master class

'Do you know when Beckett's birthday is? It's Friday the 13th of April, wouldn't you know.' Billie Whitelaw paused. 'Well, he may well have made that up. That is officially his birthday. But he's got a wicked sense of humour. He's not gloomy at all, you know.'

This year Beckett will be eighty. To mark this anniversary three short plays (or pieces as Whitelaw prefers to call them) *Footfalls*, *Rockaby*, and the narrative fragment *Enough* will be performed by Whitelaw for the first time as a trilogy in Britain.

Footfalls and *Rockaby* (both written especially for Whitelaw) have been seen in London – *Footfalls* at the Royal Court and *Rockaby* at the National. But it was not until the opening of the Samuel Beckett Theatre off-Broadway in 1984 that Whitelaw performed the trilogy. She is the only character on stage at all times.

With the Riverside production Billie Whitelaw has a problem. In New York she'd worked 'like this' (crossing two fingers tight) with Beckett and the director Alan Schneider, who died ten months ago.

Fortunately, there is Rocky Greenberg, who painted with the light so brilliantly in New York – also Robbie Hendry, who directed *Footfalls* and *Enough* at the Royal Court.

Significantly, there is no Beckett. For the first time since Whitelaw met him in 1964 while doing the National's production of *Play* at the Old Vic, she's having to rehearse without him.

'I've never done a piece of Beckett without him. The only

way I've been able to do this in the past is by sitting with him hour after hour staring at each other (he's got very pale blue eyes) and saying the whole play through together. I have to hear his voice with its slight Irish accent to get the rhythms, the right vowel sounds. I have to be able to hear the way he reads his lines, the way he uses pauses (so important in his work) in my head. That's even before I try vocalising them.'

They used to talk on the phone – not discussing the play, but reading it through together again and again, with Whitelaw returning to her native Yorkshire lilt to get the rhythms right. Now she hesitates to call him as he's had such bad flu. She tried to write a letter, but it was impossible.

She describes herself as being 'a cross between a musician and a musical instrument'. When rehearsing *Footfalls* at the Royal Court Beckett suggested to her that maybe the theatre wasn't the right place for his work any more. Where? 'Perhaps an art gallery. I think if people thought they were going to see a walking painting it would be closer to Beckett than imagining they were going to see a play.'

She points to a photograph. 'Look, in *Footfalls* I feel like a walking, talking Edvard Munch. And I look as if I'm carved out of stone, like sculpture. That is actually Beckett's favourite photo. That says it all. And out of my mouth – with a bit of luck – will come notes to match that.'

Surrounding herself day and night with her 'Beckett memorabilia', she prepares a part by a process of osmosis. She picked up a portrait of a furrow-foreheaded Beckett in Donegal-type jumper. 'A marvellously handsome, poetic face don't you think?' Another was of her in *Rockaby*, with skull-like face and dressed in strange, black-sequined finery. There was an early one of her in *Play*, with candid, youthful eyes emerging from a face encrusted in porridge substance mask ('very good for the skin').

Her battered original scripts go everywhere with her. She refuses all offers to have fresh clean ones, preferring the old ones heavily marked up with both Beckett's and her own notations.

On the text of *Rockaby* (to do with an old woman rocking herself in isolation waiting for death) she's written: 'Solitary,' 'reaching out,' 'no-one there,' 'perhaps no-one there.' And in the last section (where she closes her eyes) there's a big bold red 'Hurray!' – like a child let out from school.

Half and quarter pauses are similarly marked – almost like a musical score. 'I know it sounds dreadfully pretentious, but it does actually work,' she said, recalling the first instruction given her by Beckett when rehearsing *Play*. 'The script was filled with one word followed by dot-dot-dot, two words, dot-dot, and he said, "Billie, could you possibly change three dots to two dots?" And he pencilled out a dot. I knew what he wanted to achieve by that.'

Working with Beckett has made her incredibly disciplined, she said. 'Almost too disciplined . . . I think he demands more concentration from the actor than any other writer I know. Patrick Magee and Jack Macgowran (he used to write for the two of them) and I used to think of ourselves as the terrible Beckett triplets – but I'm the only one left.

'I remember Pat saying to me, "Ah well, Billie, we can't cheat with this man." And you can't. Because doing Beckett is utterly different from doing a three-act play, or *The Greeks* – all twelve hours – which I did at the National.

'It's as if a cook who usually has a great pan of vegetables into which he puts lots of ingredients and serves lots of people, has reduced his soup down and down until he's got this beautiful little essence and everybody can only have a tiny sip. The actual soup remains but is pared down to the thing itself. You can get away with murder if you have a big pan of soup, but when you've got it right down to nothing there's nowhere to hide.'

Sometimes acting 'the thing itself' has proved too much. She refers to the two seasons of *Not I* at the Royal Court, where at one point it was suggested she came close to a nervous collapse. 'In *Not I*, Beckett had written in a long scream, suggesting that I should do it "flat, with no emotion, no colour." But physically it was very difficult for me to do that. Because it was the scream I'd felt but never cried out for my son who was five then and desperately ill with meningitis. It was the scream that I felt for my boy then and it is the scream that is still there and that will never go.'

All parts of her body were blacked out in *Not I*, except for her 'babbling raging mouth'. It was so demanding that she feels she couldn't do it again.

In both *Footfalls* and *Rockaby* she draws on images from her own past. Her mother had Parkinson's syndrome towards the end of her life and would sit hour upon hour with a stiff expressionless face. 'I'd enter this room and see her just sitting there and think "What the hell is going on in her mind." And when I do *Rockaby* I have this picture in my mind.'

It was her mother who began her acting career by packing her off, aged ten, to Bradford Civic Playhouse to do amateur dramatics in the hope it would cure a stutter. She started doing radio work for the BBC when she was eleven, and because the money was useful (her father had died a little earlier) never saw any reason to stop. At twelve she was theatrically adopted by Joan Littlewood – a great influence on her life – and began to work a lot in Littlewood's Theatre Workshop, then based in Manchester.

Whitelaw, now aged fifty-three, says it was Alun Owen's play *Progress to the Park* at Stratford East which 'pulled me out of one layer and into another'. Kenneth Tynan described her then as 'the female Albert Finney'. (Later she co-starred with him in *Charlie Bubbles*). Soon she was playing Desdemona to Olivier's Othello.

Her meeting with Beckett was the most 'significant' of her life. 'When we met I came under a marvellous umbrella of empathy and love.' The bond was initially between director George Devine, designer Jocelyn Herbert and Beckett as they worked on *Play*. Soon it was to include Whitelaw.

Does she feel typecast as Beckett's 'great interpreter'? 'Yes . . . I've worked with him a lot. But it is only one small part of what I do. My husband Robert Muller shudders every time I go out of the front door to do a Beckett. He says I just about earn my parking fines.'

29 January, 1986   **Heather Lawton**

Coming unstuck

The questions which permeate all Bainbridge fiction are why what is so sad should be so funny, why what is fantastic should emerge from the humdrum, and why what is trivial should be so sublime.

These dozen stories* ask them all over again, and with a kind of pressing urgency. The reader is not let off with their amusement value, high though it is, he has to take stock of why he is being so entertained.

Each story begins flatly, as will the day of judgment, no doubt. We are lured into what is plainly a non-risk area before being precipitated into events from which there is no possible escape. Due to the fact that in Bainbridge country skid row masquerades as the cake walk, we are hurried to tragedy wearing big grins, like the lady on the jacket. Equally deceptive, although addicts now look round for the latest evidence of it, is the writer's defence of the standards which pop, concrete, and all the high-street moneylenders have obliterated.

The title story effortlessly evokes this lost world. Mum (short for Mrs Mumford), turbanned, dressy and loud, queens it over the regulars in the bar of the hotel in which she spent her wartime honeymoon. She is now the merry widow-companion of Mr Armitage, and the pair of them are licensed to play pranks.

However, when prim Miss Emmet enters and is forced against her will to let her hair down, something she has never done in her life, the consequences for Mum are terribly beyond anything contained in her worst hangover dreams. What she has to find out is that there are people who cannot join in.

In most of the tales the generations are crossly entangled, sometimes remotely, via a train ride, often in the home. The

* *Mum and Mr Armitage, and other stories* by Beryl Bainbridge (Duckworth)

old are cocky, the young take a hiding, and the not so young come unstuck.

Beryl Bainbridge is at her best when dealing with male immaturity and ineptness, the mates dolled up for tennis, grandad's drip of ancient cricket, fathers cringing before their huge teenage lout sons, and fumbling lovers. They are men who have been bamboozled by masculine messages sent by the media.

There is a wonderful story, a real weepy, of a pair of these men at the theatre uncomprehendingly seeing *Peter Pan* which reflects the writer's close understanding of the acrid sentiment which still lies just under the skin of much British life. The characters aren't eccentric, but ordinary creatures captured in a visionary gaze which is both comic and melancholy.

21 November, 1985   **Ronald Blythe**

The divided elf

There can't at the moment be anyone more highly regarded by intelligent movie-goers the world over than Woody Allen. He is the rich man's Steven Spielberg, a film-maker who may not make mega-hits but never seems to go entirely wrong. Actually, a more appropriate comparison would be with Buster Keaton – a brilliant comic who could make movies extremely well too, and who also had a streak of melancholy.

Keaton, of course, was neglected and driven to drink, which is not likely to happen to Allen, though one day the fashion for him too may wane. If it does he'll probably be quite happy to leave the business and concentrate on other things, like jazz and his psychoanalyst. He doesn't seem to me like a man obsessed with fame, in fact, he runs fairly hard away from it.

Perhaps that is why he is so popular, and why his films are so good. He doesn't care about the admiration of his peers, and the rave notices for his latest film, *Hannah And Her Sisters*, which arrives here next week, have taken him by surprise. He knows it's a good film but I don't think he would regard it as his masterpiece. Manhattan's Methuselah, as *Film Comment* has dubbed him, isn't satisfied just yet. Not by a long way.

Woody Allen's œuvre can be conveniently, if not wholly accurately, divided into two. There are his funny films, which are a delightful mess (*Bananas, Take The Money And Run, Everything You Always Wanted To Know About Sex*, etc.) and his serious films, which are usually funny but very definitely not a mess (*Annie Hall, Manhattan, Stardust Memories*, etc.).

Hannah And Her Sisters is claimed by some to bridge the gap between the two. It is very funny and very structured – everything you always wanted to know about Woody Allen, in fact. David Edelstein, in the late *Review* magazine, ended his very interesting tribute by saying: 'In the final exhilarating shot, the artist seems to say: "I have learned to love. I am free now to be whatever I like." He has come home at last.' Well, well.

I doubt whether Allen would agree with that. The cinema, he once said, 'is about trying to get things to come out perfect in art, because it's real difficult in life'. In *Hannah*, things do come out pretty well but perfect they are not, and nor is the film. But he is striving for something like that.

There is, in almost every funnyman, a desperate need to be taken seriously and a capacity for introspection and doubt that makes all the applause both necessary and meaningless. The only thing that's clichéd about Allen is that he is right in the mould of this stereotype. This, of course, is partly what makes his jokes and his films so interesting and so entertaining. They come out of a world that can't be understood rationally, and isn't fair at all to those who blunder through it.

Nevertheless it has its grateful moments – 'Groucho Marx, Willie Mays, the second movement of Mozart's Jupiter, Louis Armstrong's recording of Potatohead Blues', as Allen says in *Manhattan*. But these are momentary. The rest is constant, hypochondriacal struggle against the dying of the light. This isn't so much the philosophy of a genius, as of a man who knows he'll never be one. Yet Mozart, were he alive today, would probably put Allen's movies in any list he might have made.

He touches us deeply precisely because of his doubts and

imperfections, not because of his huge breadth of talent and vision. The struggle of the characters played by himself are the struggles of quite a lot of humanity when faced with sex, love, death, money troubles and a world which seems to have a baleful capacity to dump you in it at every available opportunity. Allen is imperfect man par excellence, endlessly examining his own navel.

That's him as a comedian. As a film-maker he is something else again. He has learned to make movies well through a process of trial and error, and by hiring the best to work with him. He also goes to see more of other people's movies than most directors, especially the work of those like Bergman, Fellini and Hawks, who are the real masters. He is now a very smooth operator indeed, as good a shaper of films as anyone now working in Hollywood, whose whole ethos he loathes.

David Thomson, in his excellent *Biographical Dictionary of the Cinema*, tells the old story of how Allen was studiously playing Dixieland clarinet in a New York pub when, in 1978, 'Hollywood conceded the year to him' with three Oscars.

'He avoided the awards night,' says Thomson, 'for reasons that would make another Allen movie – he might lose? he might win? It might look as if he expected to win? he preferred privacy to the cultivation of privacy? or he preferred to nurture his persona in private? He claimed shyness, and nobody noticed how oddly that sat with a film that revolves around its maker's insecure life and uses its actress's real name in the title – *Annie Hall*.'

This is a shrewd if rather bitchy comment about Allen, who tends to make a great thing about his aversion to show-biz ballyhoo at the same time as seeming to have the greatest affection for its tattiest manifestations, e.g. *Broadway Danny Rose*.

That, perhaps, is the downside – the fact that, as Thomson goes on, he seems incapable of making a picture beyond the range of his personal psychoanalytical significance. All the same, it seems a small price to pay for all the laughs, and latterly the films which give them to us and beautifully reflect the striving, hypocritical middle-class world a great many people inhabit.

Hannah And Her Sisters is the latest in a long line of work that, in relative terms, is vastly superior to 90 per cent of present-day American cinema. It is superior in both form and content, trying to be about something as well as highly entertaining. But masterpiece it is not, whatever the quotes on the hoardings will say. Allen is much more valuable for the whole body of his work than for one single example of it.

The pursuit of perfection is an entirely worthy thing for an artist to contemplate – and that is what Allen undoubtedly is. But it can actually work against inspiration and it can militate against the sheer panache of more careless raptures. There are times when I think that, if he forgot about Bergman and Chekhov and the fact that life may be meaningless, Allen would be even more precious (in the best sense of that word) than he is.

'You want to do mankind a service?' says a Martian to him in *Stardust Memories*. 'Tell funnier jokes.' Even *Hannah*, which is a kind of mixture of Allen the entertainer and Allen the artist, hasn't really found the answer to that.

12 July 1986   **Derek Malcolm**

An actor's escape from Alcatraz

It has been running now for five years or so. In a sizeable tract of land, in a remote depopulated corner of Umbria, a landscape of thickly wooded gorges and sparse fields, Dario Fo and his wife, the actress Franca Rame, have created an extraordinary amalgam of commune, court and drama school.

They have done up the scattered half-ruined buildings, among them a stone tower going back to Etruscan times. They have built a dining hall with a terrace from which you can watch the falcons wheeling overhead, see the sun set over the tangled slopes. There is a swimming pool and there are horses to ride. But pride of place – and it is visibly Fo's pride and joy – goes to the open-air theatre.

It is built on a narrow level, the land falling away in front, rising steeply behind. There is room only for the square stage and some twenty seats. A plastic canopy keeps the rain off. They use it for annual drama courses, conducted by Fo and Franca Rame, attracting students from all over the world. They also use it for particular productions, and this year a Finnish company were doing a recent play by Fo himself, under his personal direction. And apart from some French, Fo speaks no language but Italian.

The play, which has not so far been performed outside Italy, is called *Elizabeth*. It is based on two days in the reign of Elizabeth I during which she is torn between her passionate love for the Earl of Essex and the knowledge that he is conspiring against her. It ends with her signing his death warrant.

Like all Fo's plays it is concerned with the nature of power and the possibilities of freedom. It has great technical interest because Fo, while deploying to the full his formidable talent for contemporary satire and subversion, has deliberately confined himself to the stage conventions of early sixteenth-century Italy – unities of time and place, use of stock theatrical figures deriving from medieval street theatre, and in particular, in this play, the figure of the Donnazza, played by a male actor dressed as a country-woman, a combination of Juliet's nurse and Pantomime Dame.

And these conventions, which are as much linguistic and cultural as theatrical, had to be understood, of course, by the Finns, whose theatre is very young indeed and whose formalized language not very much older than the century.

There were problems from the start. The summer weather was very hot and the Finns not yet acclimatized. The play was due to open in Finland six weeks later. They had had no time to learn their lines before arriving. But they admired Fo greatly, they had all made sacrifices to go there and work with him, they were keen to make a success of it. They worked hard, rehearsing seven days a week, learning their lines between rehearsals. The hillsides resounded with Finnish.

In the early stages the directing was done by Fo and Franca Rame. Superb actors both, they are not particularly good directors, at least not with Finns. Franca Rame, alternating between assumed languor and real intensity, wanted the part

188

of Elizabeth played exactly as she had played it herself in the Rome production, down to the smallest modulation of voice, in spite of differences of style and presence between herself and Marja Sisko, the Finnish actress playing the part.

And Fo did not really understand why Finnish should sound so different from Italian. Moreover he has the inveterate habit of altering the script as he goes along, an endless process of rewriting as natural to him as breathing, but it caused a brooding kind of sorrow and finally a baffled rage in the Finns, who had been painfully learning the now cancelled and superseded lines. Every slightest change had to be translated into Finnish by the hard-pressed interpreter and written into the script. This went on for about ten days, bringing the cast by slow degrees to the edge of rebellion.

It was a rebellion of a peculiarly Finnish sort, not very demonstrative, but entirely solid. You must understand *why*, not only *how*, Fo said through the interpreter to Marja Sisko. 'Then you will not mind these changes so much.' She neither looked at him nor replied. I saw him glance at the others. None of them looked at him or said anything.

Part of the trouble was that there was no escape. The theatre was the centre of the world. We had no car. All around us were miles of wild countryside. 'Alcatraz,' Marja Sisko said one day, looking up at the steep, densely wooded slopes rising on every side. Pekka, the Donnazza, nodded. 'Yes,' he said, with all the seriousness of a Finn in full agreement. 'Yes, Alcatraz.'

No doubt sensing this malaise, the Fo's distanced themselves from the rehearsals, the direction was taken over by Arturo Corso, who has worked with Fo before and knows him well. At once things began to go better. Arturo didn't know any Finnish either but he was more patient, more skilled at explaining. His explanations were accompanied by the most amazing virtuosity of gesture that I have ever seen. He writhed and rippled all the time he was speaking. A real *maestro del gesto*: the Finns were astounded by him.

This was a deeply interesting phase of things for me, as spectator. Through the demonstrations of Arturo, the efforts of the Finns, the endlessly repeated scenes and speeches, I saw

189

the intentions of the play emerge, heard the accents of Fo's voice, genuinely dissenting, genuinely subversive, one of the great libertarian voices of our time. *Al pubblico*, Arturo urged them, always include the public, remember you are telling a story, *raccontare, non recitare*, do not interpret the part, do not apply psychology.

The interpreter, without whom there would have been no communication at all, miraculously still surviving at the centre of the storm, continued to transmit instructions. The Finns, struggling with language, an intricately amended script, and their own training – all were schooled in the psychological interpretation they were now being warned against – battled bravely on.

The stresses, of course, were registered, quickly or slowly, one way or another. The three young men in the cast, whom I thought of as the Young Finns, coming from a country where the sale and consumption of alcohol is severely controlled, were naturally drawn to the delicious local wine. They were tough, strongly built fellows all three, in the prime of life. It needed a lot of application and single minded purpose to get themselves paralytic, but once or twice they managed it.

Fo reprimanded them, gravity assumed like a mask for the occasion. They retreated to their quarters, where they played the guitar and sang Finnish folk songs about love or about stabbing people at wedding feasts.

Then a series of disasters struck. Pekka, sitting bare-headed in the sun, conning his crosshatched script, got sunstroke and had to spend the next three days supine in a darkened room. During his absence Marja Sisko had to rehearse her own scenes more intensively, spent long hours with Franca Rame, began to forget her lines, and was heard by the others crying in the evenings. Then Arturo, *il maestro del gesto*, in a fulminating, culminating gesture, wounded himself accidentally by drawing a finger nail across the cornea of his left eye.

This was the lowest ebb, the nadir of the enterprise: sunstruck Pekka muttering in his room, Marja Sisko weeping at night, Arturo stricken and immobilized with a gloomy diagonal bandage over his eye. And all around us, beyond the enclave of the theatre, the life of nature indifferently continuing, butterflies and snakes and hawks and cicades going about their business.

Then with miraculous suddenness, everything got very much better. Pekka returned from his sick-bed with fresh zest, Arturo doffed his bandage and recovered his powers, Marja Sisko stopped forgetting her lines and looked happier. The script was finalized, the scenes began to flow, words of praise were uttered by Arturo and – very valued this – by the Fo's. At dinner time the Finns began to make puns and laugh a lot. They are fond of puns, like the English; the Italians less so.

Fo made everyone roar with laughter by recounting the story of Hamlet, act by act, entirely in dumbshow. In his capacity of patron, he praised the quality of his beer and pressed foaming tankards on the young Finns. He led us all out on to the terrace to admire the sunset. One night the young Finns serenaded him and Franca Rame with their guitars. They sang one song about love and one about getting stabbed at a wedding feast.

On the last afternoon of my stay I looked in on the rehearsal for an hour or so. They were hard at it still – with two weeks to go before they opened back home at Tampere. In the last thirty days they had had just two days off. It was very hot, they were rehearsing in costume and sweating under the heavy brocades. There was a choking dust in the air, caused by visiting cars on the dirt tracks. The coffee machine had broken down.

But for the Finns these annoyances seemed not to exist. Scene flowed with scene without intervention of Arturo. The movements on stage, the timing of the lines – product of so much labour – seemed natural and inevitable now. These people I had spent a month with were lost in their borrowed identities, the priest, the courtier, the boy concubine, the Donnazza. They had finally escaped from Alcatraz.

Strangely moving, this flowing shape of drama after the blocked and resentful beginnings. The paradoxes were still present to my mind. It seemed to me that I had witnessed, in this Free University of Alcatraz, an exercise of power and control as unremitting as anything Elizabeth got up to. But some essential human business had been transacted there, under Fo's benign, impatient patronage, among those hillsides. And I was glad and grateful to have seen it.

16 December, 1985   **Barry Unsworth**

Preparing for the last act

To the Connaught Hotel in London to see Sir Alec Guinness, a most memorable and always enigmatic actor. When it comes down to it, the performances of very few actors remain for years in the memory, but I have never forgotten his playing of many parts in the film of *Kind Hearts and Coronets*, or his extraordinary Noh-like Macbeth at the Royal Court, or his personification of Smiley in the television series of John le Carré's *Tinker, Tailor, Soldier, Spy*. Now he has written an autobiography, and that too turns out to be memorable.

What a mysterious book, I said. 'Mysterious,' said Sir Alec, 'that I should have written anything.' He pressed the bell for coffee, asked quietly how I found the book mysterious, and composed himself. Throughout our talk, which lasted more than an hour, he sat upright and still on a little gilt chair, in such a way that my view was generally of him in semi-profile.

Thomas Hardy once said of himself that he was 'a man who noticed such things', by which he meant things whose presence or meaning went unnoticed by others. Sir Alec does this in a way. Once, staying with the Guthries, he found them both naked by a lakeside one morning, lighting a fire, and noticed how similar in looks they were and how identical in manner. In his book he remarks that their marriage suggested a marriage of twins.

Now that is mysterious. But Sir Alec, in grave half-profile, said he didn't think it meant more than it said. They weren't twins, but they were so identical in looks, except that Judy Guthrie was an extremely handsome woman, and very much a woman.

Then there was the matter of the young Alec Guinness's original perception of Jack Hobbs. When he was about six he

192

was dragged out on to the pitch at Lord's to shake the great man's hand. He remembers that he was kindly, but smelled of damp flannel. Sir Alec now puts it this way: 'One walks out at six or something. You're in the middle a great arena. I probably seized on whatever little strange human comforts I could find.'

In Sir Alec's sitting room at the Connaught, a waiter in white gloves appeared and poured coffee.

I asked Sir Alec if, as a young man at drama school he had really carried his shoes to save shoe leather. 'Yes, why not? I put them on somewhere when I got near Baker Street, where the school was. When one's reduced to sixpence, thinking I have sixpence I can spend on going to the Old Vic, and also realizing that the shoes I wore had got holes coming and it was going to cost at least ninepence or a shilling, you know, it becomes a toss up. To hell with the resoling. I want to go to whatever it is in the Waterloo Road.'

When war came he went into the navy and remembers that when he went before his board for a commission, the senior admiral wrote of him, 'Probably more to him than meets the eye.' I suggested this was true of him in other ways, and certainly true of, say, his performance as Smiley. Sir Alec did not reject this, but said, 'Yes, but that's the technical difficulty of seeming anonymous. It was something that hadn't occurred to me until I got down to doing it.'

A long chapter of the book concerns the active service of Lt. Guinness, RNVR. One sentence says, 'A friendly acquaintance of mine, who had been hit by phosphorus, jumped overboard and was last seen swimming deep down, lit up like a torch.' I read out part of this, and Sir Alec said he could still see it, as I spoke that word, but that it was not a thing he dreamed about. It did not come to his mind as often as his own wreck in a hurricane. He thanked God it was the only war horror he ever saw.

Sir Alec thinks of actors as unfrocked priests. Why, I asked, unfrocked? He said that, clearly, actors were not priests, and nor had they a sacramental role to play, and yet there was something priestlike – a sense of evocation and of ceremony. Laurence Olivier possessed these qualities, and so in strange way had Ralph Richardson.

As for the Church proper, he remembers as a schoolboy singing what he calls hymns of twilight or geography, Greenland's Icy Mountain and so on – but they were either melancholy or rumbustious. He cannot bear the present fashion for services with guitars strumming, or the dreary do-it-yourself language of the modern Mass.

And yet, though he liked the continuity of old ceremony, he did not grieve for the loss of the old Tridentine Mass? 'I'm appalled by the current English of the Mass, and yet I prefer the new shape.' Though, he said, he had had a doubt thrown on the preference a few weeks before, when he was making a television film of Graham Greene's *Monsignor Quixote*. He was playing the part of a priest who was concussed and sleepwalking. 'He goes into a chapel and starts saying Mass without any props at all – no chalice, bread, wine, anything. The old Latin Mass, that's been out for what, twenty years now? So I had to relearn large chunks of that.

'I probably did it very poorly, but I thought, what extraordinarily charged material it is, and I thought – as a matter of fact I jolly well know – that one or two of the chaps around, electricians or whatever, with probably not the remotest interest in any such thing, were kind of, mesmerized – much too strong a word, but totally concentrated – because of the strangeness of the thing. So, I'm a little doubtful again.'

I reminded Sir Alec that he had quoted Chesterton as saying that the Church was the one thing that saved a man from the degrading servitude of being a child of his own time. And that Sir Alec had added, for himself, that he hoped he might, with just a little more effort, deny himself the third glass of wine, or a lascivious thought. Were these things always bad?

He did not really think so, but said he saw people, including himself, getting into habits. He would hate to be in a state where he had to have a drink of an evening. If he had friends in, and they'd like a Martini, obviously. But he could see habits creeping up on him. Even that morning there had been something; he had spoiled himself pressing bells.

It struck me that the only bell I had seen pressed was for coffee, and that if you were going to stay at the Connaught what were bells for? And might it not be rather a sad day when one could see a particularly handsome woman and not allow oneself a single lascivious thought?

'Yes, I've always hoped, or assumed, as one gets on in life, that either sadly or wisely – because one doesn't want to make a fool of oneself – that those things diminish. But I remember my very wise old father-in-law, who died at the age of ninety-six, or ninety-five, saying don't kid yourself. He said – he was a well-read man – that he used to think he would sit down and read everything he had never read, and that everything would be under control. "Not a bit of it," he said; "you revert in a strange way to your younger ways of thinking. You're not past it. And the younger and prettier the girls that go by the more you think, oh it would be lovely, you know".'

Did Sir Alec instinctively like deference as a quality? I asked this because he had written that before the war it was always Miss Evans, and Miss Bradley, never their Christian names, when they were addressed by younger actors. And hadn't he written that nowadays it was the fiction of all pals together, and that the achievements of a lifetime were democratically ignored?

He asked if he had not qualified that statement. I said he had, by adding 'Quite right too,' but I had taken that to be ironical.

Well, he said, he had wanted to bring in that quotation from Shakespeare: '. . . to have done, is to hang/Quite out of fashion, like a rusty nail/In monumental mockery.'

He had kept asking himself what encounter had brought out the bitterness of that. Perhaps Shakespeare's hearing some upstart young actor, playwright, or whatever, carrying on and calling him an old has-been?

'I've known it,' he said, 'when I was a very young actor myself, I used to think, oh God, I wish some of them would die off. Now I'm an old actor I don't feel quite the same about it.'

He didn't want deference, but he thought people did not realize how tremendously formal the theatre used to be. At the St James's Theatre you used to be requested not to be seen carrying parcels in at the state door. And just twenty years ago, at the Haymarket, there was a delightful manager, now dead, who'd seen them all, who came to him one day and asked if he could speak to the younger members of the company and ask them, when they came through the stage door, to wear a tie. He had to say that he couldn't do this, that his life wouldn't be worth it. And that was only twenty years ago, when it wasn't as it is now, with that beatnik look about actors.

And he remembered that when he was a very young actor, the best nights had always been Thursdays, when it was the carriage trade and most of the stalls were in black tie. 'There was a feeling of elegance, of going out, that gave it a little extra. Though they were no more intelligent than people sitting in their raincoats, reading the *Standard*.'

Why was it Thursdays? Sir Alec supposed they went away for weekends on the Friday.

Now, he had written in his book that he had to say, at the risk of pretention, that for him the great adventure could be yet to come. What did he mean by that? 'I would love to feel, when the end of life comes, that I've achieved something in itself . . . a stability, or the feeling that life, or the latter part of it, has been well-loved, not frivolous.'

He was not talking about eminence in his profession? 'No, no, no. I have just been very lucky on that score. I have friends whom I consider wise people. I think Richardson was a wise man. He achieved something remarkable in himself.'

Did he mean serenity? 'Not just serenity. Serenity I think would be very nice and desirable. But a kind of little bow tied on life. Not too bad. And I can see myself drifting off into eternity, or nothing, or whatever it may be, with all sorts of bits of loose string hanging out of my pocket. Why didn't I say this, or do that, or why didn't I reconcile myself with someone? Or make sure that someone whom I like was all right in every way, either financially, or, I don't know . . .'

'But as a Catholic,' I began, 'didn't he . . .'

'Thank God you just said "As a Catholic". People always stick in other words and say, "As a deeply religious man". I don't know what that "deeply" is. I stick to the rules as far as I can.'

But as a Catholic, didn't he have to believe in the resurrection of the body? He said he didn't know what that meant. It was in the creed, and one trundled it out. But Jesus had said, 'Behold, I make all things new.' That was easier. He couldn't see himself at a celestial cocktail party with his friends. If eternity meant anything it meant timelessness, and he didn't see how one lumbered the body round without time. He needed a sense of worship, as he thought many did. But he had a little quarrel with Catholic attitudes to animals. He loved the animals he had at home – dogs, cats, birds – and did not want to think the human beings were in some very different category.'

Then we came round to Sir Alec's only boast, and to his only desire for revenge.

His only boast, made in the last sentence of the book, is that he is unaware of ever having lost a friend.

But that, I said, was some boast, wasn't it? He thought it a reputable one, and that he had been careful in his use of the word *unaware*. Of course he had quarrelled with people. There had been withdrawings aside. But things had always come round in the end.

The only revenge he would like, and he does not specify what sort of revenge it might be, is against Harold Hobson. In 1951 Guinness acted in and directed his own *Hamlet*. Mr Hobson wrote that, with the exception of Alec Guinness, you would never hear of any of the actors again. This infuriated Guinness. He said he had hand-picked the cast, and that with the exception of the Ophelia, poor girl, who had drifted away, and the Ghost, who was a bore, all the others became stars either in films or on the stage. All had managed to get their names above the title at some time or other. He named, as a sample, Robert Shaw, Michael Gough, and Stanley Holloway.

That notice by Mr Hobson is something Sir Alec still remembers. 'To say they would never be heard of again. The arrogance of it. Dear me.'

Then Sir Alec turned slightly away, and sat in semi-profile again. I do not at all wish to convey that this was an affectation. I'm sure that would be wrong. I'd say, on very slight acquaintance, that it is something which goes with his detachment of thought and speech. We chatted for a few minutes about Trollope, a favourite of his, the complete edition of the Pepys diaries, which he finds delightful, and the one book (a paper-

back thriller) which Lt. Guinness, RNVR, took with him when
he was obliged to abandon ship.

Then I left. 'Thank you so much for coming,' he said.
'You're the last. Did you have any props with you?'

7 October, 1985   **Terry Coleman**

Peter Stein's Otello

Peter Stein's first message to his *Otello* audience in Cardiff is
the large, plain chamfered picture frame his set designer Lucio
Fanti has inserted into the proscenium. In the middle of the
bottom of the frame two steps are cut away down to a narrow
forestage though you don't realize that until it's used. Richard
Armstrong, the conductor, launches into Verdi's astonishingly
direct, stormy opening and the flat red plush panel inside the
frame slides quickly up to reveal the bare boards of the square
stage area which suddenly fill with milling crowds, urgent and
anxious, acting as with one mind, a storm in themselves.

From Moidele Bickel's costumes and from the buildings
outlined on Fanti's flats enclosing the space, you see at once
that this is the renaissance: Verdi's renaissance, the strength
of his reawakened genius ultimately applied; Shakespeare's
renaissance revived by Boito; and Stein's too, after a ten-year
break from opera direction.

The sides of the set are decorated with the simple architecture
of paintings by the early Italian renaissance masters, but Fanti's
great flats are hinged like doors to allow instant access for all,
and an impact of speed and action that races almost faster than
the eye can follow. The focus flashes unpredictably from point
to point.

The presence is overpowering. The chorus stops, starts,
reforms, breaks with a constant sense of nervous alarm and
surprise, or assembles in a knot like a whirlpool or an animal
caught at bay, and sings with that sheer physical exhilaration
that Verdi expected and the Welsh National Opera generously
and thrillingly provides.

198

At the back, as also behind the side flats, steps lead down and away. And, as in a gallery, there stands a great canvas with a stormy sky, in front of which a jagged metallic fork of lightning points down, reflecting violent flashes of blinding, laserlike intensity. Later that canvas is switched for a night sky with moonscape, before which Otello and Desdemona hymn their love, or a blue sky with fluffy clouds for the next act, or angry waves for the council chamber scene.

Stein's picture frame is not a game. It tells of the sharp and subtle perspectives in the work and of the art with which he has chosen pictorially to honour the expected patterns, while reinforcing them with devotion and extension that in every way match Verdi's masterpiece.

This production is not just good; it is great. It wears the tradition of operatic *Otello*s lightly. If you expect to see the Moor approach Desdemona's bed with a scimitar above her head, you will. The curtains of Victorian scenography play their part: jealous red, with flame tongues, a pair of light curtains in Act 2 symbolize Iago's intrigue, and enable him to isolate his confession on the forestage.

This is a very beautiful production, both visually and in its dramatic achievement, but it is most mature and accomplished in its ability to exploit expressive elements and concepts without being hag-ridden by them. The lighting, which subtly distinguishes outside and inside and time of day, also hints at broad emotional connotations: with a threatening jealous red zone, left of stage, into which Otello immediately passes after his heroic entry at the start, contrasting with yellow on the right and blue at the back. Such hints are never laboured.

The purity of Desdemona's final scene is emotionally shattering: Helen Field, in gloriously sensitive voice, sings most of the willow song upstage, facing her mirror, a fat candle burning beside her, and then gives her Ave Maria straight out to the audience. The interior door on the right, the cold moonlit window high above it, are as Verdi directed. The Moor shuts the cupboard door on mirror and candle for his final act. Desdemona's strangling is naturalistic, horrible. Her mouth gasps, upside down. He raises her arm and lets it fall to check she's dead.

And there's perfect tact, too, in the final image, the last kiss that Otello does not achieve, as his arm tries to cradle the memory of their troth, and slowly falls away to Verdi's cadence and closing punctuation. The poised fatalism of the last act, even with Iago's flurry to escape, is the exact answer to the deeply disturbing chaos of the council-chamber scene, with Otello pacing through the crowds distraught, and ultimately physically attacking them, laying them literally flat, like the victims of some awful plague in a biblical painting, in his furious determination to clear the stage, after he has cursed his bride publicly.

Stein has accepted the challenge of pictorial theatre, and with apt reference to the method of early renaissance narrative painting – most tellingly in the great council-chamber sextet which is among the most extraordinary pieces of staging I have seen in the opera house – he has gone beyond it into a kind of expressive visual theatre which answers all the levels in this terror-struck work. The secret lies in the economy of controlled acting in every quarter, through which he has realized the fullest potential of the operatic stage. No movement, no gesture is wasted.

The line of narrative is stretched, not torn. The scene between Otello and Desdemona in Act 3 when she raises her arm in a firm gesture of honour, and then is later almost thrown off-stage, sustains a wonderfully coherent line. The narrowing of the stage area, from scene to scene, as Otello's obsession grows all-consuming provides a marvellously expressive framework for the action.

Once again WNO have triumphed. This time the triumph will be international.

Otello is not a political work. It speaks of humanity, not of society. Its great moral perception is about the nature of truth – jealousy is secondary. So this production is revolutionary only in its frightening call to face the terrifying vacuum of egotism. The truthfulness with which it presents Verdi's tragedy is only superficially conventional.

It is also in many ways a musical triumph. Richard Armstrong has never launched a new production with such confidence. Even with his Otello (Jeffrey Lawton) suffering from a cold and needing careful husbanding, he did not short-change the epic orchestral moment. His pacing and sure affection for the orchestral balance and expression make this the great achieve-ment of his long musical directorship – a happy achievement in Armstrong's final season. WNO's may not be a great orches-tra, but they sounded as rich and rewarding as far more pres-tigious bands.

Lawton looks a marvellous Otello, of imposing figure, su-perbly and traditionally made up. His voice, on form, will fill the role with distinction and taste. Donald Maxwell's Iago is excellent. He sounds better than ever, and his smiling, soft villainy is a very persuasive change from the usual brooding ham.

Helen Field's voice uses emotional vibrato with great courage and wonderful expressiveness. Wendy Verco makes much of her important scenes as Emilia, especially in her acting at the end. John Graham Hall may not have an Italianate voice style, but he cuts a very credible Cassio in appearance. There is solid work too from Jonathan Best as Montano, William Mackie as Lodovico and Richard Morton as Roderigo. Vocally this may be far from the international experience, and strictly Verdi needs more muscle in the singing. But the essentials are largely there. This is a production the theatre-going audience, whether opera buffs or not, cannot afford to miss.

1 March, 1986   **Tom Sutcliffe**

Some notes on a classical training

It is rotten to give away the tricks of someone else's trade, but here goes anyway. Be warned, any young lad auditioning for a place at Chetham's School of Music in Manchester, that the Music Director may ask you to name your favourite football team.

Do not, whatever you do, brighten up and reply 'Everton'. Or even 'Plymouth Argyle.' You will have fallen into Michael Brewer's trap. He has only asked you because you have looked so miserable while playing your set piece to him. The fact that you come alive while talking about football suggests to him that music is not your life.

It is important that music should be your life if you are trying to get into Chetham's, for it will certainly become your life once you are there. You will practise your main instrument three or four hours a day, with two hours' tuition a week. Your second instrument you will practise half an hour a day, with one lesson a week. You will play chamber music around five hours a week; rehearse with an orchestra three hours a week, sing with the choir one hour a week and undergo half an hour's aural training four days a week.

Then there are the concerts. Each lunchtime there are two or three. In addition to playing in them you may well be obliged to listen to six each term. And last week, for example, you might also have had a master class with the composer Ronald Stevenson one day; another with Denis Matthews the next. And then there were two orchestral concerts, the annual cabaret and dinner and the Purcell Room chamber concert. The orchestra will also be rehearsing for a festival in Spain at the end of the month. Anyone keener on Robson than Rossini might find it uphill work.

Chetham's began the transformation from independent boys' grammar school to a specialist music school in 1969. It has gradually expanded on its cramped site next to Manchester's Victoria Station while quietly developing a philosophy of specialist music education that is unique outside Hungary or the Soviet Union. The Menuhin School is more famous, but it is small (around forty pupils) and concentrates solely on string players. Chetham's is comparatively large (260 boys and girls) and will accept an accordion player as readily as a tuba.

Chetham's graduates have begun to fan out and make their mark. Peter Donohoe, Moscow Tchaikovsky silver medallist, is probably the best known graduate, but you could hear no fewer than nine former pupils performing in British concert halls last week – among them a Birmingham Symphony Orchestra broadcast conducted by Grant Llewellyn (1972-79 and a Cambridge soccer blue), with Stephen Hough (1972-77) as piano soloist.

Hough was the piano winner of the first BBC Young Musician of the Year competition. In the 1982 contest Chetham's pupils won three of the four sections, as well as the overall winner in Anna Markland. No fewer than eleven pupils are through to this year's semi-finals in four categories.

But more remarkable than competition successes is the regime that has been pioneered at the school – a regime which, according to Michael Brewer, seeks to find a happy balance between the slightly authoritarian rigorousness of East European schools and the more gentlemanly British approach to music education.

More remarkable still is the school's recent academic record. The sole criterion for entry is how well the applicant – who may be as young as eight – plays and performs at audition. Yet last year fifteen pupils out of forty-eight won Oxbridge places – six of them to read subjects other than music. It was, concedes John Vallins, the (non-musician) headmaster, a freak year – the Oxbridge tally is normally around five – but it demonstrates, he says, both the school's commitment to a rounded education as well as the clear correlation between musical and academic ability.

Both Vallins and Brewer spent some time visiting Hungarian schools, whose musical education is so heavily influenced by composer Zoltan Kodaly's ideas on aural training and singing. Both were highly impressed. 'It sounds sentimental, but I thought the children in Hungary were the happiest children I had ever seen,' says Vallins. 'Ordinary children really did go around with smiles on their faces.'

Brewer's experiences both there and in the Soviet Union have led him to introduce a highly disciplined tuition structure. Pianists, for instance, learn according to the 'Russian school' which lays much more emphasis on technique than repertoire. Each child is assessed each year by an external adviser who writes a finger-by-finger report on every aspect of the technique.

Peter Donohoe is a great supporter of such methods. 'At that age you don't necessarily have the maturity to cope with great music and it seems only logical that the times should be spent acquiring a formidable technique. Maturity can come later, but technique can't. I think there has been a British tendency for too long to go for "musicianship" over technique.'

Then there is the non-stop aural training designed to enable each pupil to hear a line, chord, or even entire work before he/she plays it. You only have to watch Michael Brewer warming up the chamber choir to see the result. He starts them off with an 'A' and then simply instructs them on the chords which should follow: 'We'll have F sharp minor . . . now B major . . . D minor . . . E flat seven.' Not a note out of place.

'Of course, some of them have the same adolescent reticence that any child has,' says Brewer, 'but I do believe in the importance of the "inner ear" and also feel quite primitively that when someone makes a sound at the front of their head each day it makes up their mind as well as their ear.'

Around 400 children apply each year for the fifty-five places. Fees are theoretically some £7000 a year, but almost no one pays that. Most parents qualify for mandatory grants from the DES and nearly forty parents with joint incomes of under £5000 pay nothing at all.

'What we have to guard against at audition is the well-groomed boy with ambitious middle-class parents who has been wonderfully taught,' says Brewer. 'Part of the knack is to spot the talented musician who has been badly taught. We look for six things – a musical ear, general musicianship, technical skill, creativity, performing personality and strength of character.' In amongst which the football question may or may not play its part.

For the successful, the pressures of the music training are – it is hoped – diluted by the studied normality of the rest of the curriculum and by the relaxed informality that seems, on short acquaintance, to exist. 'All of us here would think it wicked to run a school on the basis that children have made a decision to follow a career in music,' says John Vallins. 'I think we are here to educate musically gifted children rather than to turn out star performers.'

Vallins thinks there are three justifications for the school: 'Firstly, if they weren't here an awful lot of them would be dreadfully frustrated because they couldn't get the quantity of music that they need.

'Secondly, they wouldn't have the society of similarly gifted children to mix with and perform with. And thirdly, Chetham's creates an atmosphere in which they feel normal, where as in some schools – I don't say all – the exceptionally gifted child feels off or out of place.'

This last point is borne out by the testimony of a former pupil, Elizabeth Nicol, who has gone on to be head of music in a large split-site comprehensive. 'The unemployment situation puts pressure on youngsters to go for "job-getting" subjects, and music is clearly bottom of this list. In my last school, one third-year boy was so embarrassed about the fact that he played the violin that his father used to bring it in for him.'

The staff seem to be acutely aware of the dangers of too much intensity, particularly on the less gifted. One weekend in three is spent away from school, either at home or out camping or youth hostelling.

Around three pupils a year decide that they don't, after all, want to pursue a musical career and leave. Michael Brewer doesn't unduly mind such losses, confident as he is that such an education is far more than a preparation for a life as transglobe concerto soloist. 'I think you learn lots of things – social skills, concentration, the ability to cope with competitiveness and jealousy, responsibility and an understanding that great art is an important part of life and worth communicating.'

'And finally,' he adds severely, 'you will have learned that music isn't fun. Of course, it can be fun, but if that's all it is then you really have missed out.'

11 March, 1986   **Alan Rusbridger**

The 110 per cent skinny wimp

'Macho.' The nickname seems sinisterly apt. For to be sure, out there on the cricket field Malcolm Marshall's machismo is at full throttle as he looks to prove his virility by violent domination. He goes about his work with a cold-eyed, business-like, unsmiling, scary relish. He seems in a hurry to hurt. It is one thing to be acknowledged by all opposition batsmen as the fastest in the world, quite a different kettle of cower to be the most dangerously lethal.

Test batsmen have genuine nightmares only about Marshall these days – only their wives wake up with worse sweats.

Suddenly, like a revelation, the game is won or lost and Marshall's features crease into a crow's feet network of laugh lines. He is much liked around cricket's dressing rooms. People enjoy hanging their hat on the peg next to his. For one thing he whistles only the most cheerful reggae tunes. He is a whole-hearted, keen and confident comrade.

On Monday, in his home town pavilion at Bridgetown, his infectiously giggling delight bubbled all over as he cuddled, and was cuddled by, his Barbados captain Joel Garner after the two of them had laid Jamaica to waste to bring back the Shell Shield to mighty little Barbados. The Colgate-smiling, hand-slapping glee went on for an hour or so and, of a sudden, the nickname Macho had become convivial, endearing, and totally un-tense. Just as the gold chain around his neck with his name on the pendant did not look half so, well, macho or not as dangerous as it does when it glints ominously like a hired assassin's gun in the sun – or does when he turns from his mark to scud in on his toes with that short sprinter's hostility and that cruel and nasty narrowness to his eyes.

His loins girded with only a towel, Marshall looks almost ludicrously small-boned and slight; certainly he looks more of a spinner with cunning than a devilish and upsetting fast bowler. Botham calls him the 'skinny wimp'. When you talk to him, even my plump 5ft 11in towers over him by at least an inch.

To Wes Hall's Larry Holmes, Charlie Griffith's Frazier, Michael Holding's Muhammad, Colin Croft's Foreman, and Garner's, say, Carnera, he looks as small, tiny, loose and angelic as Sugar Ray Leonard at 160lbs. It is dotty to believe that Malcolm Marshall is less than two stone heavier than Barry McGuigan.

For all that, mind you, Marshall is in the whippy physical image of other legends of the fast ball – Martindale, Constant-ine, Gilchrist and that long ago founder of the faith and man of the people, George John, from some sixty years ago, who was but 5ft 9in and, as C.L.R. James said: 'All power is in proportion . . . pace and body action, he hits many a poor batsman on the inside of the knee to collapse them like a felled ox.'

This new welterweight is even lighter. Marshall's half-dozen summers so far with Hampshire have delighted him to make it his second home. But in truth Bournemouth's balmy breezes and corporation-imported palm trees patently cannot match his very nature's affinity with the bold primary colours and jangling, carefree good cheer of Barbados.

'Malcolm's real stength,' said his captain Garner above the hubbub of Monday evening, 'is that he has never given less than 110 per cent for any side he has ever played for – from school, club, Barbados, Hampshire or with us fellows in the West Indian team. Pulling his weight for the side just means everything to him.'

Garner and Marshall slapped hands in a last and poignant intimacy that we hangers-on had no business to date even understand. On Monday evening they would meet later, sure, for celebration drinks, a little music and much more laughter, but the team was off from the airport first thing in the morning to prepare for this weekend's lap of honour in Guyana so they would, they promised themselves, be early abed.

Now, nattily, crisply, and casually dressed, Marshall eases through the throng to rev up his sleek car and go home, perhaps for another change of clothing, for organizing the evening.

He revs up at the first traffic light. His countrymen recognize their silky bachelor boy hero, and shout, 'Hey, Macho, you showed 'em!' or 'You lightnin' man, Macho,' and there was not the slightest tremor of resentment that his cricket was building him one of the loveliest homes on the island.

If the Big Bird, Joel, is the working-class hero's prime minister, then Marshall is very much the one true Minister of Culture. Garner, for instance, has built himself, appropriately, the highest and most substantial house on the very foundations of the wooden shack in which his mother brought him up.

There is no surprise, when you delve into it, that Marshall loves Hampshire so. He supposes it might have started as his favourite English county when he was a ragged urchin at primary school. The Barbadian cavalier Roy Marshall was the southern counties' most dashing import when the young Malcolm was first at school, and had learned to read.

He would look up Marshall's scores, just because of the same name in the paper. Then, when he was fourteen, the other hero, Andy Roberts, joined Hampshire didn't he? Again he would examine in *The Nation* the English scoreboards every morning. When he first came to England it was almost natural that he joined Hampshire. In his debut game in April 1979 it snowed. Nevertheless, with three sweaters on he took seven wickets when he was not embracing the dressing-room radiator.

Sorry, 'ragged' was pathetically romantic. But it is not right. Marshall, they say, was always beautifully turned out for school by his mother and grandmother. First at St Giles primary, where he is now challenging Wes Hall as A1 Alumnus, then at the Parkinson Comprehensive, where he was always immaculate in his khaki shorts and shirt. He was, teachers said last week, a model pupil, a team man.

Like Gary Sobers, from across the way at Bayland, Marshall's was a matriarchal boyhood. When Garfield was six his merchant seaman father's ship was torpedoed. When Malcolm was still in his cot his policeman father died in a motorcycle accident. Dad had played for the police team. Uncle was a cricketer as well, but it was his grandfather, Oscar, who would bowl to him in the backyard every evening or on the beach on Sundays. The boy loved batting then, and he loves it best now to tell the truth. He would, he admits, dearly enjoy to match Botham, Kapil or Imran as a match-winning Test all-rounder.

It is touching that he gives thanks to the fortune of having a steady apprenticeship as understudy after his Packer-induced introduction to Test cricket in 1978 after, incredibly, only one first-class game. It followed his debut for Barbados when, just like this week, a set of pallid Jamaicans treated him like sheep for the shearing and his seven wickets got him picked for the tour to India.

Marshall was deputy then to the quick quartet and, says Joel, he was always the most cheerful and willing of twelfth men, ready with the drinks, the hot bath and laundry. A few years later Colin Croft sold his soul to South Africa, then Roberts retired . . . now Marshall is in the very pomp of fire and evil on the field. He will be twenty-eight in April, and is possibly still short of his prime.

There was a perfect example of his awesome, awful talent on Monday. It was heightened by the baying of the crowd. It was like they were at an execution. Tyburn stuff. With only an hour left and still six Jamaican wickets to fall, Marshall threw in a startlingly nasty bouncer from scarcely short of a length that reared from his ribs to graze Davidson's helmet and, taking off in a screaming fizz, cleared the gloves of the wicket-keeper standing a pitch-length back, though he leapt like Shilton. It went at one bounce for four byes.

The next fearsome ball seemed exactly the same length and pitch. This time Davidson, scared and weary, ducked his head to the level of his shins, but the ball skidded straight on, hit the nerve that joined his left bicep to his collar bone. As the batsman writhed in his crease, white-faced, he was given out. Plumb leg before, even from the pavilion it was frightening. Poor Davidson rolled away looking drunk with fear and holding his badly bruised, limp arm.

Marshall cannot explain his knack, except to say he is an athlete, with a supple, rubbery physique. He says he has worked hard to balance himself through his short run-up, so he is always at top speed as he delivers. He looks like Roberts from the ropes, and from twenty-two yards, they say, he has discovered the value of the three-speed bouncer.

Give them a few first-gear bouncers and they might get confident: throw in three times as fast and they appear in no position to play it: they are not ready. Purists at the old game of chivalry would say there is something sickening, even sadistic, about Marshall's bowling. He is confident about his defence: 'Simply, I am a professional. I play to the rules. I am lucky to have my fitness and aggression, but I do not lack sense. I am a fast bowler, this is my job; if I bowl dangerously and I'm told I intimidate, then the umpires are empowered to stop me. When they do I think of bowling differently: till then, I can only play to the best of my ability, such as it is. I am simply a man who loves cricket and happens to be a fast bowler, a keen professional and a working man with obligations to meet and a new mortgage to pay. I am a man who wants to do his best for himself and his team every time I go to work.'

The first Test in Jamaica is racing towards the English tourists. Sabina Park will probably be the fastest wicket. Yet Gower has scored a Test century against Marshall at Sabina. 'I can think of better things than facing him: he is a brilliant bowler, but it is not very nice,' says the England captain. Gooch has also hit a hundred against him at Sabina, 'but he is definitely nasty as a proposition.' Lamb has scored three hundreds against Marshall in England – 'He bounces you at will, and Malcolm must be the nastiest of them all.'

Last summer at Taunton Botham walked in at 50 for five, called for his white helmet, and though peppered by ferocious stuff from Marshall, answered fire with fire in a blazing innings of 149 in 106 balls, first dismissing Tremlett and then driving Marshall back with skimmingly crazy two iron shots over long-on or long-off, or hooking him off his whiskers into the car park over fine leg.

Exasperated, that cold-eyed look and beady fury on his brow, Marshall finally clean-bowled the blond baron of beef, and then went down the wicket with the broadest of grins, embraced his opponent, and clapped him all the way back to the pavilion.

As Botham said earlier this week, as he vanished up into the Bajam Hills, and into faraway, devious, late-night haunts with his pals Garner and Marshall: 'Of course we are friends. Malcolm and I relish the contest. He is a magnificent bowler, but he's a cricketer too. He is an athlete.

'I always say to the skinny wimp when I get to the wicket, What have you in store for me today? Malcolm is unquestionably the quickest and most dangerous man about today. He is no Lillee yet, but he is swinging it and plays it just as hard. But the point with him is everyone has a laugh and a joke afterwards.'

I asked Marshall if he would remember Botham's Taunton innings when England faced him in Jamaica this month. 'I am not sure if I will be selected,' he said modestly, and at that, from the highest corner of the dressing room, Garner stood up and laughed so much that Marshall had to join in, giggling,

and slapping a few nearby palms. Macho, sure, but a jolly nice
sportsman as well.
8 February, 1986   **Frank Keating**

Fellwanderer

We were coughing our way down from Pen-y-ghent at the time.
'Which of your guide books are you most proud of after all
these years?' 'You can't ask me that,' said A.W. 'You don't
know who I am yet.' It took a moment or two to extricate the
sound recordist from the peat bog into which he'd stumbled
during his fit of hysterics.

We were working to A.W.'s script that first filming day.
He'd arrived with a complete programme on bits of paper. I
was to be the casual fell walker who would arrive at the summit
of Pen-y-ghent to find a nice old chap having his coffee and
sandwiches. Somewhere between the cheese and chutney and
the corned beef I'd get out the A. Wainwright guide to *Walks
in Limestone Country*. 'Not a bad book,' my companion would
say, 'I know the chap who wrote it.' On the way down from
the mountain he'd take me to see the hidden limestone pinnacle,
the purple saxifrage and Hull Pot. Then in the car park at
Horton in Ribblesdale, just as I was about to leave, someone
else would slap my fellow walker on the back and say 'Hello,
A.W. good to see you again after all these years.'

'Not *the* A.W.,' I'd retort. 'You must sign my copy of your
book.' Close up A.W.'s hand, slightly shaky, making that
famous mark. Mix to end credits.

Apart from the fact that it would have taken Alec Guinness to
carry off that final showdown at Horton car park, we eventually
persuaded A.W. that there was a better way of beginning our
summer in the hills.

But it was quite an achievement to have him there at all. He
has an entirely healthy mistrust of television, the only exception
being *Coronation Street*, to which he's addicted. He doesn't like
being seen in public and will go to any lengths to avoid functions

held in his honour. When our producer Richard Else eventually persuaded him to make our series of programmes, he asked A.W. to sign a barring clause in the contract which would ensure that he didn't make any programmes for other companies for at least a year. A.W. asked us to extend the clause to two years to give him an easy out with other pestering producers. And in the last few months, 'I've got to be on standby to do some helicopter filming for the BBC' has got him off the hook of any number of dinner engagements and personal appearances.

So we set off on our travels to Mardale and Teesdale, to the Howgill Fells and Haystacks. Each morning would begin the same. 'That's the sixth cigarette you've had this morning,' A.W. would say. It took some time for me to pluck up the courage to comment that he was on his second ounce of Three Nuns. At the start, our conversations weren't easy. A.W. is, to say the least, reserved. The first couple of times the cameras rolled, the questions became longer and longer; the answers shorter. And just as I'd thought of the perfect springboard into another subject, he'd say 'Well, that's enough about that,' and wander off to stoke up with the third ounce.

It's not a reserve that's come with old age. He's seventy-eight now but has been a solitary man for forty or fifty years. During the decades when he was borough treasurer of the town of Kendal you suspect he was more at home with his copperplate ledgers than he ever was with the staff.

In the evenings after work, he'd lock himself away and work on one of the forty or more books that have carried the A. Wainwright signature. And at the weekends he'd pack his camera and his sandwiches and take the bus to Borrowdale or Buttermere at the start of a day's solitary walking in the mountains. The more famous he became, the more he avoided fellow travellers. His books encouraged tens of thousands to explore the remote Lake District, but by the time they came, he was away in some other corner of the fells preparing the next book in the series.

Out on the fell tops with Wainwright, it's easy to see why he spent all those years on the run. Despite his best endeavours, people recognize him. They stand there open-mouthed and wide-eyed in the presence of their hero, honoured to shake the hand of the man who opened the Lake District to them. He says a word or two, no more, and off they go to tell their mates in the pub and the family back home that they've met *the* A.W. When they've gone, there's a slight 'Hmph' from behind the pipe, and he changes course slightly to avoid the next group of walkers coming up the path.

The fact of the matter is that he's not very fond of people and much prefers animals. At lunch one day in a restaurant in Kendal, I remember being a little surprised when he started casting envious eyes over a bit of ham on my plate. Into a napkin it went to be taken home as a treat for Tottie. And reading Wainwright's books now, I always expect to turn a page and find a Tottie-shaped pawprint among the handwritten script and the finely drawn illustrations. This ageing, fluffy stray cat scarcely ever leaves him when he's at home. It sits on his desk while he works, it sleeps with him, and it must know the characters in *Coronation Street* as well as the cat in the titles curled up by the chimney pot.

A.W. is self-effacing to the point of rudeness, and the only time in three months that I ever saw him take real pride in his achievement was at Kapellan, the animal sanctuary near Kendal supported by A.W. and his wife Betty. Much of the profit from his books has gone into funding this little charity that finds good homes for stray cats and dogs. Suddenly the conversation blossomed. He talked for ten minutes about the better nature of animals. The next day in Kendal we took A.W. to the *Westmorland Gazette*, where more than a million of his books have been printed. He scarcely said a word except to point out that the reason the script was handwritten was to stop printers mucking about with the layout. He's never been to the printing works before despite the fact that he only lives three-quarters of a mile away.

Of course Wainwright's other great love is the landscape of Lakeland. He adores it with a quiet passion that only someone born in the confines of the terraced street and brought up in the shadow of the mill could feel. A.W. was a townie from Blackburn, and the tie with industrial Lancashire is still strong. Sheltering from the rain in Mardale one afternoon, he started to talk about his childhood. It was a bitter memory to begin with – the shame he felt when once his mother had to explain to the landlord that she couldn't afford to pay the rent. Then happier incidents. He was one of the founders of Blackburn Rovers supporters club and still tries to get to a couple of home matches a year. And then his first holiday which was also his first visit to the Lake District. He stood that day on Orrest Head above Windermere and saw the mountains, blue and grey and sharp in the distance. He never really left the Lake District after that and set about organizing a job in Kendal so he could live nearby.

Then the books came. He never intended them to be published. As he walked, he made his notes so that as an old man he would be able to relive his days on the mountains. Fortunately someone once persuaded him that they were the best guide books they'd ever seen, and the Wainwright industry began. While successive generations of novice fell walkers created a demand that has taken many of the guides into their 80th or 100th impression, Wainwright can't really use the books himself. His eyesight has been failing in recent years.

But his memory of places and vistas is phenomenal. For our final programme we battled our way through the horizontal rain up on to Haystacks above Buttermere. In that clutter of crags and hollows. A.W. seemed to remember every path and sheer drop. The weather was so bad we thought we would have to go back, and then in the mist and the rain Wainwright disappeared. We circled and searched. I got lost, the production assistant missed the path, and the cameraman walked to the wrong summit. By the time we all met up, soaked and cold, A.W. was already at the proper place and well into the sand-wiches and a soggy pipeful.

We climbed on and eventually came over the rise to the spot that Wainwright loves beyond all others in his Lake District. We were in a cleft of rock beside Innominate Tarn. There was a long silence. Not even the waterproof matches would work. 'I've already written the script for this place,' he said, 'but I think you had better read it.' It was the end of his book *Fellwanderer*, spoken into the wind and the rain.

'That day will come when there is nothing left but memories.

And afterwards a last resting place by the side of Innominate Tarn, on Haystacks, where the water gently laps the gravelly shore and the heather blooms and Pillar and Gable keep unfailing watch. A quiet place, a lonely place. I shall go to it for the last time, and be carried; someone who knew me in life will take me and empty me out of a little box and leave me there alone. And if you, dear reader, should get a bit of grit in your boot as you are crossing Haystacks in the years to come, please treat it with respect. It might be me.'

Between gusts there was the usual inconsequential chatter at the end of a successful take. 'Very good!' and 'Bloody weather!' and 'Who's carrying the tripod down?' Wainwright said nothing. He was looking towards Gable. I know he couldn't see the horizon, but I'm sure he could see a lot further.

23 November, 1985   **Eric Robson**

The King of Trafford Road

If I'd woken up one day very early and asked my fairy godmother how I happened to be in Salford, she could only have replied, 'Your father was a gutsy little Greek who was not satisfied to starve in a little mountain village in the Peloponnesos but made a zigzag way which ended him up running The King's Restaurant, Trafford Road, Salford. That's why you're here.'

My father had landed in Liverpool with not a word of English, started work as a dock labourer, became the head chef in a Blackpool hotel, opened his restaurant opposite No. 8 Dock Gates, and proudly described himself as 'late Chef of the County Palatine and Lane Ends Hotel'. But father really came into his own when, tired of the limited money that came in from the restaurant, he began to go into the docks, talk to the captains, and buy any junk they were glad to get rid of.

Money for old rope? Old rope was only the beginning. When the first world war started, my father's purchases of junk became monumental and wildly varied. A lot of the stuff had been at the bottom of the sea, torpedoed by the Germans, all brought back to Salford to be refurbished, most of it in a ramshackle yard Dad built of old timber in Aubrey Street, off Trafford Road, a few hundred yards from his restaurant.

How I wish I'd kept the photograph which showed the whole front of the King's Restaurant, the name in big letters overhead and, smiling in the sun underneath, two waitresses in white bib aprons, in between them my mother standing by the big blackboard on which was chalked day after day 'Oxtail Soup 2d, Steak Pudding 6d.' I forget the rest of the menu, but I've no doubt it, too, was unchanged day after day.

While my father was buzzing around collecting old rope or drinking ouzo in the cabins of the Greek captains in the docks, my mother was running the restaurant. Just about the time my father had been fleeing starvation, my mother was setting off from home in Macclesfield with her little tin trunk at the age of fourteen to go into service. She fell in love with my father when she was a chambermaid and he a chef.

I first realized what junk could mean when, at the age of six, I found myself on the top of a huge mountain of horse-hair dumped by my father in a deserted warehouse opposite the shop. He'd bought tons of the stuff, and I found I could leap safely from twenty feet high into a soft valley of it. For three days I arrived home anthrax-ridden and filthy, to be cleaned up by my long-suffering mother.

Junk! Miserable to handle, fascinating to look back on. Thousands of strands of soaking hemp looking like drowned blondes' hair, all hung out to dry; thousands of sodden packets of Zig Zag cigarette papers in squashy heaps. What was to be done with them? My brilliant idea meant that I spent Christmas Eve capering around in gym shoes on top of the immense boilers of the Manchester Central YMCA feverishly spreading them out to dry. Next, I typed the usual letter: 'Please note that I have for sale a hundred thousand packets of Zig Zag cigarette papers in fairly good condition.' There were no takers.

I don't know whether the Parisian pipes were sold. Ordinary looking tobacco pipes: I picked one up, wondering what the little ivory knob under the bowl was for, and discovered the tiny lens disclosing daring French pinups. They were in an upstairs room awaiting buyers, along with a lot of brand new motor bikes.

The scarcities of war brought my father a fortune. He'd go to an auction sale of torpedoed or damaged goods, buy something, and, before the sale was over, be offered a thousand pounds profit on his purchase. This made him think he was a genius. He was furious when jealous competitors called him lucky.

The war had other effects. We were foreigners. My father didn't help matters by consistently putting the German case, or what he thought was their point of view, in the little circle gathered in the entrance of the restaurant to discuss the way the war was going. 'The sword has been forced into our hands,' he would say, quoting the Kaiser.

When the customs officer, the dock clerk, and their cronies condemned the Germans for bombing women and children, my father pointed out that it was no worse than the starvation caused in Germany by the British blockade. My mother and I were scared to death by his silly nonsense but he got away with it, which told me that there was some tolerance in the English.

Not for me, though. All my life till I left home I was called a dirty dago, a greasy Greek, asked why I didn't go back home where I came from. One day, when I was thirteen, I was looking after Dad's yard. A few tatterdemalion kids came mooching around at the door. I pushed one of them back who was half way in and closed the gate in his face. In a short time there was a howling mob outside, mothers and older kids, calling for my dago blood. I came out, locked the door behind me, pushed my way through them, and ran for my life for home with them chasing me.

My father was true to form during the dock strike. He agreed to supply meals to the 300 extra policemen drafted in to take care of the dockers. As they marched into the restaurant in batches, they didn't realize that in the backyard a queue of strikers' wives was forming to have soup ladled by my mother into their jugs and bowls from a huge galvanized bathtub.

I was born in Hulton Street, just above Ordsall Park, in 1903. When I was six we moved to Trafford Road. I remember musical evenings there. The Customs officer sang 'Asleep in the Deep'. My grandmother, half full of stout, yelled, 'You can't sing it, you bugger,' and the good-humoured Mr Furse agreed, 'You're right, granny, you're right,' and gave up. When I was twelve we moved again to New Park Road, a few steps from the restaurant. It was in the bed there on Sunday mornings in between my father and mother that I first heard the Greek legends about Polyphemus and Ulysses. 'Eccy messa katty koussa . . .' sent mother and me into fits of giggles and my father into a rage, as it was the Greek national anthem he was trying to teach us.

Kids accept the circumstances around them and so did I. In fact I revelled in the Aladdin's Cave of ever-changing junk. It never occurred to me that I would ever live anywhere else.

But factors were at work that would get me out of Salford. My mother had spent some years as the 'treasure' of a household when she was in service, and middle-class gentility had got a firm grip on her. She was determined that I would never sink to the level of our poor little neighbours who shuffled off barefoot to board school every morning. Early on she found a little dame school for me. After a couple of years there I found myself at Pendleton Grammar School. Sometimes it was quite an ordeal getting there. The half-mile walk from the tram through the slums around the school gave the slum kids a chance to pick on me from time to time and knock off my maroon and yellow striped cap.

Mr Moir, the emaciated-looking, rather sadistic Scots headmaster, must have persuaded my mother that I could pass the entrance exam for the famous Grammar School, one of the glories of the city of Manchester. My mother was all for it. She was dying for me to be a little gentleman. Sent off to Sunday school, I endured more cat-calls because of the Eton collar and suit she dressed me in. My father's rascality and enterprise, my mother's thrift and hard work in the restaurant, made us comparatively well off.

About this time we took one of our occasional Sunday walks in the nearby suburb of Urmston. I say suburb: it was almost our idea of the country. We walked down Church Road in the sunshine past palatial detached villas, each with its own front garden. One of the pleasantest, Oakhurst, had a For Sale board up. My heart leapt and I whispered to my mother, 'Why can't we buy that house? We've got enough money now. We don't need to live in Salford any more.'

I had soon realized at Manchester Grammar School that I was living in a very strange neighbourhood. Although the school was almost free from snobbery, I couldn't help feeling ashamed that I lived in Salford. My mother's schemes to better me led to my nagging, which my mother joined in, to get my father to buy Oakhurst. He must have been in a good mood that Sunday for he didn't squash the idea immediately. We kept on at him until he made a date to see the old man who owned the house. The price was £800.

There was another little problem about our moving, however. Our miserable chattels were too few and too shabby to be taken to Oakhurst. So after several sessions at Oakhurst with the old brewer in his skullcap, it became apparent to my father that he was quite willing to sell everything in his house, and we soon became the owners and residents of a sumptuously furnished Edwardian house right down to the knick-knacks in the drawing room – watercolours on the walls, comfortable upholstered armchairs and, most intriguing of all, the wooden wall of the small back dining-room which could be made to disappear into the floor above, if we wanted a large salon. We got our new home, lock stock and barrel, front and large back garden, freehold for £1300.

When the sale of our few old bits and pieces in New Park Road was over, the auctioneer turned to my mother to advise her quietly, 'You're going up in the world. I know a bit about Urmston, and you mustn't be seen stoning the steps.'

We weren't quite clear of Salford yet. The restaurant was closed. My father had taken an office in rooms upstairs, so that was where I spent my days during my last few years in Salford after I'd left school. By that time, I was full of Shakespeare, novels, poetry, music, and bitter resentment at my father for not letting me go on to do history at university, which my matriculation with distinction entitled me to do. I knew I couldn't spend the rest of my life in my father's office in Trafford Road, so it wasn't long before I plucked up my courage and ran off to London to be an actor.

For most people Hollywood is a realm of fantasy: I landed up there, but found its brand of fantasy pale by comparison with my junk-filled memories of Salford; and even the fabulous Orson Welles could never displace my father as the most colourful character in my life.

15 February, 1986   **George Coulouris**

One in the eye

Hastings is where old flared jeans go to die. In the same way, Eastbourne is an elephant's graveyard of navy blue blazers and neatly pressed cavalry twill trousers. I don't know why different generations seem to impose themselves like a palimpsest upon this or that town, but in Hastings it has something to do with the unpresumptuous property prices (when we moved in, Whistler's mother's house was on the market for about £30,000 or so) and the way the nice little Georgian and Jacobean homes huddle cosily together in a frowsty comradeship in the old town. There is an air of dropping out, of dimly remembered principles of peace and love, of being 'into' antiques, of long hair and beards. There is also some dabbling in witchcraft, the manufacture of crystal balls, no doubt some smoking of pot and the echoing chords of time. Or to put it another way, where else can you hear the remnant of the Manfred Mann band providing the live music in a pub?

It means, of course, a younger class of geriatric. Poor old Eastbourne seems to sprout clean shaven, pomaded, straight-backed and arthritic retired colonels, humming tunes from White Horse Inn. In Hastings the incomers probably talk wistfully of Pink Floyd and Roxy Music.

But the town is not just the last coat hanger for the old kaftan: it is also an accretion of older ghosts. In 1918 somebody was complaining about the 'group of literary men who have come to live in Sussex . . . extolling this county in verse and prose, thus attracting other invaders'. Hastings is on the edge of Kipling's Sussex and on the other side of Romney Marsh is

Wells's Sandgate and both ambiences lap into the streets of the town. You don't have to walk far into the country to find the ash, oak and thorn of Pook's Hill.

Some of the people are straight from Kipling. 'You want to put a decent bit of oak in there,' said my neighbour, surveying the fence collapsing slowly between us. 'If you use oak, well, twenty or thirty years later you'll be poking at it and you'll find it as sound as ever and you'll be saying to yourself, "Old Mick was right." ' I never got round to showing him the last sentences of *An Habitation Enforced*.

On the other hand, *Kipps* begins over the road and down the hill a bit, where the scatter of front-room shops sell boxes of old coathangers, dusty glasses that were originally given away with gallons of petrol, sprouting onions and frozen peas in four ounce packets. 'Don't get no call for pound packets,' one shopkeeper told me. 'I buy a two pound bag, open it and sell 'em by the ounce.'

There is a man from the Sudan who sells basmati rice and packets of fenugreek, chilies, fetta and halva. 'How's business?' I asked him once. 'I'm still here,' he said. 'In Hastings, if you are still open, you are doing well.' Come to think of it, Henry James's Rye is also quite near but it hasn't left its mark on the town. Though it is rather jolly to think of him wincing as he climbed off the train and crossed the footbridge to be met by a poster urging him: 'Smile, you're in Hastings.'

It is possible to buy a kiss-me-quick hat in Hastings, but most people don't. There is a pier, a choice of amusement arcades and a trimming of ice cream, candy floss, whelk and sausage stalls and shops along the promenade but the smiles don't come easily: compared with Brighton or even Eastbourne, Hastings is small beer. If you just live there, that's a plus, of course. Brighthelmstone used to be a fishing village; when George IV helped change it into a resort there followed a net loss.

But the eastern end of Hastings remains stubbornly a beach for fishing boats; the nets continue to dry in tall black wooden huts and the plaice and lemon soles still flap freshly on to the fishmonger's slab. I don't know that anyone claims to make much money out of fishing, but the traditional full-bellied hulls hauled up on to the shingle and the detritus of cuttlefish bone, skate tails and cod heads over which the gulls fight at the water's edge remain an alibi for the town's existence in a way that a Mr Softee ice cream cart could never match.

The sea: that is why you should smile when you are in Hastings. In the morning, from the clifftops the close-mown or grazed grass shines the colour of peridot and the dawn sun turns the English channel into a sheet of electroplate. John of Gaunt must have died on the West Hill. At night the white gliding ghosts of herring gulls circle querulously over the silent town streets, erupting into intermittent explosions of communal complaint.

Sometimes the sea is invisible but you can see the mist coming off it and rolling up the town streets and climbing the hill like a palpable force (sometimes, under the street lighting, it looks like an ostentatious special effect for an old horror movie). At night the lucky commuter who has to climb the 400-foot cliff to get home sees the moon hanging over Dungeness and painting an orange or a silver stripe down the tideway to the shore's edge.

If there is no moon and the sky is clear and the ambient light of the town is masked by the hill the Milky Way, the Via Galactica, marches over his head like a highway of pearl. Sometimes when the wind is blowing he hears between the crash of the waves the large coarse shingle of the beach, all of it ground into smooth ellipses, complaining and shifting uneasily below. Sometimes the wind off the sea is so cold it gives him neuralgia. Sometimes, of course, it is raining.

When you tire of the sandstone and shingle coast of Hastings there are other worlds a bus ride away. The finest walking in southern England begins on the other side of Pevensey Bay, where the chalk begins at Eastbourne and the footpaths race across smooth grass and tiny wildflowers over Beachy Head and the Seven Sisters to the Cuckmere Valley – the valley that all the geography textbooks use to illustrate what river meanders look like – before heading into the Friston Forest and back to the Long Man of Wilmington and thence to the Polegate railway station.

Or there are the paths that run through the ancient woods

and coppices that stand, silent and a little threatening, as though they still held sprites and dryads, from the edge of Hastings as far as Battle, Burwash and Bodiam.

In such places the sense of old England stubbornly hangs like lichen. The landscape bears the patina of continuous settlement since the Iron Age: the woods have been worked by craftsmen, bark strippers and leather workers, by charcoal burners and gunpowder makers and iron workers until the last century, and every so often you note that somebody has been coppicing a chestnut stand, or layering an elm and holly hedge, or cutting logs to sell by the sack for firewood.

The other reminder that you are in touch with old England, of course, is the number of tea shops that actually resent people who ask for a cup of tea after 5 p.m. Fortunately you can always pop into the Spud-U-Like or the Kentucky Fried Chicken place in Hastings when you get back, but it's not the same. Inland East Sussex was designed by heaven to be enjoyed with scones, toasted teacakes and large round brown teapots. Meanwhile, I can't help wondering what seaside town all those people who purchase leisurewear at Top Man will choose one day over which to drape themselves, and stay, like Clingfilm.

2 August, 1986   **Tim Radford**

Prospect of London

I spend the last Wednesday morning of almost every month on the fourth floor of the Labour Party Headquarters in Walworth Road – looking out of the window at part of the London skyline. Earth has not anything to show more untidy.

I seem to have spent all my political career staring through plate glass. But in previous periods of struggle and sacrifice the view has always been much better. That may be because London *en masse* is a mess. Or previous pleasures may have been the product of the ignorance which has brought me so much pleasure over the years.

223

Once upon a time the world outside was filled by minarets protruding from other parts of the Sheffield Town Hall. When they were in my regular line of vision, I believed them to be reminiscent of the Kremlin's towers – largely because I had no idea of what the Kremlin looked like. Then, from a garret in the Palace of Westminster, I looked out on the dilapidated turrets and cloisters of St Thomas' Hospital, which I thought to be designed in the Venetian style – a judgment based on knowledge of architecture very similar to that which allowed me to confuse Muscovite *baroque* with Victorian Gothic.

At the Ministry of Defence, I could see the Royal Festival Hall just across the river, a building with origins so recent that even an aesthetic ignoramus could recognise a perfect example of the Post-War Brutal School. When I was in the Foreign Office, the trees waved at me from across Horse Guards Parade and the one disappointment of my eventual promotion to the Cabinet was that it brought me down to earth. I could still see across Horse Guards. Indeed I could watch the eponymous cavalrymen crunching their way across its gravel on the way back to barracks at eleven o'clock each Thursday morning. But the background was the old Admiralty bunker – on which life imitated a special sort of art by making the ivy-covered concrete look like wartime camouflage. But even that was better than the sight of London from the south.

Proper rooftops are one of the most romantic sights in the world. Rows of slated eaves – sloping in parallel lines up hillsides in a northern industrial town, with their chimneys smoking and rain dappling the grey with patches of silver – brings a lump to my throat far bigger than anything that can be produced by St Peter's Square, the cathedrals at Chartres and Amiens or the ruined temple of Baalbek. Granada knew what makes the sentimental heart beat faster. I have no doubt that the popularity of *Coronation Street* is wholly dependent on the title shots of that Salford cat uncurling in the winter sunlight against the backdrop of gutterings, fall pipes and television aerials.

A television shot of London from the south would result in a million knobs being switched to other channels. For it is not the sort of sight that either Lowry or Canaletto would choose

224

to paint. Against the skyline, the towers of Parliament peer out from behind a jumble of dirty brick and even dirtier concrete, and the towers of Westminster Abbey peer out, dwarfed by a trick of distance, from behind them. But the picture is dominated by the great glowering blocks of offices which tower over everything on the left – battleship grey, field grey, charcoal grey and every sort of grey except the grey of the sky into which they do not blend.

In front, there are pre-war tenements in which it may be that real people live. If I sit up straight in my seat in the way which my mother tried to teach me and peer over the window sill (in a way which has rarely been necessary since the years of my pointless posture lessons) I can just see a new housing development built in ochre brick. I would like to think that it will spread across the landscape like custard coloured lava sweeping away the domestic dereliction that stands in its path. But there is only one sign of building within the whole window frame. It is a coven of tower cranes pointing enviously from the ashen office blocks towards the towers of spiritual and temporal Westminster.

It is those huge up-ended rectangles – the shoe box cliché come to agoraphobic life – that I find so depressing. They dominate the surrounding buildings like a ghastly caricature of the old town of Sienna. But whilst Sienna is full of golden hope, the triple towers of the Environment Department and the anthracite obelisks which stand in Victoria behind them are all grey menace. The great wen is clearly an inappropriate image. For wens cannot point up into the sky. But looking at those cold grey combinations of soul-less right-angles, I know exactly what Cobbett meant. Anyone who, as Dr Johnson should have said, lives in London, must find life very tiring.

Indeed other permutations of the Johnson aphorism are possible. For the cluster of thirty-storey office blocks that cut into the sky above the real buildings of London SW1 show barely a sign of life. No smoke curls from them. No birds fly above them. No lights flash in their windows. Even the flags that ought to flutter from their roofs seem unable to flutter. In the landscapes of home, all the high buildings resemble the toppling tower of Illium. For the clouds rush behind them at such a speed that they appear to be falling down whilst keeping upright, like guardsmen fainting on parade.

There are, of course, better views of London. Looking up the Thames from Waterloo Bridge reveals, at night, a sort of Festival of Urban Light. From General Wolfe's statue in Greenwich Park, the Naval Hospital and Maritime Museum both look very much as Christopher Wren intended. There are places in Farringdon Road from which it is possible to see the half of St Paul's dome that the property developers have not blotted out. But central London – even for the people who live in it – can never look like home. And that (or at least the surroundings of home) is what I want to see when I look out of my window.

30 November, 1985   **Roy Hattersley**

The art of love

By being given a museum to himself in Paris, Picasso joins the ranks of the illustrious and the not so illustrious. Delacroix, Rodin, Moreau, Bourdelle, all have their own museums. So does someone called Henri Bouchard ('stone and bronze were his favourite materials') and the Alsation artist Jean-Jacques Hener ('in his numerous portraits he employed a very vigorous brushwork technique').

When the time comes for the blurb writers to sum up Picasso, in a line or two what, I wonder, could they possibly say: 'His mind was so active that no single style could captivate him for long,' perhaps, or 'Everything he touched turned to art,' something dull but accurate like 'The greatest painter, sculptor, print-maker of the twentieth century.'

My own summary would skip all the many relevant details of Picasso's amazingly varied career and try instead to blunder towards an understanding of that celebrated touch which lies at the heart of his art, the quality he brought to all his work, whether he was in his Blue Period or his Rose, a Cubist or a Classicist, a painter, a pot-maker, an etcher, a sculptor or even a photographer (the least known of his roles into which we are provided with several fascinating glimpses at the new museum).

My summary would read: He was a maker not a watcher. His genius lay in his hands not in his eyes. Picasso's art blurred the dividing line between painting and sculpture so that his paintings could partake of some of the hardness of sculpture and his sculpture could partake of some of the softness of painting.

There is a magnificent painting of two figures by the sea, situated roughly at the half-way point of the museum, in which this touch of Picasso's is stripped of almost all of its ornamentation. The two figures are naked and making love on the beach with extraordinary abandon. Their mouths are open, their bodies knotted together, their tongues explore each other's breath. Picasso was in the middle of what is called his Surrealist period so that the figures themselves have bodies which are rather dinosaur-like. They have small heads perched on long necks, their arms and legs are mere flippers and their eyes are tiny pin-pricks, no bigger than their nostrils.

There are those who claim to see angst and spiritual malaise in Picasso's work of this period, premonitions of civil war even (*Two Figures by the Sea* was painted on January 12, 1931). But in this case they are surely wrong. The painting is clearly a celebration of a particularly energetic bout of love-making. All Picasso's energies have gone into the recreation of the attendant sensations, the feeling of dry sand on a naked body, the colour of human skin when it is surrounded by golden sun and sand, the alternating hardness and softness of the lovers' flesh, the thrilling physicality of their embrace. To emphasize this physicality Picasso invented his dinosaur-like humans with their large thighs and small heads. He is interested in their bodies not their minds, their skin not their souls.

Extrapolate away from this painting in any direction in Picasso's career, back to the African-style nudes painted in preparation for *Les Demoiselles d'Avignon* (itself a brothel scene), sideways to the imposing series of bronze heads also produced during the thirties, fast-forwards to the late and lecherous scenes of the sculptor frolicking with his model, back even to the great series of bottles, jugs and guitars he painted as a

Cubist, and you find his same brazen hand in action, reaching roughly through the picture surface to run its fingers over the forms contained there.

The hand enjoys softness but it is hardness which makes it thrill. It is surely at this point that Picasso, the madly inventive artist, who belongs to art history, and Picasso the prodigious lover, who belongs to real life, become one and the same man.

The Picasso Museum tells the Picasso story with great energy, intelligence and insight, and in incomparable French style. It is the best museum of its kind I have visited, outstripping even the wonderful Miro Foundation in Barcelona. Sadly it also undermines completely Barcelona's own rather dreary Picasso Museum.

The Paris museum is housed within the Hotel Sale, a mid-seventeenth-century town palace situated in the Marais quarter, a few stone-throws away from the Bastille. The building makes a considerable contribution to the splendour of the museum. In particular Picasso's so-called Classical period – it was more Rococo than classical, as he painted a series of nude female bathers that could even match Renoir's in luxuriousness and downright laziness – reclines very elegantly among the stuccoed denudi and the garlands of acanthus which have been saved from the cornices of the original Hotel Sale.

The vast majority of the works come from Picasso's own collection. They are things he kept back for himself and chose for one reason or another not to sell. There is thus a kind of glorious unfamiliarity to many of the exhibits, a rare feeling in Picasso's case. Even more importantly, from the first confident self-portrait in the manner of Toulouse-Lautrec, painted as a bearded twenty-year-old newly-arrived in Paris, to the over-dressed matador, a burlesque self-portrait done seventy years later, the works Picasso saved for himself clearly have a senti-mental meaningfulness, and are thus doubly eloquent, particu-larly on the subject of love.

The museum's great strength is the skill with which it has used the tons of material at its disposal, not only the major paintings and sculptures, but also drawings, fragmentary sketches, photographs, archive clippings, books and letters, to view the artist from all sides, to present what we might call a Cubist view of him.

His membership cards to the Communist Party 1947-51 are on display and a weird drawing in which he drinks a toast to Stalin.

In two ways I think this museum significantly alters our view of Picasso. By blending into the display a selection of the works he owned by other artists, Rousseau, Degas, Renoir, Corot, and particularly his prize collection of ethnographic art, the museum makes clear just how much Picasso owed to the examples set by others, thus leavening the ridiculous aura of pure genius which surrounds him.

Secondly, by focusing on his life and his art in such close parallel, the display underlines just how wrong the Formalists have been in their view of his career, how, like all great artists, Picasso's themes were love, birth, death.

I've always enjoyed the Ernest Hemingway story about going to a bullfight at which Picasso arrived complete with an entourage even greater than the one which surrounded Hemingway himself. Seeing the old painter the crowd started spontaneously booing. When Hemingway asked why, he was told it was simply because they didn't much like his painting.

I found myself remembering the story as I toured the new Picasso Museum because the artist who emerges here is so strikingly human in his loves and his lusts, his failings and his strengths that if he had seen himself coming into that bullring, surrounded by hangers-on and wearing the mythological crown of greatness, I am sure he too would have booed.

5 November, 1985   **Waldemar Januszczak**

Legends that trip off the tongue

The people of Marseilles have a tendency to exaggerate, and you can't spend long there without hearing the story about the sardine which blocked the Vieux Port. In fact such an event really did occur during the French revolution, but the obstruction was caused not by a fish of the herring family (for the Vieux Port is about 300 yards wide) but by a ship called the *Sardine* which was placed there by counter-revolutionaries blockading the insurgents. Or perhaps it was the insurgents who were blockading the counter-revolutionaries. I can't remember which way round it was. It was before my time.

Nowadays most people have forgotten the origins of the story entirely, let alone the details, and the sardine which blocked the Vieux Port now exists mainly as a joking example of the Marseillais habit of presenting the facts larger than lifesize.

Almost as much as exaggeration, they like leg-pulling (as admirers of Pagnol's wonderful Marius trilogy will know). I was therefore more than a little sceptical when the other day in Marseilles I was told that there was a whale on the beach. Initially I dismissed the story as a piece of out-of-season April foolery. A *Poisson d'Avril*.

But there it was, *peuchère*. When we arrived, the coastguards were winching it up on to the jetty with steel hawsers wrapped around the tail. As it was on its back you could easily see the deep folds along the front that identified it as a Rorqual whale: Balenoptera Physalus, according to Madame Turon of the Marseilles Museum of Natural History.

Being a whale, it was, needless to say, enormous. It weighed ten tons and was forty-five feet long. Even so, the poor thing was only a baby. Madame Turon reckoned it was only a year old, for an adult grows to some seventy feet. She said it had died a natural death, probably as much as a month ago, having somehow been separated from its school and mother having died of thirst and hunger.

The body was scratched, presumably by having been washed up against rocks, but at first sight seemed to be in a fairly good state. The smell soon told you otherwise, and the temperature that day was in the nineties. It was an event that aroused a mixture of conflicting feelings. Fascination and awe at the close-up spectacle of such a magnificent creature. Pity at the lack of dignity with which it was being hauled from its element, backwards and upside down. Self-disgust at being part of the crowd of gawping camera-clicking onlookers.

We left fairly soon, and were glad to have missed the sequel as recorded in the next day's papers. The whale was winched onto the back of a large lorry, its tail resting on the cabin, its head hanging off the end. It was then driven to a factory to be cut up for its oils, highly valued in the manufacture of cosmetics. Taking a corner of the Corniche President John Kennedy, its decomposing tongue fell out on to the road. It caused a traffic jam that was unusual even by the standards of Marseilles and one that will doubtless go down in legend along with the sardine that blocked the Vieux Port.

The whale was not the only mammal on the Marseilles beach last week, a point that was made conspicuously by the human presence which on the Mediterranean littoral is now generally topless. There has also been a considerable reduction in the number of jellyfish this year, but there is no connection between these facts.

Another animal story currently occupying the Marseilles newspaper headlines concerns the CRS and the pigs. The CRS are the riot policemen who came to fame for the enthusiastic way in which they set about the students during the May events of 1968, a reputation they have maintained in many subsequent heroic battles against the unarmed public whose order they exist to defend.

In France, unlike English-speaking countries, the police are not generally referred to as pigs. This could well change now that it has come out that the CRS in Marseilles have been keeping pigs in their barracks. Not for constabulary duties, but for food. The CRS explain that all they have been doing is putting to good use the leftovers from the canteen and ensuring themselves a supply of high-quality pork. Even so, pig-raising does seem to be an odd way for the police to fight crime and maintain law and order.

My own feeling is that if the Marseilles police want to get involved with the animal kingdom, they would do better to be wielding their truncheons against the mosquitoes. On my first night they assaulted me on all fronts, though I should say in fairness that it was the song of a nightingale that awoke me. I spent nearly three quid on a tube of anti-mosquito cream which claimed to be 'calming and repulsive'. The instructions said that one should avoid the eyes and mouth when using it.

Presumably the mosquitoes had read the instructions too, because the eyes and mouth were where they then concentrated their attacks.

The attitude of a Marseilles mosquito seems to be Fee, fi, fo, fum, I smell the blood of an Englishman. At any rate they gave me their full attention, while leaving the natives unscathed. What the locals complained about was the *cigales* (cicadas).

Outside the house were three large plane trees which provided not only welcome shade from the fierce heat but also a home for countless of these insects which make a noise out of all proportion to their size. Ki-ki-ki-ki-ki-ki, for hours on end. Personally I like the sound, but my hosts were as irritated by the *cigales* as I was by the mosquitoes. They (my hosts) tried various ways of shutting them (the *cigales*) up, such as turning the hosepipes on the trees, but to no effect. This pleased me. What would Provence be without *cigales* pointlessly singing in plane trees under which you can sit and eat pistachios and peacefully drink pastis and pleasurably play *pétanque*?

Sad to say, the plane trees are in serious danger from a disease which could prove as devastating as the one which has virtually wiped out the elm from the English landscape. In the boulevards of Marseilles a great many of the trees have already been felled. It's a grim prospect, Provence without plane trees. As grim as the sight of MacDonald's hamburgers competing with *bouillabaisse* in the Vieux Port.

12 August, 1985   **Richard Boston**

Riviera rhapsody

Does a shepherdess in Provence – the reader with a romantic turn of mind may wonder – enjoy a life of pastoral simplicity and rustic bliss? Dressed like a Dresden figurine, as light of heart as Marie Antoinette on a hey-nonny, does she spend her time singing sweet melodies or sporting like Amaryllis in the shade?

No, she doesn't. Certainly for Brigitte, our local shepherdess in the south of France, there are occasions when life is a bowl of rather unripe cherries.

Brigitte is a sensible, down-to-earth girl. Five years ago she landed her present job through the job centre at the Centre Agricole. They gave her a few addresses and telephone numbers and she went to see a farmer in the valley. At interview, he explained that the lot of a sheep was to be fed, fleeced, slaughtered, and eaten, but while alive a sheep was entitled to no less loving care than a bishop might bestow on his flock. That having been said, it was important to remember that a sheep's place was ultimately in the kitchen oven. Brigitte had been quick to follow the farmer's reasoning and made it clear that her idea of a little lamb was strictly that of three slices of gigot d'agneau, preferably with pommes de terre nouvelles and fresh haricots verts.

I was talking to our shepherdess down by the river as I wanted to photograph her for what I grandiosely call my record of the sights and sounds of Provence. By her side she had a tame ewe that answered (by making sheep's eyes as only a sheep can – because to do it you need one drooping eyelid and one raised eyebrow) to the name of Louise. Being a sucker for looks like that, I gave her half my cheese sandwich, hoping that she would roll her eyes once more.

All she did was belch.

A single hearty belch is one thing. A volley of belches that goes on for minutes is something else. Louise either couldn't or wouldn't stop. I looked at the faces of the other sheep and sensed that there was some concern at her behaviour. Sheep have been known to stampede with less cause than this, and there was every danger of the flock taking group action.

'Que faire?' asked our shepherdess, plainly a little distraught. 'Ce n'est pas normale.'

I agreed that it wasn't *normale* at all and said (without wishing to admit responsibility) I only wished I could help. She said I could, by taking Louise to the vet in my old car. Ungallantly, I refused. The idea of transporting a flatulent, possibly manic, and probably incontinent ewe ten kilometres to St Tropez, only to be told that the vet didn't specialize in sheep, was out of the question.

I had a better plan. In the glove compartment of my car I had a pocket tape-recorder. I quickly fetched it and while Louise was in full belch I recorded several bars of her alarming cacophony. This I would go and play to the vet and see what he had to say.

Within half an hour I was explaining to the vet's secretary that I wished to have a private word with him on a pressing matter. She immediately ushered me into his surgery and discreetly withdrew. I told him that it was vital that he should listen to part of my tape of the sounds of Provence.

On being rewound, the tape objected, as tapes do, by first offering unwanted pieces from the repertoire – nightingales singing, cicadas chanting, and Les Jolly Boys de Sainte Maxime giving their regional rendering of Frankie Goes to Hollywood's 'Relax'.

'*Mes excuses, monsieur.*' As I apologized, Louise's stentorian belching began. At that moment the secretary put her head around the door but again rapidly withdrew. The vet himself put a hand to his brow and listened intently, rather as a concert goer might listen to Stockhausen.

Suddenly it came to him. That was a sheep, he pronounced. Moreover it had wind, a great deal of wind, much more wind than was right and proper in a sheep. There was, however, no cause for dismay. He would let me have some strong purgative tablets that would eliminate the problem in no time.

The thought of getting a sheep to swallow a tablet didn't appeal to me and I said so.

There was, he told me, an alternative method of adminis-tration, but at this I demurred. I could well envisage what a French vet's alternative method might involve. Under the circumstances I settled for the tablets. Four of them. They were enormous.

Back in the car I began asking myself how I could persuade Louise to take them. The solution was staring me in the face. There above the dashboard was a Mars bar. I broke it in two and deftly pushed a tablet into each half. It couldn't fail. I drove back with speed and confidence to our shepherdess. She was waiting for me in the meadow, Louise belching by her side.

'*Tout va bien,*' I told her, voicing the triumph of a man who has thought of everything.

I handed her the Mars bar and the two remaining tablets and proceeded to make a fuss of Louise. Five seconds later our shepherdess was smiling at me with gratitude.

'*Merci infiniment, monsieur. C' était delicieux. J' adore les Mars.*'

There would, she assured me, be no difficulty in getting Louise to take the two tablets.

5 April, 1986   **Patrick Heyworth**

A wonderful experience

Surgeons are natural performers, hence the phrase "operating theatre". The surgeon in *Hospital Watch* (BBC1) carried a kidney in its own little hairnet. ("It's in this sock, which is my major contribution to British surgery") from its bed of ice to the patient, James Dalglish, and began the transplant.

"Can you see the colour changing to a delicate pink rather like a salmon? What was no more than offal is now a living organ." He pointed suddenly with a pallid rubber finger to the kidney and nearly shouted, "Do you see that?" See what? "Marvellous stuff. Marvellous!" The kidney turned a rosier, appreciative pink. "It's really one of the seven wonders of the world. A few minutes ago it was a nasty grey organ and now it's beautifully pink and look – making urine!"

Meanwhile at home Mark Dalglish was weeping. He had not seen his father for years but the next day at his bedside he described the moment when the kidney turned pink and began to drip urine. "It was a great moment. I was very happy for him and tears flooded to my eyes."

And somewhere someone was crying for the kidney's donor, a young woman killed in an accident.

Urine and tears. A fatal crash, a bedside reconciliation, a long lost son and offal in a sock. It makes you look at playwrights with pity. They wouldn't dare.

Mark's simple reaction – "I took the day off specially" – was the ultimate justification of *Hospital Watch*, a twice-nightly live documentary about two Portsmouth hospitals. He saw something that changed his mind. Ian Sandeman, whose colon was hauled out in handfuls, particularly asked the BBC "not to hide what happens" because he had found that if he talked to people plainly about his operation they sympathized and supported him. Ian's body wastes will now be discharged through a stoma in his stomach into a bag. He is only a young man.

People are afraid of what they think they will see. Ian's surgeon, burrowing away, said: "The thing that makes people pass out is the initial skin incision, makes you go queasy. And the other thing is watching legs being sawn off. Guaranteed to upset people."

The actual operation is like plumbing with soft pipes. The area of the operation is bathed in brilliant light and everything inside shines with a silky phosphorescence. Sometimes you come up with a sparkling gallstone. It is difficult to remember that there are a pair of feet sticking out of one end and a bath hat the other. There seems to be nobody there at all.

An orthopaedic surgeon drew a big black arrow pointing firmly to the hip, and said: "I'm going to write HIP to be sure we don't do your KNEE." He added, being a punctilious man, a firm full-stop. The patient smiled.

The really impressive thing was the patients. How patient patients are. With surgeons whose humour runs to the rollicking, with reporters who want to see their babies born. As *Hospital Watch* rolled on through the week, developing its own momentum, I felt increasingly silenced by something that was not quite courage nor cheerfulness. More like beautiful behaviour.

Mrs Grace Jones had a pacemaker, which looked like an old-fashioned turnip watch, popped into her breast as if into a breast pocket. She said: "Thank you for letting me come and have such pleasant company. I've really enjoyed it. A wonderful experience." Maggie Philbin, who was seeing her first operation, went pink like a kidney.

The best advertisement is to be banned. By cancelling *Another Country* (*Red Herrings*, BBC-1) last month because a group of charities had bought newspaper space to promote it, the BBC will have gained a very healthy audience for last night's viewing. Better yet: by not telling critics it was cancelled, they will have ensured two sets of enthusiastic reviews. Sometimes you think the BBC is blundering about with a bag over its head and sometimes you think it must all be a brilliant plot.

The beautifully made little programme by Chris Lent about the homeless young which was wittily and painfully intercut with the BBC's own *Bleak House* deserves all the attention it can get.

21 February, 1986   **Nancy Banks-Smith**

The up and down staircase

The last full Saturday programme of the football season takes place this afternoon. Essential questions should be answered before the grounds are returfed, or, increasingly, re-Astroturfed, and the national winter sport, still, just, resisting the snooker take-over, makes way for the summer sport, the Mexico World Cup. It has been the season of the footballing apotheosis of Thatcherism: the great divide between the haves and the have-nots, between the south-east and the rest of the country; little Englanderism; survival of the fittest; the wiping away of traditional footballing practices; the emergence of successful footballing small businesses; even products of youth training schemes finding places in league teams.

A quick survey of those relegated or likely to be so underlines the parallels between economic recession and its soccer equivalent. The West Midlands, which enjoyed prosperity until the late seventies and then suffered rapid decline, has experienced unprecedented footballing failure. West Bromwich Albion, Birmingham and Coventry are at or near the bottom of the first division, while the plummet of the once great Wolverhampton Wanderers has continued into the fourth division. South Wales sees all three of its league teams, Cardiff, Swansea and Newport, at the bottom of the third division.

Contrast this with the success of the Tory south. Swindon, at the heart of prosperous silicon valley, are fourth division champions at a canter, while nearby Reading have walked the third. And, most significantly, while the football elite have talked super leagues and excluding the minnows, these same tiny clubs have quietly won matches before minute crowds and are coming up to join them. Wimbledon, always better known for tennis and strawberries, and, Charlton, so destitute they had earlier this season to put together a ground share scheme with Crystal Palace, are heading for the first division. Being part of the prosperous south-east has proved more useful than history.

Fortunately sociology remains no science and Liverpool has retained its unique ability to defy economic and political logic. The two exceptions to footballing Thatcherism, Liverpool and Everton, are likely to finish first and second in the first division, (unless West Ham rise to the thesis) and will contest next week's Cup Final. Merseyside always triumphed in adversity, perhaps because it has known it longest.

3 May, 1986   **Leader**

An odd couple

The banana cake and pretzels have gone, the notes and curling photographs have been taken down. The rehearsal room down on 19th Street that had become home, has been left behind. This week, Jonathan Miller's *Long Day's Journey into Night* comes to life on stage: Duke University. Washington – then Broadway.

It is referred to as The Great American Play. ('Played with great reverence, very slowly, often with what is regarded as poetic fiction,' is how Miller defines that.) It is the account of Eugene O'Neill's own family: the vain, neglectful, stingy actor father; the awful, morphine-addicted mother; the two sons, drunken, weak, sick. Undercurrents of ferocity and tyranny; a quartet totally bound together.

238

Last week, after the month's rehearsals in that big, downtown space were over, Miller sat the actors down and played them a tape of Beethoven's 'Grosse Fugue'. 'Having made them like that,' he says with delight, 'they suddenly understood what it was that they were like.' Doubtless, at this moment, Jack Lemmon either looked at his boots, fidgeted with his bag or silently went over his words.

Friendship takes many forms; it is mostly, with adults, to do with work. The worry-ridden, brow-furrowed Dr Miller from London with his intellectual wizardry; the golf-playing, fly-fishing actor from Beverly Hills with his tales of Hollywood. An odd couple, indeed. ('I don't even know what par means,' says Miller.)

Lemmon was Miller's choice, the reason he took it on: the play, he says, had become embalmed. 'It needs to be renovated in a way by being given to an *interesting* rather than a sparky actor.' The Lemmon of *Missing*, of *The China Syndrome*, knew about ordinary men, bewildered, frightened, watching the dis-integration of their world. O'Neill's Tyrone, for all his bombast, his theatrical manners, has that quality too. 'I always try to choose actors who are very close to the people they're playing,' says Miller. 'I don't believe in spectacular feats of dissembling. Jack is a timid man – he's really quite frightened of things. I don't know why.'

At first, it is hard to see what Miller means. Jack Lemmon comes into rehearsal looking, in some curious way, inescapably Californian in this puddle of earnest, tense New Yorkers. Is it the jeans, the loose gait, the odd tweed hat, the beautiful and over-tailored sweat shirts? He is very touching as Tyrone, and if he so much as notices the two young actors flexing and bristling, hears their cracks about that being what he gets the big bucks for, he pays no attention. ('They are ferociously and carnivorously ambitious, those two boys,' says Miller with his most mischievous goblin look.)

But it does show: the way he holds his neck, stiff; the way he holds his head down and stares up with his dark eyes. The thin lip, the too quick smile, the careful modesty: a man keeping his chin out of the way of a punch. 'Respect is what you get if you're an old poop and last long enough,' he says,

239

making much of his need to peer through tiny, gold-rimmed spectacles. 'I'm sort of like a butterfly compared to O'Neill,' he says. 'Well, Jonathan doesn't think that way – bless him.'

Miller has stayed in a dusty, rambling but not too clean, hotel on the West Side, opposite the Natural History Museum, its bookshop and volumes on evolutionary theory. Jack Lemmon with his wife, Felicia, has been at The Lowell: small, East Sixties, charming, beyond reproach, full of stars and celebrities such as he, long, black, stretch limousines waiting outside.

He is sixty-two years old, has been married for twenty-four years, been in films for thirty years, and has forty-six film credits: classics such as *Some Like it Hot*, *Days of Wine and Roses*, *The Front Page*, *The Prisoner of Second Avenue*. Mistakes, too: *Luv* ('a bumeroo'), *Alex and the Gypsy* ('I don't know where that one went').

People in the hotel recognize him; there is that pleasure of hailing the famous, of being attended to in return – for Lemmon, is above all, a courteous man. 'I don't think there's anything to be proud of because you're famous,' he says. 'But there is something to be proud of about how you got famous. I've seen it over and over again. Careers dwindle because they start to make deals – instead of just taking a crack at it. The satisfaction has not been that I'm a star – whatever that goddammed word means – but that I'm an actor. I don't think failure does anyone any harm. I think fear of failure is lethal. It keeps you from doing things.'

He talks of his children, his actor son, Chris, by a first marriage, Courtney, his daughter with Felicia, now at college. 'You pray a lot, you cross your fingers a lot. I've seen more kids go right down the bloody tubes. Ninety per cent of having famous parents is negative for the kid. Chris is sensational and at thirty-one he may be my closest friend – but he was a crazy, flighty kid in his teens. And if it does happen for him as an actor, when the biggies start coming in – it will be delicious, just delicious.'

He is the most likeable of men, and also the most hidden. Such unflappable charm, such niceness – there must be more than that. The clues are there, though, long ago but deep within him: John Uhler Lemmon III, born in Boston, Mass, Phillips

Academy, Andover, Harvard. He has tough American fibre, controlled, professional. Of course he squirms when Miller dissects the guts of the play, the soul of characters and actors.

Lemmon must spend his life trying to keep at bay all the chaos and insecurity of the world in which he, an only, privileged, upper-class child, has now chosen to live and work. Everything about him is to do with control and distance, with not losing faith – except, that is, in the moment of acting.

'There's dinner and testimonials, a feeling you get of recognition when you're a middle-aged dinosaur like me. But it's plenty, I think.' And then: 'But God knows, it often doesn't seem like plenty.' He remembers the Broadway play in the sixties that was a disaster: 'Not one good review. It's like God was whispering in my ear: "You can get clobbered for a performance, but it doesn't mean you're a rotten actor".'

Interesting, though, it is the failure he brings up – not the year on Broadway, a decade later, in *Tribute*, his Broadway Drama Guild Award for it, his Tony nomination. 'I'm attracted to flawed characters,' he says 'to characters that have to exist under the pressures we all have to do with. If actors start playing a heavy, they usually make him a shit. Tyrone thinks of himself as a put upon man – and, basically it's true. But whether it's true or not, I make him care deeply because he adores his wife; he does absolutely adore that shell of a woman.'

He says it with such feeling: who knows from where, under his gentle, craggy, familiar face, that feeling comes: 'People think I'm a nice guy,' he says. 'I'm petrified. I'm afraid of a one-on-one confrontation. I cannot stand temperament for the sake of temperament. The star bullshit: there's no room, absolutely no room for that anywhere.' How unexpected that, when it comes to it, he is just another of Jonathan Miller's band of good troupers.

19 March, 1986   **Linda Blandford**

To the manna born

Some people make a solemn ritual out of breadmaking but for me it is sensual, almost sexy – right from the moment when my sticky batter turns into soft, pliable, fragrant, spongy dough. Next comes the squeezing and kneading and then the lovely, rounded swelling as the dough rises – only for me to punch it down again. (I don't really punch; I slap with the back of my hand.) And then another rising and finally the ineffable smell of baking bread that fills the whole house.

I'm only a beginner of a year's standing and I enjoy it more and more. My wife and children were sceptical as the only other things I can cook are French omelette and spaghetti bolognaise. They complained about the mess (flour + water = glue) that has to lie around for one and a half hours while the dough rises, waiting for the second kneading.

I grew tidier with practice and my family have now gone right off shop bread. They disagree over which of my loaves is best: my wholemeal-rye mixture with caraway seeds, my creamy white, almost a Jewish *cholla*, with milk and eggs, glazed with poppy seeds, or my latest sour dough – an attempt to capture the intoxicating taste and feel of German rye.

My aim was to escape from shop bread. This has vastly improved since the fifties, when plastic factory-white and factory-Hovis had a near monopoly. But even now your supermarket 'wholemeal' and 'granary' are flabby, anaemic, boringly repetitive and insubstantial compared with the crunchy, more fragrant and infinitely variable bread you can make. My ambition was, and remains, to make German-type rye, but that needs sour-dough techniques I'm only just starting on.

Home-baked loaves are about half the price of shop bread, and the promotion of bread into a delicacy makes it even more economical because bread is practically a meal in itself. I am not fussy about the flour: any stoneground wholemeal will do. Sainsbury's do a good one; also a delicious granary mix. All the health shops sell various kinds. Use strong white flour for white bread. I also use a branch of Marriages, the grain dealers, for bulk quantities.

Nor is bread time-consuming. A complete two-rise process takes about three hours for up to six loaves (a bit more for up to twelve: you can freeze your bread). But this time is mostly taken up with long intervals of waiting, during which you can do something else. My Sunday dough is rising while I am writing this. Equipment is minimal: a mixing-bowl and spoon and a few baking tins which can cost less than £1 each.

Bread at its most serious can be learned about by taking a Yarner Trust course with Pam and Nick Rodway at their farm (Welcombe Barton, Bideford, Devon), a house which was listed in Domesday Book. They will teach whatever they do, which includes cheesemaking, shoe-making and living off the land.

Taking the one-upmanship of bread to its limit, they grow their own wheat, mill and grind their own flour. Pam observes a minute's silence before she starts with the bread, but I find I can manage without this. For my taste her own bread turned out coarse, but this is due to her choice of coarser-milled flour than is commercially sold. Her technique has a religious purity and indeed she uses a natural-leaven method given to her by the French L'Arche community.

Kindly, she gave me a sour-dough 'mother' to take home in a plastic bag. This, like a yoghurt-starter, is renewed and stored indefinitely. I intend using mine for the rest of my life and passing it on to my descendants.

Bread-making is a trend. Jane Inglis, for instance, sent this page her pamphlet *Bake Your Way to a Better Diet* (Oakroyd Press). Her method is as simple as you can get: the bread rises only once, cutting down the time and the mess. I know from other peoples' bread that this can work without loss of lightness, but two risings are said to be healthier. A weakness of her pamphlet is that it doesn't tell you how to knead. All it says is 'knead, pummel and pound,' which isn't right. In each movement you rotate the dough a quarter-turn, fold it back and press it down. So: turn, fold and press are the correct magic words.

The classic is still Elizabeth David's *English Bread and Yeast*

Cookery (Penguin £4.95), a marvellous read even if you never bake bread. My own little bible, unbeatably practical, is Glynn Christian's *Bread and Yeast Cookery* (Macdonald, £2.95).
3 January, 1986   **Walter Schwarz**

St Bob and Old Nick

When a man in Slough once pressed through the crowd to declare to Bob Geldof that Jesus would say the Kingdom was open to him, Geldof was, it is reported, horrified. 'Being a saint, which I'm not,' he has said, 'is a pain, to be honest.'

Yet the tales of the man and his works must grow. Of how from early beginnings as meat factory worker, pea canner, and youth organizer for CND, he was translated into King of the Boomtown Rats. Of how his following grew, in spite of his declaration that he had nothing to teach or preach, that he had no wish to lead anyone, and that most people went into bands simply and entirely to get laid, get famous and get rich. Of how he once silenced a mob by saying to them: 'I'm not going to be insulted by you assholes – get out!' And of how they did. Of how he asked the world whether the people of Ethiopia knew it was Christmas and of how that record became a record-breaker.

Already then, a year ago, there were people who reached for their typewriters and called him saint. There was talk of miracles; a likeness was detected to John the Baptist. And then there was Live Aid, the global jukebox, the greatest show on earth, and the Archbishop of Canterbury thanked God for it. 'It's either vilification or sanctification,' says Bob Geldof, 'and both piss me off.'

But maybe his time for being a mortal has passed, and he has become instead a legend, a hook for any projections that people need to send his way, offering – like all the best saints – something for everyone. 'The world feels a better place when we see a true Brit with true grit doing something for himself and his country.' That is perhaps rather an odd thing for a British Prime Minister to say about a Dubliner. But maybe it's not odd at all when you imagine what Mrs Thatcher might like people to say of herself.

It isn't the man's personal following, for his professional star was on the wane before it all began. It isn't even just the cash, for all that he has spun the gold from his name into lorries and supplies, and Live Aid has inspired Fashion Aid and Classical Music Aid and who knows how many smaller rattlings of tins. If the feeding of the world is the miracle in view, as the Live Aid banners declare it to be, then it's going to take more than those millions, and we all know it.

Yet what Geldof-the-legend has brought is the hope that some lightness at least could be brought into a darkness in which the earth itself seemed turned against humanity. That global jukebox forged a link between Western perplexities and the place that Homer called the end of the earth, that the Greeks knew as the home of dark power ever since Phaeton's chariot careened off-course and slewed the light from it. It forged a link between who knows what light and shadow in ourselves. And the message came not from the great and the good at all, for the power to fire the imagination seems to have gone from them altogether. It came from King Rat, from the underground of the counter culture.

The established order has hardly been slow to draw comfort from that. (Football hooligans, national disgrace, civic disorder, Law and Order Bill – yet let no one say that young people today. And so on.) But as Geldof-the-legend effs and blinds his way across the world, he's not going to let them get away with it. There's a kind of glorious innocence in that opening salvo in Ethiopia: 'Minister, do you mind if we cut the crap?' And 'Why don't you get your act together?' To slag off the Common Agricultural Policy as 'the crowning idiocy', to bawl out the Prime Minister for allowing that butter to mount, to say of the EEC bureaucracy 'this place needs a laxative'. Like the boy who laughed because the Emperor was bollock-naked, like the jester at court, he says what countless others wished they dared. He chucks away the niceties that oil the diplomatic wheels, and turns order upside down.

And who's to say we don't need something of that in a world grown weary of what it has wrought of itself? It wasn't just the simple coincidence, perhaps, of television's horrific messages and shrewd commercial sense that brought Band Aid to birth at Christmas. For what have the December festivals ever been about if it isn't bringing new light and hope at the time of greatest darkness, of life where there was death, the overturning of the old order with the energy of the new? Come saint, come sinner, the greatest show on earth is the death and resurrection show – the greatest of miracles, the deepest of magics.

And there is precious little either miraculous or magical about these days. Not like once upon a time and long ago, when it was open season for both all the year round, with no shortage of wonderworkers and magicians to mediate them. Saints, they used to be called. Time was when you could just create them as you needed them to carry your hopes and your fears. It wasn't until the thirteenth century, after all, that Rome brought the making of new saints under its order, and not for four centuries after that that it got the company sorted to its satisfaction. Even sixteen years ago there was thought of pruning, cults being seen to get in the way of proper attention to the great rhythm of the Church's major festivals.

But before Rome and the Reformation got their very different sorts of hands on them, as Keith Thomas shows in his marvellously rich *Religion and the Decline of Magic* (Peregrine Books, 1978), saints were what the people wanted. They didn't just intercede for you with God and leave the outcome to Him, which is what theology would have them do, calling it religion. They did the trick themselves, and that is magic.

They weren't just dealers in white magic, either. 'We worship saints for fear,' wrote William Tyndale in the early sixteenth century, 'lest they should be displeased and angry with us and plague us or hurt us: as who is not afraid of St Laurence? Who dare deny St Anthony a fleece of wool for fear of his terrible fire, or lest he send the pox among our sheep?' Magic was a tricky business in those days: it wasn't even unknown for priest to turn sorcerer and say a requiem mass for someone still alive in the expectation that they soon wouldn't be.

And if saints were most often preservers of life and health, they could be death-dealers too. What about St Wilgefortis, a bearded lady to be found to this day in Westminster Abbey?

The *Oxford Dictionary of Saints* asserts that she never existed at all, far less being granted her beard and her martyrdom when God heard her prayer for preservation of her dedicated virginity and her father had her crucified for repelling her suitors. But try telling that to the women who called her St Uncumber because, if you slipped her a peck of oats, she would will unwanted husbands to drop dead.

The Reformation may have got rid of that sort of thing when it threw the images of the saints out of the churches, when Protestantism simultaneously denied its people their protection and emphasized the power of the Devil. (In Norwich in 1558, the annual procession of St George's Guild had to do without its patron and his companion St Margaret, but the Dragon was still allowed to frisk along.) Yet wonderworking and magic aren't stamped out as easily as that, any more than the Christmas festivals can be stamped out by Act of Parliament, for all the attempts of the Puritans. Take, for maybe the best instance of all, St Nicholas, patron of Russia, Manhattan, and Great Yarmouth, to name but a few: Santa Claus, Old Nick himself.

The best thing of all about St Nicholas for yarnspinning purposes is that, although one of the most venerated saints, very little is known about his life. Certainly he started well: so pious a babe was he that he refused his mother's breast on Wednesdays and Fridays. His life was as exemplary as his infancy, and he became Bishop of Myra in Turkey (in the fourth century, this). Even after his death the odour of sanctity clung about him: from his eventual tomb in Bari wafted the scent they called 'myrrh' and unguent makers took him as their patron. So did sailors: the first church in Liverpool was dedicated to him. So too did pawnbrokers hang up their three golden balls in his honour and young girls pray to him as proprietor of a sort of celestial dating agency, because one of his few recorded acts was to slip three bags of gold, secretly by night, through the windows of three maidens about to be sold into prostitution. And if he saved them from a fate worse than, he once saved three young boys from death itself, by fishing them piecemeal from the barrel of brine in which a dismembering butcher had stowed them. He put them together again, good as new.

It took the people of New Amsterdam, even then blessed with a keen eye to commercial potential, to translate St Nicholas into someone nearer the figure who beams on us today. But theirs sounds to have been something of a Superego Santa Claus, for it was only the good children who got presents from him on his feast on December 6, as their parents and grandparents had in the Low Countries. In Europe, too, there are stories of how young nuns would hang their stockings outside their doors on the eve of his feast, for the abbess to fill with favours. But as to expecting him to slide down chimneys, far less park reindeer atop them or roister about in bibulous geniality . . .

'In comes I, Father Christmas, welcome or welcome not,' says the character in one of the English mumming plays – a tricky customer, evidently, in those days when he kept company with the likes of Beelzebub, the Turk, and St George. But then nothing and no one were quite as they seemed when the guisers donned their disguises and men dressed as women and women as men and the Abbot of Misrule rumbustiously misruled. (Even in Scotland the Abbot of Unreason had his fling until defrocked by Act of Parliament, the Scots being, as an ecclesiastical historian observed in 1830, 'a staid and holiday-hating people'.)

Such meetings then of the sacred and the profane! Such was the level of smutty jokes and parody of holy order among the lesser clergy when the Boy Bishop ruled around Holy Innocents Day in Notre Dame in twelfth-century Paris that the sternest of decrees had to be issued. Yet here they are again with their Fool's Pope three centuries later, singing dirty songs in the choir during holy service, gobbling their greasy snacks right beside the altar, hopping about all over the church. Established order turned upside down and inside out. (Minister, can we cut the crap? This place needs a laxative.)

Somehow the Christmas television Specials and the office party don't have quite the same ring in these days when, so we're told, it's open season on licence all year round. But then, too, the medieval world was a whole lot nearer to the great December feast of the Saturnalia, when a criminal or slave was king, crowned with ass's ears and mock-sacrificed – or maybe the ass for real – with a blow from Saturn's sacred holly-club to ensure nature's own rebirth. In those seven topsy-turvy days, people bathed early so that they could feast uninterrupted; masters served their slaves in memory of the golden age; the apparatus of order – the law courts, the schools, commercial and military operations – was suspended altogether.

And where the old dark gods are, it's not really much of a surprise to smell a rat, for the underworld is where rats have ever been at home. There's a Romano-Gallic stele from Rheims of the Celtic Curnunnos, The Horned One, Lord of All the Stags, with a rat crouched atop his throne to show his underworld power. He carries a bag of gold, spilling over his lap, this god of prosperity and good fortune. The Romans later called him Pan, god of all nature; the Christians later yet called him the Devil. Old Nick himself, with his sacks of gold.

Yet of the making of Father Christmas there is maybe no end. If the gods have travelled up from the south to Britain and Ireland, then they have travelled down from the north as well, and they have their links with reindeer-land itself. We have our echoes of Yuletide too, the northern festival of the winter solstice, the yule-log blazing to conjure the rebirth of light in those dark lands. 'A boar's head in hand bear I,' goes the English carol, and if Frey, the Scandinavian god of plenty, rode on a golden boar to his mid-winter festival, then a boar was sacrificed too in those days as the Twin of the Sacred King, to ensure new life.

But the greatest of all the Northern gods, and so later the devil himself in most powerful guise, was Wotan. And there are those, like Ean Begg in *Myth and Today's Consciousness* (Coventure, 1984), who see in him Father Christmas himself. We have our links. It was to Wotan that the Angles prayed before they set out to invade Britain, as ancestor of their kings. In Germany, where his was the most powerful cult of all, the early Christians so feared him that they expunged his name from the weekly calendar altogether. In Britain, we kept it, and on his day Christmas falls this year.

Wotan was orderer of fate, the god of the spiritual life. Not grand with it, though: he liked to wander about in his great cloak and slouch hat to listen and learn among the mortals;

those who drank with him, it was said, would never get a hangover. In darkest guise, he was lord of all rage and violence, thundering on his eight-hoofed horse across the sky with his great troop of Berserkers, warrior-phantoms all, the archetype of power whose fury, some would say, has been unleashed twice already in Germany this century, the stronger for its repression, and threatens yet on global scale.

But Wotan was also lord of wisdom and poetry. For him, no substitute sacrifice would do, and he chose to suffer for himself the ritual of death and resurrection, hanging for nine nights on the great world-tree Yggdrasil, its roots stretching into the underworld and its branches, decked with reindeer, into heaven. The English missionary St Boniface, it's said, introduced the fir into Germany to take people's hearts and minds from sacrificing in memory of Wotan's own ordeal. It took something like 1100 years for the Germans to bring us back our Christmas tree.

That is not our only legacy, for Wotan the frenzied, the all-wise, was lord of the shamans too, of the priest-magicians of that universal ecstatic cult which in the west spread from Asia and Siberia up to the northern lands of the Eskimos and even, perhaps, across to North America.

The shamans got their power to heal, to mediate with the spirits of the upper world and the underworld too, through their own harsh initiation by a ritual experience of death, dismemberment and resurrection. They decked themselves with puppets as their spirit familiars and wore crowns of reindeer horns; they could summon the spirits to descend through that smoke hole in the yurt on the pole that stood for the great world-tree itself. And as they knew the underworld, so too could they fly to the upper one, leading their people in a drug-induced frenzy of release and healing, masters, and mistresses too, and sometimes both in their sexual ambivalence, of the transformation of Middle World consciousness.

Remember St Nicholas's re-membering of the boys in brine? And who is Santa still but the chimney-descending spirit, sky-flying on his reindeer?

'In comes I, Father Christmas, welcome or welcome not': we used to know to be wary of such power. Like a shaman,

Santa on the Victorian Christmas cards is decked with dolls and puppets, his familiars peering out of his pockets, perched on his shoulders. His red and white robes are still the colours of death and resurrection. Some nurses shun the colours yet when they come together in a bunch of flowers for a hospital bedside, and each participant at the Russian Orthodox Easter celebration may still be offered one red flower and one white. These are the colours, too, of the fly agaric mushroom, the sacred shamanic drug, which some identify with the ancient Vedic Soma, which was also the god, some say, who became Dionysus.

So Santa as shaman, and shaman as showman, too. In *The Death and Resurrection Show* (Blond, 1985), Rogan Taylor weaves a fascinating spell of his own as he shows how the shamanic tradition has lived on in that other place of transformation: the theatre.

'All the old gods are devils', said Tertullian. 'Dionysus the old god is god of the theatre, therefore the theatre belongs to a devil, *the devil*'. Centuries later, the English Puritans would echo their Amen to that. So the dark wealth of the underworld became the Hell of damnation, and theatre people its servants. And so the shamanic tradition took to the roads, its players not strolling at all, but running for their livelihood and their art.

When they pitched their tents, it was the shamanic rites they re-enacted. In the mummers' tale the early traditions of clowning and the cross-dressed pantomime, they gave you again, ladies and gentlemen, the greatest show on earth: the tale of death, dismemberment, and resurrection. They flew through the air, too, and with the greatest of ease, those daring young trapeze artists; they walked the tightrope just as shamanic initiates had braved the crossing of a deep ravine; they walked on redhot coals and they swallowed fire and swords just as their forebears had. Seasonal fare to this day, just as it was when the Abbots of Misrule brought the old traditions erupting into the new order.

'Laugh? I could have died' the comics still tell us, and on the nights when control dissolves the actors still corpse their way through the show. Yet the tradition has stronger echoes yet. Where else have the ecstatic fanatics gone but into the crowds of fans who follow their cult-leaders in the haze of consciousness-transforming drugs to the beat of popular music? 'Showbusiness', reckons Rogan Taylor, 'is the major therapeutic event of the modern age; it has risen in response to our new sickness – our loss of soul to science.'

'The oracle has spoken, we cast the perfect spell' sang John Lennon, whose martyrdom is celebrated just two days after the Feast of St Nicholas. 'No one I think is in my tree, I mean it must be high or low', he sang. Wotan himself could have cried the same.

'What am I anyway? Some kind of Messiah walking around? If I thought we needed a new religion I would start one,' said Bob Dylan.

'It's either vilification or sanctification,' says Bob Geldof. Pissed off he may be. But then doesn't the book of Band Aid bill it as 'the greatest show on earth'?

24 December, 1985   **Ann Shearer**

Index